WHEN WE WERE GHOULS

Thank you for reading!

Amy Wheller
December 2021

AMERICAN LIVES | Series editor: Tobias Wolff

When We Were Ghouls

A Memoir of Ghost Stories

AMY E. WALLEN

University of Nebraska Press | Lincoln and London

The essay "When We Were Ghouls" was originally published in the *Gettysburg Review* 29, no. 1 (Spring 2016).

Library of Congress Cataloging-in-Publication Data
Names: Wallen, Amy, author.
Title: When we were ghouls: a memoir of
ghost stories / Amy E. Wallen.
Description: Lincoln: University of Nebraska Press, [2018]
Series: American lives | "The essay 'When We
Were Ghouls' was originally published in the
Gettysburg Review 29, no. 1 (Spring 2016)."
Identifiers: LCCN 2017037691
ISBN 9780803296954 (pbk.: alk. paper)
ISBN 9781496205384 (epub)
ISBN 9781496205391 (mobi)
ISBN 9781496205407 (pdf)
Subjects: LCSH: Wallen, Amy—Childhood and youth. |
Wallen, Amy—Homes and haunts. | Authors, American—
Biography. | Right and wrong. | Grave robbing. | Memory.
Classification: LCC PS3623.A3599 W45 2018
DDC 818/.603 [B]—dc23
LC record available at https://lccn.loc.gov/2017037691

Set in New Baskerville ITC by E. Cuddy.

Designed by N. Putens.

To my family,

who taught me to believe in ghosts

To Eber,

who believes in me

Ghosts and Fashion

Although it no longer has a body
to cover out of a sense of decorum,

the ghost must still consider fashion—

must clothe its invisibility in something
if it is to "appear" in public.

Some traditional specters favor
the simple shroud—

a toga of ectoplasm
worn Isadora-Duncan-style
swirling around them.

While others opt for lightweight versions
of once familiar tee shirts and jeans.

Perhaps being thought-forms,
they can change their outfits instantly—

or if they were loved ones,
it is we who clothe them
like dolls from memory.

—Elaine Equi

CONTENTS

ILLUSTRATIONS

Dear Reader, I changed some but not all of the names of the people herein, not to protect the innocent, as no one is truly innocent in this story, but out of respect for privacy. If you think you recognize yourself, or others, it could be only an illusion. These memories, after all, are ghost stories.

When We Were Ghouls

> Drab Habitation of Whom?
> Tabernacle or Tomb—
> Or Dome of Worm—
> Or Porch of Gnome—
> Or some Elf's Catacomb?
>
> —Emily Dickinson

A COFFIN IS JUST TOO LONELY. AN URN, WITH ALL THAT porcelain, is too cold. Graves like giant steamer trunks, that's what Buddhists, Egyptians, and Incas have. This is my preference. A big hole in the ground filled with all my belongings, packaged food, remembrances, and even a companion—like a family to-go.

This Family Plot, I'm unearthing it rather than burying it. I'm going six feet down, maybe farther, to collect all the pieces, my inheritance for the afterlife.

I will start in a Peruvian ghost town.

I remember miles and miles of sand dunes. Everything on the surface is broken to pieces. To find anything whole, I have to dig. Deep.

I don't believe in the afterlife. But I do believe in ghosts. Which I know makes no sense. I believe in ghosts because, while I may never know when they will show up, or whether they will ever show up again, I know they can and, on occasion, they do.

But why ghosts when no one is dead yet?

Let me start with a memory that takes place at this gravesite.

This is that memory:

I squatted just on the other side of the sand dune, knees sticking up pointy like chicken wing bones. This way I could sift through the melty sand around me, scavenge for pieces to take home. The dunes were scattered with bones and clay shards, and I thought this was the best ghost town my family had ever explored. A real ghost town.

A pre-Inca graveyard.

I heard my brother Marty's deep voice on the other side of the dune. He was talking to Sarah Riley, the daughter of the family friends who had come with us to explore this ghost town. To me, Sarah was too flirty, had too big a crush on my brother. He was mine, not hers. He was seventeen, I was eight.

At first I heard their voices like a radio tuning in a distant station—in and out, in and out. Then they were gone. I climbed over the ridge, hoping to spy on my brother and Sarah. The sand dunes splayed out all around me were reminiscent of Saint-Exupéry's *The Little Prince* when the pilot's plane crashes in the Sahara. Only I was not in the Sahara; I was in a graveyard near the beach north of Lima. The sand warmed my feet up to my ankles, but the air blew cool and constant. I looked out over the swell of the dunes and tried to see the invisible wind, see how it swept the sand into waves. I spotted the picnic set up where we all just finished lunch. Everyone mulled around, picking up the remnants, the scraps, leaving the heavier bottles and baskets to weigh down the blanket, to keep it from getting carried off in the fierce wind.

With my short and pudgy eight-year-old legs, I trudged back over to the far side of the deep sand dunes to hide. Hiding was what I did. Hiding was a place I could be by myself. Where I *chose* to be alone. I also hid hoping my mom would come looking for me. She never did, but I still tried. I also wanted to see a ghost. I figured if I were alone a ghost was more likely to appear than in the noisy crowd on the other side of the dune. I didn't know whether I would be afraid if a ghost showed itself, but I wanted to find out. A ghost would be so much better than the pottery shards and bones lying around. I imagined a specter would be there for only a moment, then disappear, leaving only my memory. I would have to convince everyone or save the vision for my own. Maybe it would be better not to share the experience, because the adults would only convince me it wasn't true. That I hadn't seen what I'd seen. My family was always doing that. Telling me it couldn't have happened that way.

"Check this out!" I heard Marty call, then he quicksanded his way over the soft crest of the tall dune, Sarah Riley right behind.

In his hands he held up a skull.

"A skull," I said. Human skulls were scattered everywhere, so I didn't really see the point in getting excited.

The dunes were so littered with bones you could barely walk a few feet without finding a clavicle or rib or ulna. "It's not *just* a skull," Marty said. "Look." He held the skull skyward with his left hand, and then with his right he attached the jawbone, making it whole. Now that was a find! Even I knew the jaw always got lost; rarely could you find a human skull with its mandible intact. Nothing held the two jawbones together except skin, cartilage, and muscle, which easily disintegrated under most circumstances. Marty had a real find. I'd never seen a skull intact, in all my eight years of ghost town scavenging. Something about this place had kept the skull whole. Something about this place kept the bodies embalmed. Something prevented decomposition.

"It'll make a great lamp," my brother said.

"Really?" And for the first time Sarah Riley backed away from my brother.

"A great lamp!" I agreed, my love for him monster-sized. This is my favorite part of the memory, because it's just as weird and macabre as my brother and me.

He held the skull out to show me where the wiring could come in from the base; the bulb would sit right behind the eye sockets so they'd light up. I nodded. I recalled another bedside lamp in his room where I sometimes slept when he was away at boarding school, so I could smell the stinky, sweaty boy smell on his sheets and imagine he was not so far away as Switzerland.

Sarah headed back toward the picnic area. Marty and I followed behind carrying our treasures; I had a pottery shard with monkeys painted on it, and my brother his new lamp base. Two dunes over, the land flattened out. The wind was blocked on one side but came from the other direction, creating a barrage of sand and grit whirls. This was where the parents were now, standing next to a large opening in the ground. My mother stood at the farthest edge—a tiny woman in espadrilles, navy blue slacks, and a matching striped blouse. I wanted to be next to her, but she was out of reach.

By the time my brother and I joined the group, a square area the size of our Toyota had been staked off by the diggers. Three young Peruvian boys had come over the dunes after we had driven into the area and had offered to help. They carried shovels, mattocks, adzes, and iron rebar longer than they were tall. My parents and the Rileys had hired them, and with the iron pokers they prodded at the earth until they found a spot that gave. Dirt fell through, and they shoveled and dug.

When I was five years old and we lived in the Sierras of Nevada, we would drive our green Buick Wildcat out into the little mountain mining towns, and we'd find pocketfuls of blue glass bottles caked in dirt. My mother taught me original glass has a seam. Medicine bottles from the Old West in Nevada, abandoned artifacts, these she'd polish and place on shelves in our home. A whole bottle, not just a shard of glass, was a good find. A dented pot and its lid—a treasure. A woman's wooden-handled hairbrush with its bristles intact—pure luck. Intact artifacts were rare, but she taught me to value their completeness, to make sure they had no chips, no cracks, no missing parts. My family did not have much, and our tacky treasures lined the windowsills and shelves of our home.

Two years later my father's job in oil exploration moved us overseas, but we still visited ghost towns. Our demographic changed, and the demographic of the ghost town we visited also changed—the treasure much bigger, someone else's treasure, and it wasn't so much a ghost town as a graveyard.

As I remember standing graveside in Peru, the memories start to cave in on me. How had we ended up here? Had we happened upon the site during our weekend expedition? Our peripatetic life had peripatetic weekends.

Had my parents done it knowingly, dug up a grave? Why is my brother making lamps from skulls? Why are human bones scattered everywhere?

Who were we?

The scattered human bones and artifacts on top of the ground? In my conscious mind, the image seems unbelievable. This is more than just a lost memory; it feels more like a phantasm moving in and out. The memory is not slipping through my fingers, it's sliding around on my amygdala.

I begin to dig for more proof of my memories. I feel unsteady, as each stone I overturn reveals something more gruesome.

I google "Pre-Columbian gravesites Peru." The images on my computer screen closely resemble the artifacts in my parents' house in Texas and even a couple of pots that sit on top of a cabinet in my own house. I frantically click on links and come across a piece of embroidered fabric with red cord trim and mythological creatures like ants on their hind legs dancing across the band—it is just like a piece we had taken from the grave, which my mother now uses as living room décor. A French gallery website shows the same type of pot my mother put on a wrought iron stand in their hallway and filled with dried cattails. Our family home is definitely not a French art gallery. It's a Texas ranch-style surrounded by bluebonnets with a buckskin-colored pickup truck out front.

The gravesite, where were we exactly?

My memory's graveyard seemed so much bigger than, say, the grassy, parklike setting where my grandparents were buried. Where exactly was this graveyard? In my search, I encounter a *National Geographic News* article from 2002 that describes the major problem in Peru with looting and smuggling of antiquities, and how the mummies of the Puruchuco pre-Columbian gravesite are strewn on open ground, denuded and stripped of ornamentation. Puruchuco. The name does not sound even vaguely familiar to me. I am certain I do not have the right necropolis, despite the familiarity of the artifacts. One line reads that Puruchuco is the second largest gravesite. That means there is a bigger one.

This also means my family were looters—a word my family had never used. I am frightened at the prospect. I am afraid of what I will find out, but I am caught in this tug-of-war: the family story and what now looks like a crime.

I scour maps on the web and finally pull out a name that rings a bell, "Ancon." "When we went to Ancon . . ." my mother's voice echoes through my dusty memories. I google "Ancon": "a seaside resort for the wealthy." I zoom in on the map, looking for a cemetery, but don't see one. Did our graveyard get built over with a tourist attraction? We didn't go to the beach very often when we lived in Peru. I remember only one time after an earthquake, we went to see the giant tidal waves. That's what my family did—we'd go to the tsunami, we didn't wait for it to come to us.

I email my eighty-year-old mother hoping she'll reveal more.

"Where were we when we dug up the grave?" I type. This is how we talked about it—*when we dug up the grave.* As though it was the same as the day we had a picnic on Wheeler Peak in the South Snake Mountain range in Nevada. But how long has it been since I have heard anyone tell this story? Twenty, thirty years? No one mentions it any longer.

"Was it Ancon?"

While I wait for my mother's answer, I watch a video on the *National Geographic* site of an embalmed, pre-Columbian Chancay body being unwrapped from its linen embalming cloth by archaeologists. Do I remember that same gauzy fabric? My doubt is fading as fast as my heart is racing. Do I really remember the same peeling back of the layers? My memory reemerges simultaneously in my mind as the film reveals the mummy on my screen.

As I stood graveside, I watched each layer of fabric sticking to the layer below it, like an old Band-Aid. The grave now deeper than the diggers were tall. The gray-brown linen peeled back from the forehead revealed the skull. I remember the unraveling of the cloth that kept the body embalmed in the dry earth for 800–1000 years. The unwinding like the slow peeling away of a giant gauze bandage revealed eye sockets with bits of dried, brown skin still clinging to bone, a toothy, lipless grin, his arms crossed, his legs tucked up to his chest, his feet folded over one another.

Watching the video makes me feel I am watching the unveiling of a relative. I have a creepy feeling I will recognize the corpse that clearly when they peel off the thick cotton.

And I do.

The same face, the same empty eye sockets looking shocked and scared. The same dried, curling skin as the video skeleton. The same melancholy spread of teeth, as though he was glad finally to be dug up. Relieved, maybe. Is he asking, "But what afterlife is this?"

I question my memory. Maybe the video just seems real because I want it to be. Power of suggestion. Maybe I want to be someone who has witnessed such things firsthand. Does that make me an ogre?

The only part I'm certain about, absolutely dead certain, is the scene with my brother and the complete skull, jawbone intact, and the contents inside the grave.

Could the dunes really have been covered in pottery shards and random bones, human bones, femurs, ulnas, and clavicles? Why would bones and pottery just be scattered about? I've always assumed the story we tell, *when we dug up the grave*, has elaborations. It's how my family tells a story. We are Southerners from birth, after all. But I'm starting to fear what is true, what is fact. Who is the family who traipses through a place like this? With an eight-year-old in tow? Maybe I've just imagined it. My own elaborations.

But even the omniscient Wikipedia refutes my imagination and insists what I've seen was true. I type in "Ancon" and find this description of the indigenous history:

> In Ancon the ridges of gravel and sandy soil were littered with skulls, bones, and remnants of tattered handwoven cloth.

Wikipedia might fudge the truth, but it isn't a mind reader.

Then I read, "Beneath the surface, grave robbers found mummified bodies with all the accompanying grave goods in shallow graves."

Grave robbers. Naw, I don't want to use this label. I have a good family. Not the kind who would decimate remains for their own sake. Greedy and selfish? All my family members might be a little weird, a bit too fascinated with the dark side, but they aren't body snatchers. Nor corpse thieves. Grave robbers? Looters, maybe. I'll stick to looters.

MY MOM'S EMAIL RESPONSE ABOUT THE NAME OF THE LOCALE arrives a couple of hours later. She's asked my dad:

We're both trying to get our brains around it, but so far . . . I think it had three syllables. It's rattling around in my head. If I think of it, I'll email you back.

Since I am pretty sure Ancon sounds right, and my googling has unearthed another word that sounds familiar, I pick up the phone and call my folks, anxious to know what they can fill in, what I can't retrieve from my memory. When my mom answers, I don't say hello. I ask, "Was it Chancay? It doesn't sound familiar to me, but it looks right."

My mother replies, "Chancay? I don't know." Then another phone in the house picks up on her end. "Jaime, is that you? Was it Chancay?"

"That's the culture," my father says. "Chancay were the people. It was their gravesite."

"Do you remember the body?" I ask first. I want to know about that *National Geographic* fellow I watched unwound. I don't want to prompt my dad too much, but I want to see if his memory matches mine, if it matches the *National Geographic* video. "Was it wrapped in the fabric that we have on the wall?"

"*Tela*," my dad corrects me and feeds me the Spanish word for "fabric." Their house is filled with *telas*. Framed pieces of ancient cloth line one wall in my folks' house. Intricate geometric designs on camelid wool the color of dried blood, in small woven pieces, about the size of a license plate, hang on another wall. These are surrounded by the oil paintings of Texas Hill Country bluebonnets my dad has created since retirement.

"*Tela*," my dad repeats. "Yes, the body was in that position, that knees-up-to-the-chin—what's that called?" He's eighty-four, and his memory is disappearing for the things said over and over like "fetal position," although he can remember the Spanish word for cloth and the name of the culture that thrived north of Lima from 1000 to 1475 AD before the Inca conquest. He has always been the family member who recalls all details. Some of us even say he has a photographic memory. When his memory goes, so will the story archives. This is why I want him to confirm my memory of the embalmed body.

He has become frustrated that he can't remember the word. Then he recalls the right phrase, and we are off to the rest of the story.

"All the bodies were buried in the fetal position. Embalmed and wrapped in the cloth." Yes, just as the *National Geographic* websites concur. "The ground below their bodies would be stained where the fluids had leaked out. And the cloth stuck to their skin. Like taffy. Remember how the skin was like taffy the way it clung to the bones?" I can hear his smile as he describes it.

His memories can be overlaid with mine without too much slippage. To me, this makes them facts. I've seen a ghost—the body we dug up. It is true we dug up a grave. It is true that my family members are grave robbers. My nerve endings push themselves to the surface, make me want to slough off my own skin. I want to find a new body. I don't know where I belong. The body in the grave, the body we dug up, is now more recognizable than my family.

"We didn't find a body, did we?" my mother says. "There was no body."

"Sure, there was a body," I reply. As much as I don't want there to be a body, as much as the realization that my family were grave robbers has me wanting to seek cover, to find a new place to hide, her denial of the truth unearths more in me. It's ludicrous she doesn't remember a body. Now I am certain the body was exactly the way I remember it.

"The body was all wrapped up on that shelf. The shelf built into the wall," my father says.

"I don't remember a body," my mother says. "We were even more ghoulish, if we dug up a body."

Did she really not know? Her contradiction confounds me. Didn't we always say, *when we dug up the grave?* What's the main ingredient in a grave, if not a body?

"I don't remember the shelf." I evade my mother.

This is my memory of what happened graveside next:

The skeleton in the ground looked just like all the other skeletons my father had taken me to see at the Peruvian museums. With the body unwrapped, the diggers almost danced around it. I didn't see what there was to make all the hoopla about. All squatty and balled up, like the skeleton was afraid of being beaten.

"Look how long his hair is," Mrs. Riley said. The long black hair of the dead man had grown down around his pelvic bone. He could have sat on it in the school bus, as I could my own hair. But his hair was black and matted, caked with dried mud in places.

"The hair and fingernails keep growing after they die," my dad said. He always knew those kinds of things.

I craned my neck around the diggers who had gathered around the body now and tried to catch sight of the dead man's fingers. His hands curled in under his chin, so I couldn't see whether his nails were long like his hair. One of the diggers reached down and grabbed a handful of the black tresses and lifted the skull, separating it from the rest of the skeleton. Then, like a lasso, he twirled the long ponytail of black hair and the wide-eyed skull over his head a few times before tossing it out of the grave they had dug.

Mrs. Riley and my mom screamed, as the skull sank in the sand. I followed suit with a scream, until my dad laughed, then I laughed too. I don't recall being terrified like a normal eight-year-old might have been. This corpse was more of a specimen to me after all we had seen since moving first to Africa and then to Peru. A museum artifact, or it could have been.

Now I scramble to the edge to see what's inside.

"Jaime, you tell them to put that right back where they got it." My mom's jawbones manacled together as they did when she told me to stop doing whatever I was doing that was getting on her nerves. I watched closely, because in those days I wanted her never to be unhappy. Her elbows splayed out from her hips, her face shrunk inward. I wanted to stand by her, but, well, a grave breached between us.

My dad shouted in English, "Hey, go get that. We want it." He pointed to where the skull had landed. When the diggers turned around and saw my dad point, one quickly scrambled out of the grave hole and ran for the skull.

"MART, OF COURSE THERE WAS A BODY," MY FATHER ARGUES with my mom while I'm on the phone.

"We didn't have any respect for the dead. None. We were ghouls." She lets her own memory flit from one thought, one belief, one ideal to the next. Whatever suits her. Or does she? My own memories seem to decide on their own when to show up, so maybe hers do too. I listen to her deny the pile of bones we unearthed, but I also fixate on the word "ghouls." Something about me likes the idea of having a family made up of looters, grave robbers, and ghouls. The Munsters incarnate. When I was young, I knew my mom was every bit as beautiful as Lily Munster, my dad as goofy as Herman. It's funny, at first. Then maybe not so funny.

"I didn't know what we were doing," she repeats. "I had no idea." Her denial is vexing. *Denial*, the finest form of forgetfulness. She will insist she had no part in it until we agree with her. It's what she does. She wants it to go away. I would normally give in to her. Want her to see how loyal I am. But this story I cannot give away. Especially now that these memories are coming back to me like white horses pushing me under. I need to know all the facts. I need to start at the beginning, know how we got here. How we got there.

I ask how they knew where to go, and my mother replies, "Someone told us about it at the dinner party the night before."

"And they had said it was a burial site, so what did you think we were doing?" my father queries her.

They had a lot of dinner parties.

This is what I remember:

I stood on the toilet lid, leaning over the sink, trying not to block my mom's reflection as I gazed at my own in the corner of the mirror. My cheeks were pudgy. So I looked at my mom's face instead. She was prettier. She sprayed her frosted, blonde hair into a flip on the ends. The ladies at the beauty parlor did a much better job, but she tried to repeat what they did the next day, her hair always a little flatter, even though she slept on a pink, satin pillowcase. Sometimes she even wore a Shirley MacLaine wig. Short shag style, all the rage right then.

"What are you looking at?" she asked me.

"You," I admitted. "How much longer till the party?"

"Ten minutes. You can come down and say hello, but just until dinner." She took a sip of the drink that had been sitting in the metal cup holder where dangling toothbrushes surrounded it. It was a Salty Dog. She liked the bitter grapefruit taste. She licked her lips and left a coral lip print on the glass rim.

"Will the Nelsons be here?" I asked.

"No," she said. "It's not that group. It's the Rileys and some Peruvian and embassy friends."

"You're pretty," I told her. She took my face between her manicured fingers and kissed my forehead. Then she walked out of the bathroom, drink in hand. I looked in the mirror to check out the lip print on my forehead that matched the one on the rim of her glass. Throughout the evening, the ladies who came for the party would plant more lipstick kisses on my face. I wouldn't wipe them off. Instead, like a stamp collector, I gathered them in their different shades and imprints.

Later after the dinner party, where I stayed the whole night because my mother didn't notice, and my dad didn't tell, I stood on the toilet seat again as she brushed her teeth. I stared in the mirror at her. She'd been crying. She cried at parties.

"Americans are show-offs, aren't they?" I said.

"Pretty much," she said, "for the most part."

"I don't want to be American," I said.

"Not much you can do about it," she said. And she spit into the sink.

The next morning we packed the car to go on an excursion. It's what we did every weekend, went for a drive, a picnic, anything that got us out of the house, no matter where or what country we lived in. We drove in the Buick, the Land Rover, or the Toyota to out-of-the-way places. This weekend it was up *carretera Panamericana Norte*, the Panamerican Highway, to a location outside Lima their friends had talked about at the party last night. The Rileys were going with us, and my mom thought Mrs. Riley would pack a better picnic basket than she could. This was probably true, but I told her that whatever she packed would be better.

"WHEN WE FIRST ARRIVED, WE HAD TO DRIVE OVER THE TWO split logs. Remember that?" My father still tromps down cemetery lane.

I don't remember that detail at all. "Sounds scary," I say.

"No, no, they had a sense of humor. The Rileys' car wouldn't go over the logs, but ours would so we all piled in our car and drove over. Then we came around a corner and had to stop because there was a big mound of dirt. On top of the mound was a mummified skeleton propped up announcing the entrance to the cemetery." He laughs, he likes this part. We both do. Our dark senses of humor are complementary.

I should be writing this down, I think, but I don't, not yet, because I want to just listen and ask questions, to sift through the silt of memory and find mine, and see what matches, what doesn't, what might fit together, like a skeleton.

"There wasn't a body in the grave," my mom says again. "We never found a body. I would remember." I again have the vision of her yelling at the diggers to retrieve the skull they flung out of the grave.

"Sure we did," my father says. "Remember, I kept the skull for years. A prince, he had that silver band around his forehead."

I hadn't remembered the silver band until he mentions it on the phone call. But now I recall how that was the determining factor that the body we had unearthed was valuable, was a person worthy of respect. Or, I guess, respect during his lifetime. A crown—silver, or maybe it was tin—meant royalty. To us.

"Oh gads, that's right," my mom says. "We kept that skull in the pantry." Her memories come in lightning bolts, like mine.

"No, that was Marty's skull," I say. "He found it and kept it to make a lamp. It sat in our pantry until it didn't."

"Marty wasn't there," my dad says.

My mind comes to a jolting halt, as though while shoveling sand I've hit titanium, and the blow jars me. Marty is the beginning of my tale. He was always the part I knew was true. Why is my brother in my memory so clearly? I know I heard his voice over the sand dune. Why can I still see how he held up that skull and showed me the jawbone? Why do I remember him, if he wasn't there?

"But I remember him there," I say to my parents, expecting them to come around to my perspective.

I remember his traipsing over the sand dune just like the memory of the mummy I so distinctly recognized, and which my father confirmed. No, I don't want this memory of Marty to go away, to not be true. I need him to be there, otherwise I would have been alone. I would have been hiding on the other side of that dune with the scattered bones all alone. Who would have come over the dune to find me? I make the decision I will keep this memory. A truth exists inside that memory that I am not ready to relinquish. A ghost I saw that I will keep to myself.

"We were ghouls," my mom announces. We have been leaving her out of the conversation, and she wants us to pay attention. "I know it's hard to believe that I didn't know, but I didn't—but if I had, I wouldn't have—I couldn't believe we were doing that. Digging up a grave. If I had known—"

I can't stand her faux denial anymore. "What?" I ask her. "If you knew, you wouldn't have taken all the pottery home and used it to decorate the house?" My tone is sharp, too sharp. She will excoriate me for this, but I've lost patience and want to stop her repudiation. I can picture her living room where the pieces of fabric are framed behind museum-quality glass, the pottery is filled with dried cattails and lines the hallway to the bedrooms, and the Nigerian mahogany hand-carved chest is stuffed with silks from Asia that she bought to sew dresses and pantsuits, but that still lie folded, unstitched, fabrics never used. Carved ivory tusks sit on ebony pedestals on the chest next to the giant thorn carvings.

"We were ghouls," she repeats, a sting in her voice. "Hideous people."

Hideous. She does not refer just to herself. She refers to the past. And to the present. I will pay for disagreeing, she warns. She refers to all of us. We are all hideous. None of us innocent.

I carry on with my quest. My quest for what lies between innocence and guilt.

"Didn't you have to bribe the movers to get all the stuff out of the country?" I ask my dad.

This is how I remember the story:

A bribe was given to the moving company so we wouldn't be reported to the Peruvian government for stealing national artifacts.

"I took the *tela* and the pots to the British Embassy the next week," my mom says, "and asked whether we shouldn't have this stuff, but the woman there, the muckety-muck, what was she?"

"British Embassy liaison," Dad fills in.

"Yeah, that's it," my mom replies, "and she said, 'Good gosh no, the Peruvian government has warehouses of that stuff. They don't want it.'"

In my inquiry, I had come across a *Washington Post* article detailing the court case of an inheritance, of a man selling Peruvian artifacts, of jail time served. "Portions of coastal Peru are so rich in ancient gravesites dug up by robbers that 'from an airplane, it looks like the area has been bombed,' the consul general said." "Humanity," the article argues, "is who owns these antiquities, not individuals."

Humanity. Hideous. Who are we?

I repeat my question: "But didn't you have to bribe the movers?"

"Naw, I just gave them that skull and told them it was theirs if they packed the pieces really well so nothing broke. I didn't want any of it to break."

"We were ghouls. We had no respect. If had known——." My mother won't quit pleading her innocence. Won't quit declaring our guilt.

What I didn't know when I squatted at the graveside, but found out later, was that the hair and nails don't keep growing. It's the decomposition of the layers of flesh and the plumpness of skin deflating that make the nails and hair look like they have grown. It's all a matter of perspective.

Years ago I heard a *Radiolab* podcast about memory. Hosts Jad Abumrad and Robert Krulwich interviewed scientists, and these are snippets of what I learned: Memories are not stored in filing cabinets or hard drives in our brain. Memory is a bridge over a chasm. It's a physical thing made of proteins. A cellular construction. Re-creating the memory, the act of remembering, is an act of creation. It's an act of imagination. What you're remembering is the memory reinterpreted in the light of today. Each time you remember it's a brand-new memory. Every time you remember, you rewrite it. The more you remember it, the less accurate it becomes. All you have is the most recent recollection. The more often you tell the memory, the more it becomes about you, and the less it becomes about what actually happened.

Memory, I realize, is also a decomposition, a revised perspective.

"DO YOU REMEMBER HOW THE BODY WAS WRAPPED?" I ASK again. If my brother was missing from the original story, I have to confirm the essential ingredient—the body. The body my mother wants to deny, the body I want to confirm. Now a headless body. "I have a memory of layers and layers of *tela* wrapped around the body, and we peeled it off." Or, maybe, it occurs to me, I want to erase the memory. I want my father to deny it, so that like my mother, I can say it never happened.

One phone line clicks off. My mother has hung up. Her absence itches like an old yellow jacket sting.

"That's exactly right," my dad says. "They peeled it all back to reveal the body. But remember, it was on a shelf, the embalmed body sat on a shelf with bowls of food laid out like an offering, like it was supper for the gods." This supper triggers more mental images for me.

"Remember the dog?" my father says.

I recall the dog:

I was crouched again on the edge of the big hole they'd dug. If I fell in, what would happen? I teetered with my rubber Keds, toes on the brink, waiting, hoping my mom would say to get away from the edge. I carefully watched her standing next to the opposite side. I was afraid it was she who would fall into the grave. I scooted back when they rolled away a big, flat stone like a car tire and underneath lay a flattened, little skeleton—a dog.

"Sending the dog to the other side with its master," Mrs. Riley said from where she stood next to my mom, too close to the berm.

I stood up and took another step away from the dusty, sunken edge. Pebbles crashed into the tomb. I didn't want to fall into a hole where they killed the dog to bury it with its master. I couldn't quit staring at the dog skeleton, lying on its side, as though it napped in the sun. If I whistled, I thought, it would lift its head, its ears would periscope around, searching for a familiar voice. It'd have spots and wag its tail. We'd had to give away our dog when we moved overseas, it was either that or a six-month quarantine for the twelve-pound poodle. I still remember our pooch looking at me out the back window of the pickup as his new owners drove off with him. I didn't understand that, and I didn't understand this dog buried with its master. Who does this?

Often my mom spoke about her belief of going to the next life; she read about it in her Shirley MacLaine books. She believed in reincarnation. She told me about being buried with what she would need or want. She never mentioned me. I wanted her to say she would take me with her into the next life. Now I saw how the dog's life was shortened, and I realized how it would have to work.

I had never thought about body and soul as separate from bones because I couldn't get my head around how the dog skeleton could still be there if the intent was to go to the other side. If it had traveled to the next life with its master, wouldn't the spot under the rock be empty? Wouldn't the grave be empty? The pots serving supper should have been whisked away to another place, not still be there waiting. Killing the dog was an abortive attempt at what was merely a belief, an imagining, and this realization had me scrambling to get as far away from the threshold of the grave as I could. I wished I could grab my mom's hand and yank her away too. I wanted my mother to exist in this realm only, with me. Both of us living here and now forever, together.

"THEN UNDERNEATH THE BODY WERE ALL THE REALLY BIG pots with rounded bottoms," my father tells me on the phone. "The pots sat better in the sand as ovoids." My dad the geologist loves this kind of history. "Inside each pot, dirt was filled to the brim, but encased in the dirt were corn kernels, dried corncobs, teensy bird bones, or guinea pig bones, or tiny animals served as food. We left those carcasses on the ground, but loaded the car with the pottery and fabric."

I remember the pots with the tiny bird bones. Tiny skeletons the size of my thumb:

In the smaller bowls were bird and guinea pig bones. Food for the afterlife. Now it was pretty clear to me that there was no afterlife because this fellow we dug up didn't take any of this stuff with him. The dog: a wasted sacrifice. Proof the afterlife didn't exist sat waiting loyally in the grave. The Peruvian boys whom my parents and their friends had hired hoisted the pots onto the graveside. The hole was dug six feet deep, and the boys, not tall enough, had to stretch in order to hand the pots out to Mr. Riley, my dad, my mom, and Mrs. Riley, who each laid them out on the ground.

I once again crept to the edge and sat on my haunches. I wanted to be close to the excavation, to not miss anything. The dirt underneath me crumbled into the grave, tiny landslides from the weight of my bum. I knocked in more dirt, hoping my mom would look my way. I checked to see whether the ground was steady beneath her crepe-soled shoes. She gaped at the relics being lifted out, pottery as big as me and as small as a communion cup. Sculptures of monkeys and ants. Cloths that smelled dirt-dead.

"REMEMBER THE CAR THAT DROVE BY SLOWLY WHILE WE were digging?" my father asks. "The boys went running off over the hill and out of sight when they saw that car coming. They didn't want to get in trouble. It was against the law what they were doing." But weren't *we* doing it, I wonder, but don't say. "The boys returned as soon as the car was out of sight."

My dad continues. "Then remember when we got in our own car, and as soon as we drove off, the Peruvian boys took off as fast as they could over the sand dunes back toward the grave?"

"Yeah," I say, "I remember." I remember, because this is the part my folks always told at the end of the story. Despite my mother's rant of denials about that day, they used to tell this story often. I did too, years ago, before I understood what we did. But do I really remember the boys running off? I don't. I imagine it. I have a visual of the young men, dashing away from the cars, up and over the sand dune out of sight.

"We figured they were heading back to get the really valuable stuff buried deeper—the gold." Dad loves that part, the part where we got rubbed by the ruse.

I don't believe that part. I don't think there was anything buried below. But everyone else believes it because the band of silver around the skull indicated the embalmed body belonged to a prince, an elite.

"Probably the gold was underneath the body." My dad is certain the corpse lay on top of gold.

"Probably," I say, because it's his memory, and it's best not to erase any of them, true, false, ghoulish or not.

THE CARS WERE LOADED DOWN. WE FILLED THE RILEYS' STATION wagon and our Corona's trunk with pots and fabrics. The adults split the treasure, decided who got what pot. They divided it equally. You get one pot, we get one. You get a bigger pot, we get a pot and an extra *tela*. Mommy liked the pot with the sculpted monkeys on the handles. Mrs. Riley wanted the extra-large pot that wouldn't fit in our trunk, the pot the size of a chubby sixth-grader. Maybe we traded it for the skull. But no, I suppose Daddy was the only one who wanted to keep the skull. We drove back on a dirt road that spilt out onto La Carretera Panamericana. As we waited at an intersection to pull out, to reenter Lima's city limits, I watched the traffic, examined the seven-foot concrete walls bordering the wide road, and breathed the soot-filled air. Fanta and Braniff ads were painted on the walls, both in brilliant but dusty orange. Then I noticed red letters as tall as could fit on the wall. I had to sound out the words, "Yan. Qui." Painted sloppily, ¡Yanqui Go Home!

DAYS LATER I READ ANOTHER *NATIONAL GEOGRAPHIC* ARTICLE from 2005 that says the Peruvians who built houses over the graves of another pre-Columbian graveyard are beleaguered by illness. They believe they are cursed by the *huaca*, the ancient Inca state of being after death, or spirits. Scientists say it's the bacteria from the groundwater that leeched contaminants from the graves.

I call home again. I share my new information with my mother first. "There's a curse on those who messed with those graves like we did."

"That's why I have all these allergies," she replies, matter-of-factly. She is allergic to everything from paper to pickles. She is not allergic to potatoes. Fortunately, vodka is made from potatoes. And my mother believes in curses.

I hear a mumbling in the background. "It's Amy," she says.

Then to me, "Your dad's home. I'll let him talk to you."

"Thanks," I say, appreciative of the approval.

"There's a curse," I tell my father first thing through the phone. "Digging up the grave means your life is cursed."

"My life cursed?" he sounds surprised. "You mean, instead of just one Cadillac, I could have had two?"

MONTHS LATER, STILL GRIPPED BY THE NEED TO FIND OUT what parts of the story are true, I google Peruvian graves again, and this time I watch a 2007 YouTube video "Looting Inca Graves—Peru."

I recognize the iron prods the looters use to poke at the soil for places to dig and to find artifacts. I know the hillsides and gravelly sand dunes. The arid landscape. The video explains the underserved Peruvian population loots the graves to supplement their income, that agriculture has fallen off with the drought, and by looting they find gold to sell. So there really was gold. In 2007 the looters still find gold, so my dad's ending—the diggers' race for the real treasure— was more than likely the truth in 1972.

I call my brother to find out the truth about the skull. What happened to it?

"They kept it in the pantry, and then they gave it away. Dad promised it to me. I was going to make a lamp," he said. I remembered it in the pantry. In the depths of our big, walk-in pantry, the skull sat eye-level with me, staring out at our kitchen area. "But I wasn't at the gravedigging."

"You weren't there?" I say, disappointed. It feels as if I've awakened from reality only to find out that my brother is part of a dream instead. But while he speaks, I also hear that the giveaway of the promised skull is a betrayal. "Dad promised it to me." But our father had given it away so easily, as though it were the piece of the treasure that didn't matter to him, the piece he could use as barter to make his favorite pieces, the most valuable, safe.

My family, our treasures, who we were before we moved overseas, to Africa, to South America, we each hold on to what we want, what we need. No matter how fortunate we become, we are all still scared we will lose what was never ours. I know I have clung to every person, every story, every memory for dear life.

Are we ghouls? Are we hideous? Are we cursed? Am I?

I have to start over. I have to go back to how we got here. I have to examine my own perspective. Because this wasn't my first dead body.

PART 1

NIGERIA

I believe in everything until it's disproved.
So I believe in fairies, the myths, dragons.
It all exists, even if it's in your mind. Who's
to say that dreams and nightmares aren't as
real as the here and now?

—John Lennon

FIG. 1. Amy, seven, in Ely, Nevada. Courtesy of the author.

Redneck Arrival

> If there's anything in the world I hate, it's
> leeches—filthy little devils!
>
> —Charlie Allnut played by Humphrey Bogart in
> *African Queen*

A FRAMED PHOTO OF MY DAD SITS ON A NIGHTSTAND IN MY
parents' guest room. The photo, black and white, depicts the jungle
in the background, colored over in green crayon by my artistic seven-
year-old hand. Or at least that's what my mom told me—that I had
childishly defaced the photo. My brother said it had been a photography class project, and he had marked it up. Whoever it was, the
interpretation is spot on: my dad's face and neck are colored in with
a vermillion crayon. In the summers my dad always had a farmer's tan,
which my mother claims as proof we were rednecks. My father stands,
one leg on the bumper of a Land Rover, one elbow on his bent knee,
holding a cigarette. A Winston, I can promise, because that's all he
ever smoked, no matter where we lived. He wears khakis and a T-shirt.
And Justin Roper boots, the one true sign of his Texas upbringing.

My father's aspiration was to own his own Phillips 66 filling station
in Uvalde, Texas. He was a man of determination and hard work,
so to get his proverbial foot in the door, he took a job with Phillips

Petroleum Company searching for places to drill in oil-rich Texas and Louisiana with the local seismograph crews. Over time the company offered him a new job in worldwide oil exploration, and his gas station became a small, forgotten dream. Resembling John Wayne in both character and looks, he never looked back when offered the opportunity to explore the Everglades, the Sierra Nevadas, and eventually the African bush, Amazon jungles, and the Andes.

But before we went overseas, my dad worked for Kennecott Mines in Ely, Nevada. In Ely, the console TV's bigger screen only magnified the mountain reception's staticky picture. So we preferred the tiny twelve-inch in Mom and Dad's room. The little TV was the television on which we had watched the first moon landing, so maybe we had a soft spot for it. My folks had a little sitting area around a fireplace in their bedroom, and on snowy nights, which could be 365 days a year in Ely, that was the coziest spot in the house.

When Dad called to say we were being transferred to Africa, we were watching *The African Queen* starring Humphrey Bogart and Katharine Hepburn. That's the anecdote the family has always told, although now I find it too coincidental to be true. Still, I share the same anecdote, and I add how I remember it: The movie had reached the part where Humphrey Bogart peeled leeches off Katharine Hepburn as they sat in the eponymous steamboat. Or maybe it was Hepburn pulling the leeches off Bogart. It doesn't matter, leeches are leeches, and my skin crawled.

Watching *African Queen,* my mom sat on the black hard-backed chair she'd antiqued with early American eagle appliqués, and Marty lay on his stomach with his chin propped on his fists on the red shag carpeting. My sister, Suzanne, sat in the big cushy chair Mom had reupholstered herself using moss green, nubby fabric and thumbtacks as rivets. Suzanne sat sideways in the chair, leaning against one round arm, her legs hanging over the other arm. I was either splayed out on the red shag carpeted floor next to Marty or hanging off the end of Mom and Dad's bed.

When the aqua Princess phone on the nightstand next to Mom's side of the bed rang, I answered it. I answered every possible call that came in, dashing to the phone, hoping it would be Dad on the other end. But anyone was good news.

After I first said hello, I heard the long delay, then the swoosh swoosh like the call passed underwater, which it did. The words distant, like the ocean waves inside the pink nautilus shell Mom kept on the toilet tank in every house we ever lived in. I knew immediately who was at the other end of the line, whose voice I waited for. I held my breath because any sound I made could interrupt the response, could send back another round of echoes. I pictured the telephone cable as thick as our living room sofa laid down across the ocean floor, my dad's voice undulating all the way across the vast Atlantic, then across the United States to get to us in Nevada. It both came too slow and too quick for as far as the voice had to travel.

"Amy . . . how would you like to live in Africa?" he said. My father always asked questions like he was elated about the idea.

My mom stood next to me; I had waved her over when I heard the long, transatlantic pause after my first hello. "It's Daddy," I had mouthed. He had left six months before, gone to see about a project, is all I knew. He often went on business trips, to the mines or to visit the drilling crews. I wanted to give my mom the phone, let her answer his question, but he was waiting for me. "Amy," he had said. He had asked *me*.

Would I have to leave all my friends again? All I knew of Africa was Tarzan, the boring Sunday afternoon TV show. And leeches.

My mom snatched the phone from my hand before the right question, the right response, could form in my head, before it could navigate all the way back to him.

WE WOULD TRAVEL FROM ELY, NEVADA, A SMALL SILVER MINING town over six thousand feet above sea level with a population of 2,500, to Lagos, Nigeria, as close to sea level as you can get without drowning, with a population of over eight million people.

We sold all our belongings. Not that we had anything valuable.

Mostly yard sale items appliquéd and reupholstered. We were allowed to keep our more sentimental possessions. My most paramount possession was my Barbie doll collection. I had never played with baby dolls, but Barbie didn't even go in the shipment. I packed Barbie and Ken in my Samsonite Naugahyde carry-on, slung the shoulder strap over my head and across my chest, and lugged them through all the airports between Nevada and Nigeria. Moving was unnerving enough; getting rid of all that was familiar was downright scary, so my family of twelve-inch dolls and the microcosm I had created for them would not be left in the hands of Mayflower movers.

Like Barbie, my mom retained her figure. Mom liked to point out that her own ballet-length wedding dress, now in the cedar chest, had an eighteen-inch waist. And Mom still had her eighteen-inch waist. The cedar chest filled with our baby mementos, winter sweaters, and her wedding dress, would go to Mommom and Papa's, Mom's parents' house in Uvalde.

I would no longer receive king-size bags of peanut M&Ms from Papa. Papa had kept me well stocked in the candy he claimed he picked from trees. He wrapped the M&Ms in brown paper sacks folded over and over then sealed with masking tape, my name and address written in blue-ink scrawl inside the square boundary of yellowed tape. Any packages sent to Nigeria would have arrived, if they arrived, long after any expiration date, so no one bothered mail anything other than an aerogram or thin, airmail envelope. When I was told my M&M supply would be cut off, I felt double-crossed and wanted to rethink this transfer to Africa, the land of no peanut M&Ms.

Mom chose her Singer sewing machine to take to Lagos and packed the Christmas decorations in better boxes to be shipped. Dad sent his hunting rifles to Granma's house in Texas. And we took our first ride in a jet airplane.

I didn't know it yet, but my family of five, all lined up in the middle seats of the 747 jumbo jet, would slowly disperse. Maybe I had a sense of their pending disappearance because I kept that Naughahyde carry-on, Barbie's tomb filled with all her belongings and companions, tight against my chest for the entire trip.

My father's new contract was with an Italian oil company, Agip Oil. In order to absorb the time and fear of flying in a 747 for the first time in our lives, the first time for us even to be on a plane, my mother decided we would learn Italian, and so she bought a phrase book. I learned one phrase on the last leg from Milan to Lagos: *non lo desídero.* I do not want it. To this day, it is all the Italian I remember. The first time I used it was after my mother pounded on the airplane bathroom door.

"Amy, what's taking you so long?" I could hear her panicked voice through the flimsy door.

"I'm doing Barbie's laundry," I replied. That miniature sink, the tiny faucets, the whole room Barbie-sized, I couldn't resist. Barbie sat spread eagle on the small, stainless steel counter watching me rinse out her ball gown.

"Amy!" my mom said. She tried the knob. I had failed to lock it. Her head popped in, and her eyes nearly popped out when she saw the damp Barbie clothes spread out around the room. "There's a line out here! You have to come back to your seat."

"I'm busy," I told her. I still had a couple of pantsuits to wash. The flight was terribly boring. Shouldn't Mom be glad I'd found something to do?

"Amy," she said first in panic and then from between gritted teeth, "the line is down the aisle. You need to come out now." She snatched up my carefully arranged, damp laundry and naked Barbie, then grabbed my wrist.

"Non lo desídero!" I told her as she pulled me from Barbie's Laundromat.

THAT WAS, MORE OR LESS, HOW WE ENDED UP LIVING IN Lagos in 1971. My father says it was where, as Southerners, we had our eyes opened. But Mom says redneck eyes take forever to open, if they ever do. For me, there's a sliver of time when my eyes wouldn't close, even to blink, but not out of any kind of search for understanding. I wasn't that aware. More out of fear, of being afraid that if I blinked, one more person would disappear.

TO THIS DAY, I CAN'T SMELL DIESEL AND NOT BE REMINDED of the drive from the Lagos International airport on Lagos Island to our house on Ikoyi Island inside a compound that consisted of two large two-story houses for oil company families, the Griffins' and ours. In the back of the compound, behind a tall wall sat the servants' quarters. The Quarters, we called them. Our previous houses certainly had never had The Quarters, but instead were rundown rentals lucky to have a yard. Like the one-story, three-bedroom, one-bath house in Nevada, the greatest luxury being the new linoleum installed in the bathroom when the pipes burst one winter. To brighten up a dingy room, my mother made a lampshade from a coffee can spray-painted white and decorated with plastic daisies.

But here in Lagos, Portuguese for "lakes," we were on the western Africa coastline, made up of islands in the Bay of Guinea in the Southern Atlantic Ocean: Victoria, Ikoyi, and Lagos Islands. Our house was a two-story glass-sided contemporary complete with a gateman, a night watchman, a steward, a gardener who mowed the lawn with a machete, and a nanny. The latter just for me. Built-in babysitter. *Non lo desídero.* "It's not necessary," my mother told the oil company escort. "We're used to doing things on our own. We don't need help." By "help," she meant assistance, not servants. But they came with the house. We were no longer the beans-and-cornbread-for-supper Wallens.

My first nanny was our steward, Phillip's wife, Okinaya. She was so shy, she would hide in the servants' quarters and not come out, so I didn't really have a nanny at all. Then Mom hired Martha, who finally had to be fired because she drank all of Dad's whiskey, which was hard to come by. He bought bootleg from the slick Nigerian man who drove his long, black Chrysler New Yorker into the compound.

Standing in the hot, Nigerian sun, my father and our compound neighbor, Mr. Griffin, and other men gathered around the long trunk of the Chrysler and picked out cases to stock their supply of booze and cigarettes. I stood off to the side, peering into the trunk from afar, watching the clandestine act. Intoxicated by the nicotine from the cigs they'd lit up and the wafting aroma of whiskey as the J&B Black Label was tested, I watched my dad joke with his buddies, negotiate for an extra box of cigarettes or bottle of booze, and surreptitiously hand over rolls of quid. To my young eyes, something sneaky was going on. Where there's an American will for liquor in a Muslim country, there's a way to buy it. We had a new way of life, and it didn't include the Piggly Wiggly anymore.

My next and last nanny was Alice. I loved Alice, her bosom so deep, I would fall inside when she clutched me tight, and her bottom so big it jutted out like a table behind her. Alice could make me laugh even when there was nothing to laugh about.

It was Alice who looked after me. Here we'd landed in the land of perpetual summer, and I was not allowed to go barefoot. I was given a pair of flip-flops, and Mom told me never to leave the house without them on my feet or I would get hookworm. And a spanking. The hookworms, my dad explained, make their way from the soles of your feet, through your blood stream to your heart. Then they travel to your intestines, where they dine for years. Even under the threat of a spanking and little, yellow hookworms burrowing through the pink soles of my feet, I tried to get away with going barefoot. So, whenever I left the house sans shoes, Alice chased after me waggling the rubber thongs in the air. She would make certain those worms did not drill into my heart.

My Baptism

There's always a light at the end of the sewer.

—Tudy Wolfe

THE OIL COMPANIES PAID TUITION FOR THEIR TRANSPLANTED employees' kids at the American International School Lagos, but the grades went only as high as eighth grade. My brother and sister were starting the eleventh and twelfth grades, respectively, so they were to attend The American School in Switzerland, a boarding school thousands of miles away from me. *Non lo desídero.*

This is when the disappearances started.

My siblings leaving for school was more than just something I didn't want. Their absence resembled a tearing in two of my world: a world I remembered in the States and a new world from which something very essential had gone missing. The world I would now live in had no ties, except my mother, to the old life. The life I'd had with my brother and sister at home, or coming home any minute now, was over. I would now become an only child. With a more-or-less single mother.

LOSING MY GRIP ON MY FAMILY FELT TEMPORARY AT FIRST, time that had been stretched not to my liking. My dad had always traveled for work, so "gone to the bush" most weeks wasn't much

32

different from "off on hot shot" in Louisiana. But my siblings away at boarding school, albeit speckled with holidays home in Lagos, confused me. No more coming home from school and sharing peanut butter sandwiches. A time warp of sorts had occurred. Like they'd gone to school, only it took so much longer for them to come home. Months. They'd gone to school halfway around the world. It seemed as though I was perpetually waiting. The days appeared tilted in the wrong direction. I didn't understand distance like "halfway around the world" yet. Time, when you're seven, is in increments of play vs. boredom.

"Come on, Amy, let's go." I heard my favorite words from my brother. I followed Marty everywhere. Any moment spent with him was pure mirth. It was the day before their first departure. Marty and I left the compound with its red hibiscus bushes growing taller than the bamboo fences, umbrella trees shading the grass, and big, fat bumble bees buzzing around the elephant ear bushes. We entered Omo Osagie Street, which swam with people, Nigerians on their way to market, tradesmen going house to house, sandals slapping the soles of pink-bottomed feet, bicycle bells dinging. Nigerian women balletically towered along the side of the asphalt, wearing brightly colored *lappas*, yards of fabric wrapped around and around their bodies, and baskets filled with you-name-its balanced perfectly on their heads. In contrast, the open sewer on either side of the road teemed with all of humankind's detritus, both fecal and random household trash. Debris piled high against the concrete walls of the surrounding compounds. Even here in the most exclusive part of Lagos, Ikoyi Island, with the green, yellow, and orange tropical birds fluttering, the palm trees fanning overhead, the ocean air just a few blocks over, nothing could escape the jungle heat, making the sewer's smell swell in the oxygen we inhaled.

We headed toward the marina, walked around the curve at the end of Omo Osagie Street, and turned right onto Awolowo Road. We walked along the marina's wide sidewalk, bordered on one side by lapping bay water and a busy city street, cars honking, on the other.

The water slapped against the short concrete barrier on the other side. In the distance, greasy and unkempt oil tankers sat side-by-side with a few cargo ships stained black with soot from their smokestacks and the seeping oil buried deep in their bellies. All that separated Marty and me from the water was a short but thick concrete wall. The wall was so short even I could lean over and dangle my hand, if I wanted to, that is. In the water, thick bunches of paper and rags and old plastic cartons, all wrapped in seaweed, bumped up against the edge of the marina wall. The refuse's rank smell was outdone only by the Awolowo Road's diesel and tire rubber wafting in the heat.

As we looked over the edge of the wall at the trash, Marty said he was going to throw me in. I knew he wouldn't do it, but the idea of it scared me, and I loved being scared. I liked for my stomach to flip-flop, like when we watched scary movies together. It meant I was daring like my brother. My older brother crush was so big I would have swum ten miles in that polluted water for him. His eyes, dark brown like mine, lit up when he smiled. His smile revealed a front tooth broken in half at a diagonal. He said that when he was older he was going to have a gold cap made for that tooth. I knew that would make him only more handsome. Alas, he became an English literature professor rather than the gold-toothed rock star he perhaps longed to be.

Marty leaned farther over the edge of the seawall. "Look," he said, pointing toward a big clump of wet dreck. I thought he was just trying to draw me closer, so he could pretend to throw me in. I was on to his shenanigans. It wasn't that I thought he would really do it, I was more afraid of the prospect that he could make a mistake, and I would fall in by accident. By accident, the possibility of this was what scared me most.

"I don't see anything," I said. I didn't want to lean too far over, still worried it was a trick, and he would try to push me. I had to be at the ready for anything he might try, yet I was giddy with excitement. I wanted my brother to know how much I loved him.

"You're not leaning over far enough," he told me. "You can't see it from there."

I leaned just a little farther. "What is it?"

"A body," he said.

Then I saw it. The body of a Nigerian man bumped against the side of the wall, same as the water slapping the rest of the offal. Mixed with trash, gray and brown and bloated with yellowed edges, his whole body appeared to be heaving.

We didn't speak.

Marty leaned a little closer, and so did I. I knew he wouldn't throw me in. My hands clutched the gritty concrete, and the odors slid up my nasal passages, colliding with the part of my brain that holds memory, my ears overloaded with traffic roars and honks, while my eyes burned with stain.

I looked up at the horizon. Past the ships, past the long bridges between the islands, and out of sight were my school and the execution amphitheater.

"Day before yesterday Daddy said a man was executed by the Nigerian army. Do you think this is the guy who was executed?" I pictured a firing squad and wondered whether the man was a criminal. Was this moment menacing or ghoulish? A kind of shame in not knowing the right thing to say about a dead man moved around in me. I wanted Marty to see me in the best light. I scooted an inch or two closer to him.

He didn't move when my forearm rested against his. "No, this guy's too swollen," he said.

I looked at my brother for what to do, how we did this. We weren't supposed to stare, but he was staring. So I stared.

Once we'd come across a tiny bird on the sidewalk. I squatted next to it. A baby bird. But not a little bird. It appeared naked to me without feathers. Its skin so translucent I could almost see the bones.

When I reached my finger out to touch it, Marty said, "Don't. It's dead." Like with the man in the marina, I wanted to understand what had happened to the bird. "How did he die?" I asked. "He fell." We both looked up to the sky to the tree overhead for a nest.

The marine layer had rolled into the bay. Gray clouds would

dump tropical rain in an hour. I knew this man did not fall from the sky. But so many similarities existed between him and the bird. The twisted and limp neck. And while this man didn't have the same bright yellow beak, his lips were white and stood out against his gray skin. The bird's skin had glowed translucent and rubbery. No feathers except the tiniest inkling on the wing: minuscule, wet, and black, they were the size of my smallest hair clips. The only color had been the bright yellow beak and the black wings. A crow, my brother had said. He knew. He was smart. Was that my first encounter with something dead? An embryonic raven?

Throughout my life I had come across dead animals. My friends would squeal and avert their eyes or walk briskly away. Not me. I'd poke it with a stick. This is what I did. It was dead, after all. What was I to be afraid of? Was I attracted to death? Did I attract death? Dead bodies.

I had never watched anything die, just come across things already dead. If I found something dying, like my friend who found the sick baby squirrel, took it home, and nursed it with a bottle, would I do that? Or would I poke it with a stick?

THE FLOATING MAN'S LEGS WERE LONG AND NAKED, KNOBBY-KNEED like the bird's. Trash wrapped around his feet. Newspapers, etc. The body fascinated and grossed me out. Like the bird, I didn't want him to be dead. But he was. Did I know what dead was at that age? Did I understand the stillness was so much different? Was it in my DNA? When I think back, when I'm counting the dead bodies in my head now, I am aware I could not have known the difference between sleeping and dead. I would have poked either one with a stick. I hated it when my mom took a nap. I'd stare at her the same way. I'd poke her to see if she'd wake up.

But it wasn't just the bodies. It was the Biafran war, the stories about death that I listened to like other kids might hear princess stories. I couldn't care less about being a princess with long, golden hair fit for tossing out a window for a prince.

The waves flipped the body over and a piece of *The Sun* newspaper wrapped around the dead man's neck.

"He's been here awhile," Marty said.

Then the corpse was heaved under by a wave. When he bobbed to the surface again, the straps of half a rubber sandal adorned his wrist.

I didn't look at his eyes. I knew they would be turned inside out, the white parts tinged orange. I was glad that Marty wanted to stare, because I wanted to stare too.

EVEN THIS WASN'T MY FIRST DEAD HUMAN. I HAD STEPPED over them in the street when Mom and I walked to the market. The concept of a person being dead, gone forever, hadn't fully formed in my consciousness yet. How was I to make sense of a state of being, or not being—a human being like any other lying prone on the sidewalk, up against the curb maybe, or curled up against a concrete wall? My mother's way of dealing with it was to barrel through, to not look down, to yank on my hand signaling me to hurry it up. My way was to look at everything, to figure out as much as I could, as fast as I could, before I was told to stop.

"Mommy, what's wrong with him?" I asked as we stepped over the legs of a man appearing to lounge against the wall.

"Don't stare," she said. "He might just be sleeping." But I knew you didn't sleep with your tongue hanging out and your eyes rolled.

So many things to stare at in Nigeria, and I was so rarely allowed to stare. But if I couldn't look, I couldn't understand.

"Are they really dead?" I asked as we traipsed through Bhojson's grocery store parking lot, me holding her hand tighter, she squeezing so hard my knuckles crunched together. When I remember the pressure on my knuckles, I suspect she was more afraid than I was. How could she have had any idea where she would end up with this move from Nevada to Nigeria? Her seven-year-old charge not letting her ignore the setting.

"They probably just fell asleep and didn't wake up," Mom said.

It wasn't just corpses. It was also the beggars, the poor and starving, who ran between cars with their hands outstretched. "Madam, madam," they said. "A shilling, madam." She scooted her handbag up onto her shoulder more securely. I pulled my long braid around to the front of my neck, afraid a hand would yank it from the back.

Their eyes could be sunken, or even missing, and yet they smiled at me. The boys with festering wounds on their arms and legs still shoved and played with their fellow beggars. Sometimes they could be so physically grotesque with limbs so infected that, despite my curiosity, my eyes would divert themselves.

"Please, madam, please, just one shilling."

The beggars on little wooden carts zoomed between the lanes of cars and sidled up beside me with only the slick click, click, click of the ball-bearing wheels on the asphalt. I'd heard at my folks' dinner parties that they rode on carts because their legs had been chopped off. Their parents or they themselves axed off limbs for more sympathy, for more shillings. What kind of parent did that, I remembered thinking? The toughened, callused pads that had grown over where their knees should have been were black with grime and grit, but it crossed my mind how much more fun it would be to be a beggar on a little cart with wheels. I mean, if one had to be a beggar.

The beggars stuck an infected arm in my face, grabbed at me— their way of getting more sympathy from Mom, of trying to shock for money. If they had no hands, they reached with their callused foot, which felt hard and crusty on my skin, and I cringed. Mom yanked me away, whispering in my ear, with what sounded like anger. "Don't let them touch you."

"Mommy, can't we give a shilling to this one?" I'd pull on her arm, fully engaged with the urchins.

She crunched my fingers together tighter, focused on getting to the front doors of the air-conditioned grocery store. "No, Amy, we can't give any shillings. They'll just swarm."

I sucked in my breath. To hinder the odor of staph, yes, but the held breath was like a pause button—it kept their world from entering my world. To be dead was one thing, but to have to live and suffer was another. Of the beggars, I was most afraid. Not afraid of them doing anything to me. Afraid I could catch what they had, could so easily become one of them. And if I became one, I would die a horrible death. Weren't *they* the hideous people with their boil-covered skin?

I hurried in the air-conditioned Bhojson's with Mom.

I STARED AT THE DEAD MAN IN THE MARINA, MY ARM AGAINST Marty's. I didn't think about how the man could have died. I looked at how his black skin was turning a powdery gray, how his lips were gone, how the little fish nibbled at the thin threads of algae on his elbow.

"I'd rather die in my sleep than be executed," I told Marty, trying to sound smart. "They execute you if you do anything wrong here." My parents never worried whether I was in the room when they talked with their friends.

Marty looked at me with a question on his face. I wanted him to know that I knew about these things. Looking back, I know I didn't know, but I thought I sounded as if I did. "Not like Saudi Arabia where they just cut your hand off." I'd heard that at one of my folks' parties too, so I repeated it.

A small smile crossed his mouth, then he nodded. He'd do that, if I said something a little absurd. He'd take it in and then seemed to understand it. Understand me. He didn't rush me away; he didn't squeeze my knuckles till they hurt. He had a familiar expression, a brief glance, as though he were just checking in, checking to see if I was okay. Because of this expression, this look, I sensed he kept an eye on me when it seemed no one else did. Like somehow he knew me.

I smiled back. He poked me in the side, which never failed to tickle me, as all anyone had to do was to come at me with wiggly fingers, and I'd fall on the floor. My brother and my father, for that matter, always resorted to making everything funny, to trying to make me laugh when scary or sad presented itself. Nothing is a better cover-up for fear and sadness. I was being taught not to be afraid when I looked and to laugh when I turned away. Mine was a different kind of callus. Humor provides a certain salve, if only for a moment.

"ReeRee!" Marty said. ReeRee was our code word for riotous laughter. We headed back in the direction of home.

"ReeRee!" I said back. Now maybe we could go back to having a carnival of a good time before he had to leave. "ReeRee!"

"ReeRee," he said. We held hands as we continued on Awolowo Road's sidewalk, closer to the cars now instead of the water.

When we got back to Omo Osagie Street and approached the gate to our compound, I pointed up to the Andrews's house in the compound next door. "They have a pet monkey," I whispered.

"Really?" he said. "Are you going to get one?"

"ReeRee!" I said. That was silly. I didn't want a pet monkey. I wanted the shaggy, inbred poodle, Boudreaux, that we had had to leave with another family when we left Nevada.

In front of our gate, Marty let go of my hand, and with one big leap he jumped across the green, slimy, open sewer. When midair, his legs spanned the width of the trench. He landed on the small strip of grass along the compound concrete wall. Not more than a few feet away, a Nigerian in flip-flops had unzipped his fly and peed into our compound's slimy moat. A woman in her orange and brown geometrically patterned *lappa* squatted with her skirt pulled up around her thighs. The sewer was really just a big public toilet.

"Come on," Marty said from across the gully. "Jump!" He waved his arm and smiled his crooked tooth grin. If he said I could do it, then I knew I could. He wasn't teasing.

I was good at squat jumps in PE, so why not a leap across a five-foot green and slimy gulch? I tried to ignore the stench. As I crouched into my leapfrog position, Marty hollered, "You can do it." I never wanted to disappoint him. I pushed off the edge, looking not down at the oozing muck, but up at Marty, his arms wide.

Halfway across, midair, I could tell jumping wasn't a good idea. In fact, it was a very bad idea.

I missed the other edge by inches. As I slid down into the slime,

I heard him say, "Grab my hand! Quick." But all I could grab were the long, slippery strands of silky, green algae that rained down the concrete side of the sewer wall.

Marty yanked me from the thick sewer water. I tried stifling the cry bubbling out of my throat, not just because I didn't want to cry in front of Marty, but I was afraid to open my mouth.

James, our gateman, and the neighbor's steward, Winston, came running through the gates. "So sorry, Small Sister!" they hollered. "So sorry, so sorry," they repeated as they wiped down my slippery, little arms.

So sorry. I knew the phrase from when I fell off my bike and anyone passing by would say, "So sorry." I got it. "So sorry" wasn't an apology, but a compassionate and empathetic cry for me, for my plight. So sorry I was for the beggars. So sorry for the dead man in the marina. So sorry for the plight of all the poor people of Lagos, as I entered the white gates of our well-kept and guarded compound. So sorry.

My mother stood in the doorway to our house. She must have heard the commotion.

"Go straight to the bathtub," she said.

As I went up the marble stairs of our house, I tried not to touch anything. If I got green slime on the banister, Mom would be "madder than Old Billie Hell," as she would say in her Texas accent. Marty had disappeared, probably hoping to avoid the wrath of Mom when she saw her green daughter.

While Mom gathered cleaning supplies from the kitchen, I undressed. I piled my red shorts and T-shirt along with my Keds, now gunked with sewer crud, in the corner. I knew better than to get the goopy mess on any of the pretty pink bath rugs Mom had decorated with. As I stood naked in the bathtub waiting, I winced at the wet, sticky long hair plastered on my skin.

"The water's going to be hot," Mom said, as she arrived with a bucket full of supplies. I spied a scruffy pad, the brown bottle of hydrogen peroxide, and the giant green bottle of Phisohex antibacterial soap. Today Phisohex is sold only by prescription, and the FDA recommends it be used only on occasion to flush out severe infections. It has a tendency to cause convulsions. People with the severest forms of acne and boils use it, but otherwise it's avoided as a cleanser. We bathed prophylactically with it every day in Nigeria. It stung like the dickens under normal circumstances. The shower hose attachment in hand, Mom rinsed me off from top to bottom like a dog, and then lathered me up. Rinse, then repeat. In addition to the scruffy pad she'd brought from the kitchen, she kept turning the water up hotter. Now with the steel wool, scalding water, and Mom's scrubbing me all over like an iron griddle, I had to hold my breath to keep from succumbing to the sting. I didn't cry until she poured the hydrogen peroxide onto my raw, pink skin.

"You're scrubbing too hard!" I screamed. I hoped to keep at least one layer of skin after this bath.

"We have to make sure we get it off you," said Mom, her face pinched. "Hold still!" She hosed me off again. She didn't want a daughter who came from the sewer. She liked a nice, clean, sweet daughter. I must stay clean, not grow necrotic like the beggars.

My body felt like one giant sunburn, like when we went home to Padre Island, Texas, for summer vacation. Mom would soothe my sunburn sting with cool Noxzema all over my back and shoulders.

Just when I thought she was done sloughing off the sewer sludge, she drained the water from the tub and started over again. When she finally finished, she told me to close my eyes and mouth tight, then poured rubbing alcohol all over me. She poked around inside my ears, underarms, and between my toes, checking for green slime.

This bath, I remember it as if it were yesterday—Mom doing all she could to keep the gruesome outside world from seeping into my pores. But try as she might, I know she failed to get all of Nigeria out of me. I would never be the clean little girl I was before. What I'd seen, what I touched, tasted, smelled, and heard, that would never come off.

MARTY LEFT FOR BOARDING SCHOOL. POOF! HE WAS GONE.
A few weeks later a letter arrived in a red-and-blue airmail envelope
addressed to me. Return address: TASIS Switzerland in his tall, slant-
ing handwriting. I ran up to my room, closed the door, and lay on
my yellow bedspread, scooting right up next to the air-conditioning
unit. While the refreshing cold air blew on my face, I pulled the thin
onion skin paper from the envelope. The onion skin cost less to mail
overseas and was so light and so thin, like sheer gossamer, if held up
to the light it was translucent. The entire single page contained only
this typewritten message: "ReeeeReeeeReeeeReeeeeREEEEEEE!" Over
and over. I faced the wall, the cold air conditioner blowing on my face.
Falling into hysterical laughter, I read every last ReeRee on the page,
while the ghostlike paper fluttered in my hands. Then I hugged the
thin page to my chest and let the air conditioner turn my tears sticky.

ALL OF THIS IS TRUE. ALL OF IT HAPPENED. ALTHOUGH THE
part with my brother along the marina with the dead body, that part
has holes in it. The fall in the sewer, no doubt it happened that way. I
can still feel the slime. All the other dead bodies, they are true, exactly
as I remember them. But the memory of Marty and me at the marina
with the dead body, I will not call home to confirm it. Unlike the
memory of Marty being at the graveyard with the skull, this memory
cannot be taken from me. Unlike the skull, this memory was given
to me. This memory is mine to hold onto.

   That I relish these memories, does that make me a ghoul? I suppose
it does. There is no one to call and ask because they are all ghouls
too. I am not obsessed with death—okay, maybe I am a little—but I
am obsessed by something else.

   I am afraid of the consequences.

Under the Dogonyaro Tree

> How do you think we can fight when our
> own brothers have turned against us? The
> white man is very clever. He came quietly and
> peaceably with his religion. We were amused
> at his foolishness and allowed him to stay.
> Now he has won our brothers, and our clan
> can no longer act like one. He has a put a
> knife on the things that held us together and
> we have fallen apart.
>
> —Chinua Achebe, *Things Fall Apart*

THE AMERICAN INTERNATIONAL SCHOOL WAS CONCRETE block buildings, Quonset huts, and a dirt field surrounded by coiled, barbed wire–topped chain-link. This was no Exeter. No ivy-covered walls. Just razor wire above chain-link fence. Next door to AIS sat more Quonset huts of the Nigerian army base. Just beyond the huts, green and white painted oil drums, the colors of the Nigerian flag, stacked two and three high, created the backdrop for firing squad executions. Only the tall chain-link fence separated our school property from the military base where public executions took place. Zoning laws weren't prevalent in Nigeria. I have to assume the Americans who built the school in this location thought the semblance of military security took precedence over bloody executions. In fact, we got Execution Days just as we had Snow Days in Nevada, although not all executions took place at the firing squad arena.

THE PARTICULAR DAY IN MY MEMORY WAS A WEDNESDAY. I remember the day because Mom got her hair done on Wednesdays, and when she came downstairs with her limp, unwashed hair, she startled me. "Don't worry," she said. "I'm going to the beauty shop in an hour."

Dad had left for the bush that morning, so it was just the two of us. And the staff. I ran out the front door, happy to hear the toot toot of the little vw school bus come to pick me up.

On the road to school, I stared out the window at the thick, caramel-colored air. The Harmattan winds off the Sahara blew hot and sandy, making the sky dense as cornmeal.

About midway through our day, we had Nigerian culture class. Mrs. Nwoko, the Nigerian culture teacher, always dressed in a Sears polyester jumper and wore her hair well coiffed in a smooth, turned-under, Western style. Many Nigerian women opted for Western-style dress instead of the traditional wrap-around *iro* skirt and the *gele* wrapped like a wonton on the head. Mrs. Nwoko laughed a lot and looked around as though wondering if she were in the right place. I empathized with her. Her job was to come to class each week and teach us how to cook Nigerian foods or construct other arts and crafts representing the Yoruba, Igbo, or Hausa. I liked Nigerian culture class because it usually involved eating food or using glue, two things I was good at.

On this day we worked on our calabash painting project. The large, pumpkin-shaped gourds were dried and halved for us to make masks, wall hangings, or ornaments. I had chosen one the size of a split basketball. In the midst of painting what I considered to be a unique design that I'd seen embroidered on Suzanne's hip-hugger blue jeans back pocket—a red, white, and blue peace sign, Miss Abby stepped into our room.

The air conditioning had gone out. Wiping sweat from her neck, she told Mrs. Nwoko to take us outside.

"I will teach them the Igbo dance," Mrs. Nwoko said.

That's how we ended up on the playing field under the forsaken dogonyaro tree. The middle of the field lay barren but for that tree and a few dried-up patches of grass, which right then during the dry season were the same color as the dirt.

Sometimes at recess we'd see and hear the Nigerian soldiers dressed in green fatigues marching in formation on the other side of the chain-link. But today only our class had come outside, and it was quiet stillness.

The dance started off like ring-around-the-rosy. We held hands and skipped in a circle around the dogonyaro tree. I held onto the French girl's hand. Mrs. Nwoko held the other sweaty hand of the French girl as we hopped one way in the circle, then the other. Twice around the tree. Mrs. Nwoko demonstrated the next hop. "My people, they skip with a bow," she said, pulling her hand free and placing it at her waist. As she bent forward, the tip of a branch snagged the top of her hair, while we all shuffled a few steps along.

Her wig dangled from the branch until she realized what had happened. She must have felt the warm breeze on her head, the titillation of her skin in the electric Harmattan air, and the tittering of the kids as we saw her scalp bared. She screamed and crouched with her hands covering the tiny pigtails braided all over her head. She cowered as though ashamed. With her tiny braids, she looked young like a girl and more Nigerian than her American TV–inspired look from *Room 222*. But she crouched in humiliation and embarrassment when her real self was revealed. I wonder, did she think the Western clothing and wig made her beautiful? Did she think she was ugly otherwise? The Western world, the desire for anything American, was creeping into third world nations.

She snatched her wig off the branch and gave a quick, stern look at any gigglers as she replaced her false head of hair and readjusted her snug dress. "My people," she said with a stern voice, "dance with a bounce." And she gave a kick and another tuck at the waist. We followed. A kick and a tuck. I spied Mrs. Nwoko checking with one hand to make sure her wig was in place. Kick and tuck. A kick and tuck. Around the dogonyaro tree we go.

"My people," she said, "dance with their hearts." Her voice was lifted by the wind and drifted off. Only the sounds of our soft, dusty kicks padding on the dirt touched our ears.

Maybe it was the ferociously dry air from the Harmattan wind that day, or maybe we were all busy concentrating, but the playground got deathly quiet as we bent at the waist and touched the ground. When we reached for the sky with our little white hands as Mrs. Nwoko demonstrated with her dark brown ones, the Harmattan howled. Our tiny ears perked up. The circle tightened around the dogonyaro tree as we grasped hands again. Then a long shriek pierced the thick air over our heads.

The circle froze.

My skin prickled; the wail sounded close enough to brush my bare shoulders. The troubled ululation had come from the lunch hut near the front doors of the school. Then it came again. Another long moan, just as the janitor jutted out from the hut, and right behind him the cook.

In the hot, African sun, I saw a glint flash off a long, silvery knife, more than likely a machete. The janitor didn't wear a shirt. He never did, the African heat too hot for American tees. Small rivers of red trickled in the dust at his feet. On the playground, we scuttled around Mrs. Nwoko's polyester hem as the janitor screamed again. He ran past the teeter-totters and dodge ball court, still howling, now at the cornmeal sky. The cafeteria cook sprinted right behind him, red blood turned purple against the dark skin of his arm. It clashed with the faded Orange Fanta T-shirt he wore. The knife in his hand, then in the back of the janitor, waggled between them. As they returned along the chain-link fence, I saw the gash in the janitor's back between his shoulder blades. The dark blood turned bright as it hit the cook's white apron. The cook was the most hysterical, acting as though *he* had been stabbed in the back, *his* life stolen from him. The janitor screamed again, and the cook spewed curses in Yoruba or Hausa, I didn't know which.

Not one of us let go of our handhold, and we pulled in closer to the center of the circle, as the possessed men rushed and stumbled onto the field. Mrs. Nwoko kept whispering, "get down, get down," like she was afraid they'd notice us if she were too loud. So we all squatted as they passed us and left a trail like tar in the dust.

More teachers came pouring out of the school building. In my opinion they were too late. They shooed us inside, keeping us in queue while looking over their shoulders shouting whispers. Mrs. Nwoko's eyes were wide, wig askew, her hands too busy holding ours to check her coif. She seemed especially frightened, dressed in her smart Western wear, her jumper from Sears. Instead Miss Abby, the principal in her maxi skirt like a giant quilt around her legs, marched up and down in front, steering us inside. "But we hadn't finished learning the dance yet," Scott Curtis shouted. Miss Abby leaned over the rush of kids and shushed him. The little French girl, who had been holding my hand for the Igbo dance and never let go, buried her face in the skirt of Miss Abby's quilted maxi.

Just as we approached the lunch hut, I turned to look back. The janitor and cook had worked their way around to the far side of the playground, moving toward the Quonset huts and then the firing squad amphitheater. The chain-link fence topped with razor wire would be their dead end.

Back inside at our desks waiting for the teachers to quit whispering in the hall, we could still hear the yelling and cursing of the janitor and cook, their howls of agony swirling around the dogonyaro tree, until they ran out of blood to shed.

I sat at my desk; my glossy red, white, and blue peace sign calabash stared at me, and I at it.

Tribal differences, Mrs. Nwoko explained. "My motherland is broken." Again she adjusted her wig. "My people are still fighting the war."

I wanted to be the little French girl with my face buried in Miss

Abby's patchwork skirt. Only I didn't want it to be Miss Abby. I wanted it to be Mom—my only person left. I wanted to bury my face, to climb into the folds of the skirt, to wrap myself in the quilted cushions of padding, in soft, muffled fabric, in a cradle of peace.

I GOOGLE "BIAFRAN WAR." MY PEOPLE STARTED THIS WAR.

My people, the white missionaries, brought religions. Then the white man came back to take the oil. My people. The countries with red, white, and blue flags. American culture class—*my* motherland, my family. Entitlement, is it part of our culture? What culture do I belong to? Did I become initiated by birth or by experience?

THE LITTLE BLUE AND WHITE VOLKSWAGEN SCHOOL BUS carted us kids who lived on Ikoyi Island to and from the gates of AIS. After the crazy day at school, I didn't pay attention to the other kids on the bus as they were dropped off one by one. Instead I watched the afternoon thunderclouds building in the sky. Once the other kids finally had been dropped off, Samson, the driver, let me sit in the front passenger seat next to him, since I was the last stop. Dad always sat in the front seat with the driver when we rode in the oil company Mercedes Benzes or in taxis.

Samson and I sat alone in a traffic jam. The air along the road smelled of diesel and something especially rancid that should remain nameless but was probably a combination of defecation and decomposition.

Every day was a traffic jam, but today in particular something up ahead had the cars at a standstill, bumpers edging into spaces that weren't theirs. Outside the minibus, the city was in chaos. Arms reached out car windows, shaking fists, or better yet, open palm shoved into the air, the Nigerian version of flipping someone off. Samson remained calm, probably as instructed by his Western bosses. I watched out my window as ladies walking along the sidewalk, up and down the curb, made their way through the cram-packed jumble. With baskets balanced on their heads, their bare breasts bounced against the orange and brown fabrics of their *lappas* wrapped around and around their ribs, the fabric flowing down around their floating feet. Inside the vehicle, I felt a muffled safety, but it was taking so long to get home to Mom that I thought she might be worried.

"A beggar run over in the road," Samson said. I craned my neck to see, but there were so many cars, so many pedestrians, all trying to get around the mess, I couldn't catch even so much as a dismemberment.

The vw bus coughed, and I tired of looking at the constant throng jostling to get through the jam. I switched my eyes to Samson instead. Samson never seemed to mind if you stared at him. Or at least he never told me to stop. His tribal status probably gave him an air of superiority that I wasn't attuned to, but I stared because he had long, thick scars on his face. Three horizontal lines on each side. Long, deep, straight lines, like the skin was split open then healed. Which was exactly what was done; a knife was drawn across the cheek, then charcoal and coconut oil were rubbed in the skin to darken it. My dad used the word "cauterized" when he explained how it was done. The sound of that word, "cauterized," captured my attention, the way it sounded like what it did. Nigeria was like a scratch-n-sniff *National Geographic* magazine come to life.

Originally, I learned, the markings were sliced because of the excessive communal wars and the slave trade. Families would get separated, and the scars were a way to identify one another. For those taken away as slaves, it was a way of holding family ties. The scars were a way to find their relations, no matter how long the family might have been separated. My family was separated, but would scars be enough to keep us in touch?

"Does it hurt when they do it?" I asked Samson since no one else was on the bus with us now.

"Do what, Small Sister?"

"Cut your face."

"I was small boy, like your size. My mum says I was brave and did not cry. I was awake the whole time." He held his head high, as though he thought he was very handsome. And he was. Traditionally the

markings were also a sign of beauty. I wanted to touch them, see if
they were as smooth as they looked.

"Why do they do it?"

"It is the sign of my tribe. My father is Yoruba chieftain. He wears
the same sign. Now everyone know I am my father's son because I
have chieftain sign on my face."

I was so glad my dad was just a geologist.

"Can't they just paint them on?"

"No," Samson explained, "scars are for life. I will always be my
father's son, and my son will have same markings." He took his eyes
off the struggling traffic for a moment and smiled at me. "Small Sister
want my tribal markings too?"

"No thanks," I wiggled in my seat.

Samson would always be his father's son. Would I always be my
father's daughter? My mother's daughter? My brother and sister's
annoying little sibling? I worried about Suzanne and Marty off to
boarding school, my dad in the Niger Delta. We had no identifying
marks to keep us in touch.

My family had no physical scars. I wanted a link. I desperately
needed a link. I wanted to see, to feel, whom I belonged to. My soli-
tude had only just begun.

Eventually we pushed through the diesel-fumed boulevards, crossed
two concrete bridges, avoided more beggars and street vendors, and
pulled up to the gates of the compound where I lived. Samson honked
the horn long and hard. "James, Hausa Tribe. He open gates for
chieftain's son."

I understood enough at this point to know that each tribe wanted to
be the boss of the other tribes. This jostling for power, for government
control in the former British colony, these boundaries are what caused
the Biafran War just before we came to Lagos. The interior borders
were drawn by Lord Mountbatten, the same fellow who did such a great
job drawing boundaries between India and Pakistan and for Israel.
Who doesn't know that drawing a line is an instigator for aggression?

When we'd gotten the call from Dad, I asked my mom where the

jungle was and whether we could we visit—I would write letters to my
friends. But there would be no jungle visits in 1971. The Biafran War
had just ended, and it was not safe to travel outside the city. This war,
I knew as Mrs. Nwoko explained, was why the janitor and cook on
our playground still fought.

"You'd think the civil war was still going on," the adults would
say at my folks' cocktail parties where I liked to sit and watch them
get potted on lime-green daiquiris. "Britain gave the Nigerians their
independence, and then they fight among themselves. Why can't
they just be happy?"

The children we'd seen on the TV/stereo console's snowy screen
in Ely, the Igbo children with the extended bellies, the flies around
their eyes, the reports of them dying every hour, that was the Biafran
War I knew, but only through the television screen. I didn't connect
it to the Nigeria where I now lived.

As I'm retracing that memory, I research Biafra. How the Igbo
territory in the South segregated from the rest of Nigeria. How the
children were starving because the Hausa and Yoruba cut off the
resources to Biafra, where the Igbo tribes lived. How oil was discovered. The United States, Britain, and France hadn't wanted to help
Biafra, but then they changed their minds when they wanted the oil.
An American advertising agency created the propaganda ads about
the pot-bellied children with flies crawling on their eyes to sway the
American public that we should go in and assist. We should go in and
help get the oil. We should go in and help turn Nigeria into the most
corrupt country in the world. Okay, the last part wasn't part of the
plan, just the detritus from the plan. The consequences.

Oil, my people's blood.

But I was too young to think this. I was still just my father's daughter.

JAMES HURRIED TO OPEN THE GATES, BUT I KNEW IT WASN'T
because a Yoruba chieftain's son wanted him to. It was because Small
Sister had arrived. James was teaching me how to ride my bike since
the training wheels broke in the shipment. We would have a lesson

when I finished my after-school snack. The sticky plastic of the bus seat snapped at my thighs as I bounced in excitement and waved back at him.

Alice waited in front of our pink four o'clocks and greeted me as Samson drove to the back of the compound to drop me off.

"Today was a scary day at school," I told Alice.

"Yes, always scare," she said with a big hug, as if she already knew what I must have seen. Did she know, or did she discern that any day could be dangerous? "Tomorrow is new day." She lifted my chin with her finger, wiped at my runny nose.

"I have a cold," I told her, embarrassed by my mucousy upper lip.

"You don't feel cold," she said, putting her hand to my cheek. Her interpretation of English wasn't always the same as mine, so I didn't know if she was being literal or if she was just being silly. I laughed because either way, inside the compound, inside Alice's embrace, I was somebody's.

One Without the Other

> "'Poor little monkey!' she at last exclaimed;
> and the words were an epitaph for the tomb
> of Maisie's childhood. She was abandoned to
> her fate."
>
> —*What Maisie Knew*, Henry James

MY MOTHER IS WHO CALLED US "HIDEOUS." BUT MY MOTHER was far from hideous physically. She is petite and blonde. Well into her seventies she wore stiletto heels, the most stylish cocktail attire, and always had her hair and nails done immaculately. I was very proud of her wide smile that showed her gums, her straight teeth, and her well-coiffed hair in the latest style—shag, flip, or French twist.

My mother's talent for piccolo reached such great heights in high school that she was awarded a music scholarship to Southwest Texas Junior College. She had been on her way to becoming a concert flutist. She loved us, but oh, what could have been, she reminded me often, if she had never gotten married and had children. The fact that I wouldn't have existed if she had really gone that route never occurred to me. The fact that that route probably never could have existed for a woman in 1952 was never mentioned. My mother and her dreams were all that mattered. "I raised all of you to be

independent so that you wouldn't make the same mistakes I did,"
she tells me to this day. All of this, I suppose, is why I played the
flute in junior high band, even though secretly all I ever wanted
was piano lessons. I thought it best to be like my mother. Then she
could love me completely.

When my second-grade teacher at AIS, Mrs. Lavigne, asked my
mom to be Room Mother, my mom replied that she had already
done her time as a Room Mother with her two older children ten
years ago. Mrs. Lavigne said, "Oh, Mrs. Wallen, you definitely don't
look old enough to have children ten years older than Amy." People
were always saying that to my mom, not just teachers trying to sway
her to bake cupcakes. Somehow that statement made me feel like
she didn't fully belong to me. That our relationship was tenuous if
she got a better offer—concert flutist, another more elegant life. A
less hideous family.

"I am a petunia in an onion patch," my mother once told me. She,
the petunia, her family, the onion patch. It was becoming clear to
me that I couldn't be like her—I was never petite, I had no musical
inclinations, and I wasn't even sure what a petunia or piccolo was.

Moving to Africa may not have been my mother's idea, and from
her point of view, she may have had no choice in the matter, but
she seemed to fit into the social scene just fine. She threw daiquiri
parties that rivaled all the other oil company expat fetes. She knew
instinctively how to dress the part, as though we'd always been high
society, dressing in tailor-made clothes and having barefoot servants
who passed canapés on silver trays.

The slipcovered garage sale couch and coffee-can and plastic daisy
lampshade in Nevada—long forgotten.

After we moved to Lagos, and SwissAir had flown off with Suzanne
and Marty, and the houseboat on the Niger Delta was Daddy's home
away, my mom and I did everything together. This was just fine with
me. I wanted more than anything to live up to her expectations, and
this was my chance to watch her closely, examine her ways and learn
how to become like her.

VISITORS DIDN'T KNOCK ON OUR FRONT DOOR; INSTEAD THEY walked up to the sliding glass windows along the living room wall, placed their hands on either side of their face and their nose up to the glass to peer inside, then tapped on the pane. Either of us might be sitting in the living room reading and then sense someone was staring at us, or we'd hear the slap, slap, slap of leather sandals echoing an approach in the carport. But if we didn't realize someone was peering at us, they'd rap, rap, rap on the glass.

If a trader came, they'd want to see Mom. "Tell Madam I have new thorn carvings. Momma with baby on back, the way she likes."

While I or Philip, our steward, went to get Mom, they'd lay out their display of wares on a big piece of greasy fabric in our empty carport. Thorn carvings, mahogany furniture, ivory tusks carved into faces, all of which they'd transported on their heads. Mom always bought something. She could never say no. "They went to so much work," she'd say, "to show me everything, to lay out all their art."

But the traders always wanted her to buy more.

The diesel fumes from Omo Osagie Street wafted to our carport where Isaiah had laid out his wares in front of our door. Rows of masks, animal statues, thorn carvings like tiny Nigerian action figures (dentists drilling on a patient, coconut harvesters climbing a palm tree, and tiny buses with miniature figures spilling out of windows just like the jam-packed to overflowing buses on Awolowo Road), and ebony jewelry boxes with ivory inlay. "This one, Madam," Isaiah said, grabbing the ebony mask she had picked up but rejected. "You buy today. Tell me price, Madam."

"No, no," she replied. "This statue is all I want." She pulled out her cream-colored American-made billfold with the brass clasp.

While she pulled out the right money, I examined the remaining artwork. I liked the thorn carvings the best, the intricately detailed, two- to four-inch images of Yoruba men and women in daily tasks, such as dyeing yarn or mashing yams for fufu. Each image was carved out of the light buff and dark brown thorns of the ata tree and the pink thorns of the egun egun tree.

Over the weeks, she bought the canoes carrying several passengers with baggage and jugs of palm wine, a nativity set complete with black baby Jesus the size of a bead, and a chess set for my dad and Marty to play when both of them came home, whenever that may be.

I loved the ebony pieces too, the black surface polished like a marble wood.

"Please, Madam," Isaiah pleaded. "I need to sell more today."

"But this is all I can afford," Mom said, setting the mahogany antelope statue at her feet, then pulling pound notes from her billfold.

"No, Madam," Isaiah held up his hand to stop her. "You are rich lady. You can buy ebony face." And he held the mask closer to her.

"Isaiah," Mom shook her head. "I am not rich."

"Madam not rich?" Isaiah acted shocked. He was teasing her, but he knew something more. To Isaiah, Mom was lying, which she did sometimes, like when she wanted me to get ready for school quicker so she'd flub the time. But rich? To me, rich meant Uncle Nick, vice president of a Houston GM car dealership. But his house in Houston was smaller than our two-story with umbrella trees, fruit bats, and bumblebees. Rich meant swimming pools, and we swam at the Ikoyi Club. Were we rich? "Madam," Isaiah said, his forehead creased, "you are very rich." The black dirt around his pink nail beds accented the cracked calluses across the tips of his fingers. "You can buy all my carvings." He knelt next to his display and now fanned his empty black-stained palm across his wares.

"Isaiah, that's just not true."

"Madam, please do not tease me." He looked down at his chest. That, I thought, was putting it on a bit heavy. His baggy crepe pants had worn through at the pocket. The wad of Nigerian pound notes he carried poked through, revealing the Nigerian face on the bill: a man, machete held overhead, hard at work.

Nigerians often called us rich. I wondered what it would be like for the traders, Isaiah or Justus or Friday, if Mom did buy all their artwork in one day. Would they feel rich that day? Could they buy the solid yellow mangoes at the market and not the small dented brown ones? But when I mentioned it to my mom, she said that if she bought everything, then they wouldn't have anything to sell to anyone else. She looked at me sideways. "What would they do?" she said. I thought maybe they could take the day off, rest, or maybe they had more stuff at home they could sell. But I didn't say anything more, because apparently my idea was dumb.

Isaiah stacked all his statues and other wares in the middle of the cloth then pulled up the corners into a big knot. With one big heave, he hoisted the whole bundle onto his head, the sides sagging around his ears like the bottom of a giant pumpkin. Even with the load balanced, he still managed a small bow, then ambled down the drive and out the front gates.

TRADERS CAME BY OUR HOUSE DAILY SELLING THEIR WARES. On Wednesday, Friday the tailor came through the gates with his black Singer sewing machine balanced on his head, carrying a leather briefcase. From inside the briefcase, he pulled patterns and detailed drawings of dresses and laid them out in the carport. On Friday, Justus came to sell thorn carvings. I always thought it would make much more sense if Friday came on Friday and Justus on Wednesday.

Friday opened one leather-bound binder filled with brilliant fabric swatches in African prints and rich solids, then opened another with pages and pages of the hand-drawn embroidery fretwork of flourishes and frippery. Mom and I chose fabric and thread color, pointed to pantsuits, dress, or tunic, and within a week my mother had a new wardrobe. She wore maxi dresses and pantsuits for entertaining and minidresses for everyday teas and daytime events at the Ikoyi Club. Occasionally she would pick out a pattern for me. In my red pantsuit with stitched frippery across the bodice, I pretended to be one of the ladies at a daiquiri party, my hand holding an invisible stemmed glass.

On the other days Mom and I shopped at Jankara Market, Lagos's largest, open-air bazaar. In one section trade beads were sold, or slave beads as they were also called because they were used as currency for slaves and services during the sixteenth to nineteenth centuries.

My dad likes to point out that Nigerians had slaves long before the white man came along and shipped them crowded in the belly of the vessel. He says this as though it excuses Southern plantations, cat-o'-nine-tails, and the tearing apart of families. When I was little, I nodded wide-eyed, taking it in as if fact. As I grew older, the nod gradually became a shake in disbelief and shame at my lack of questioning two wrongs.

Strings of glass beads dangled from the walls of the Jankara Market booths. Baskets of loose beads spilled out from the front. Mom would string her own combination of round, tubular Krobo or brass beads. Some looked like red-and-white striped peppermints, others like chocolate Tootsie Rolls or caramels or whimsical, painted tubes or coins. I never got my own beads, but I helped her pick out combinations, long strands hung around her neck matching the dresses Friday made for her.

In Jankara Market anything could be bought, even juju potions and powders. We squeezed through the crowded rows of vendors. People wove through the aisles, women in long *iros*—rectangular fabrics wrapped around the waist—with *geles* wrapped around their hair, often holding baskets filled with purchases on their heads, while we carried ours in shopping bags dangling from our arms.

Mom and I were the only cohesive part left of our family. I missed Marty with a vengeance. But Mom and I had each other, and we were ladies shopping. She may not belong to me, but I belonged to her. We were inseparable.

Or so I thought.

A new trader came to the house one day and brought wood and ivory tusk carvings. "Ebony, Madam," he swore about the black wood. "Ebony. Not fake, Madam." She pointed to a foot-tall carving of a man—I could tell because he wore a loincloth. The trader picked up the statue along with the one next to it—a woman with long, pointed breasts.

"Just the one," Mom said.

"No, Madam," he said, and shook his head with vigor. "You must buy both."

"I just want one," Mom said.

"Real ebony, Madam." He handed her both dolls, "They go together. See." He held the male and female carvings side-by-side, identical except for mammary glands and sex organs. "Twins, Madam. Twins are killed by Igbo, Madam. They think they are evil. When twins are born, they throw them in the woods. These are replicas for mother of her babies."

"They kill the twins?" Mom asked. I pictured the mothers coddling the wooden statues like baby dolls, as replacements for the babies they had to throw away. I grabbed Mom's arm, and without saying it, she knew I meant, *you have to buy them both, you have to keep them together.* "Okay then, I'll buy both." She seemed reluctant and disbelieving, but she liked a story that came with a purchase. I liked that she wasn't giving up one without the other, that she realized they belonged together. I laid my head on her elbow.

She placed the woodcarving on the shelf above the living room couch. After a few weeks under the air conditioner running full blast, the wood dried out then cracked at the base, the pink, fleshy wood peeking through the outer black shoe polish. I watched the splintered "ebony" open wider and wider each day, until I could stick my pinky inside. But I never said a word. I didn't want Mom to know she had been cheated. I didn't want her to know one wasn't as good as the other. If she knew, she might throw that twin away. One shouldn't be without the other. I stood tiptoe on the couch and placed one statue just behind the other twin so the pink crack wouldn't show.

OUR TRIPS TO THE STUFFY AND CROWDED PHONE COMPANY to wait our turn to make an international call were a curiosity to me. Even now looking back, these *special* days spent waiting and sweating on Naugahyde make no sense to me. I know we had no telephone or television at the house; no one did in Nigeria. To make a phone call required driving to the public utilities building downtown. At the front desk a clerk took a reservation, then we waited in the unair-conditioned lobby until the call was placed. As we waited hours for our call to go through, I watched the fruit bats hanging in the giant umbrella tree out front.

That's how I remember it: that we went to make phone calls on a semiregular basis. But when I call my sister and tell her I remember going down to the phone company to call her and Marty at boarding school, I find out that again my memory had it all wrong.

"No one ever called me during the school year when we were in Switzerland," Suzanne replies.

This stings. Why had no one called Suzanne and Marty once they'd left home? Sent so far away, and our parents never called them?

"No one called?" I say.

"Not once," she says. "My roommate and I became close. I made friends; that helped."

I don't ask my mother about this. I know the answer, and I'm too broken-hearted. She will say that it was too expensive, too difficult, that it just wasn't done. Instead I ring my mother and ask who it was we did call in the memory I so clearly have in my head of when we went to the phone company and I watched the fruit bats.

"We must have been calling Mom," she says, referring to her own mother, my grandmother, Mommom. A telex came. "She had gotten sick, so we called home." My mom pauses for a moment. "She died during my flight over, before I got there."

A familiar pang of sadness for her rips through my gut—losing her mother while she's trying to get to her. I want to hug her. If only my mother were closer. If only she didn't live so far away. I miss my mother for who she was, for who she is. My memory erases, and my thoughts shift. If I squint my mind's eye, if I look through the kalei-doscope of stories—my sister's, my mom's, mine—I see a montage of family each surviving in her own way. I see my eight-year-old self coloring in her *Places I Have Lived* book. That little girl doesn't know that this giant, seismic shift in cultures, this upheaval, isn't normal. She doesn't comprehend time, abandonment, or death.

I say to my mother on the phone, "You left me in Lagos alone, after everyone else was gone when you went to the States." I don't accuse. It's a statement. I only say it with the hope she will respond with remorse or regret. Or awareness. Maybe she'll want to hug me too.

"I left you with the Griffins," she says, matter-of-factly.

I should have realized the placed call from my memory was an emergency because Dad was home from the bush and not at the office. I recall that he paced the floor in front of the counter.

The Nigerian women, professionally dressed in Western seersucker dresses and neckerchiefs, looked up each time Dad stopped to ask how much longer.

"Your telephone call must travel many miles," the bouffant-do'd lady behind the counter replied.

"We've been here two hours already," he told her.

"Yes, Master," she replied. "We too have been here four hours, still your call has not gone through."

"We just put the call through when we—. Never mind." He resumed his pacing. The illogic in the woman's response irritated him, but he knew it was no use. The women continued to put up with my dad's complaining for the rest of the afternoon. He was John Wayne waiting behind the saloon doors for the gunman to show up.

"Jaime," my mother said each time he griped, "they can't do anything about it."

"You think we should just wait until they get around to it? We'll be here for a month." It felt like a month already. I sat on a hard plastic chair with nothing to look at except the dangling bats out the window, the linoleum floor, or the red telephone booths lined up against one wall.

Finally when our call had been placed, Mom and I both crammed into the red Naugahyde-covered phone booth. Tight and hot from the body heat of previous callers, the snug, unair-conditioned box was oppressive. The phone booth reeked of sweaty, stale body odor and pomade. But I didn't care as I sat on Mom's thigh, my hand holding onto her knee, her skin always soft like kid leather. My ear glued to the backside of the receiver, I just heard a squawking buzz come through.

International calls in those days were a hassle, the sounds so distant and the time it took one voice to travel to the next so long you inevitably talked over one another. The price was exorbitant and not much could be discussed in the short time and tiny air space.

This must have been what happened: On our end, my mother relayed her arrival date and time. She would be going to the States, to Texas. Her mother was deathly ill.

I remember nothing of the events leading up to the day she left. I am certain though that I stood at her side as she packed her Samsonite suitcase. I imagine she filled it with Nigerian souvenirs for her sisters, strings of beads from Jankara, funny thorn carvings of dentists pulling teeth, ebony and ivory bookmarkers—trinkets that fit easily inside a suitcase. No room for a seven-year-old girl. I don't remember a single thing about her preparing to leave, perhaps because I didn't understand or just didn't want to believe it.

But I do remember clearly the day she left.

I hid behind the curtains, looking out the sliding doors, and watched through the decorative cuts in the carport's concrete block as Pious, the Griffins' driver, put Mom's suitcase in the trunk of the blue Renault. I grabbed the blue-and-orange African print curtains that hung the length of the living room glass wall. A bigger cry than I had ever cried pushed itself up from my belly. I know what "wracked with sobs" means because of that day. I was not a crier, but from my hiding place, I dropped to my knees, grabbed hold of the rough curtain fabric, and covered my face. I pleaded. I sobbed.

She waved as she slid into the Renault's backseat. She'd spotted me! I reached up with my little hand, smudging the glass. I pounded my balled up fist, rattling the glass. The car backed out. I banged harder, the glass shimmying in its track. I couldn't catch my breath from bawling. I ached with each gulp and wail.

And she left anyway.

I blubbered. I bawled. I wailed. I rolled myself up in those curtains.

Snuffling, I wiped my nose on the orange bird print. Maybe I did know something from those long-distance calls at the phone company. Maybe I comprehended the essence of the calls. Maybe I knew that even though Papa told me about the deer he'd shot, or how next time I came to visit he'd have M&Ms for me, that something had shifted. Maybe I sensed what traveled beneath all the aunts' and uncles' sepulchral echoes through the transatlantic wires lying at the bottom of the ocean.

I stared at the empty carport, at the grease stain where a car should have been. I hiccuped, trembled out more sobs, dried my eyes on the scratchy orange-and-blue curtain. If I kept staring, I thought, she might pull back into the carport. She might get out of the backseat of the Renault.

She might realize she had forgotten something.

I watched. I waited. I sat on the cold marble floor clinging to the curtains.

She was gone.

Dad had returned to Port Harcourt in the Niger Delta, and he could call only when he had shortwave radio reception.

This meant one thing: now my family was just *me*.

BEHIND ME I HEARD, "SMALL SISTER, MAY I COOK PANCAKES?" It was Philip. I peeled my face away from the curtain. "Do not cry all day," he said.

Why not? I wondered. That's what I wanted to do. He reached out his hand, his pink palm bigger than my little hand. He helped me get back to my feet and find my way out of the curtains I'd wrapped myself in. He had tissue for my eyes. I didn't like for anyone to see me cry, so I quickly swiped away the snot running down my chin.

"Pancakes, Small Sister?" he asked again. "Will this help make you not so sorrowful?"

By pancakes, he meant crepes, thin, holey little flapjacks smeared with, worst of all, this new jam we had on our table—orange marmalade. All foreigners liked pancakes, so he assumed our family would too. By all foreigners he meant British people. We were

IHOP and Denny's Americans. Where was the Welch's grape jelly? Or the maple syrup?

"Syrup?" I asked Philip. "Can we get syrup for the pancakes?" If you smother anything in maple syrup it tastes good.

"Yes! Small Sister, we have." Philip was a master at people-pleasing.

I sat at the modern Danish teak dining table, seats covered in white leather. The scene in my head now is like one of the cartoon character Richie Rich, the Poor Little Rich Kid—the richest kid in the world with no companions.

"Syrup for Small Sister," Philip said, and he put the Karo corn syrup on the table. My tears slowed, but only to explain that the kind of syrup I wanted was brown, not clear. He returned with a bottle of *dark* Karo corn syrup.

MY ROUTINE STAYED THE SAME. EXCEPT FOR ONE THING.

Philip made sure my meals were all served hot and on time, and the house was kept tiptop. After school Alice sat with me while I read or drew in the map book I was making of all the places I had lived so far—Louisiana, Alabama, Mississippi, Louisiana again, then Nevada and Nigeria. Other days Alice ironed and watched out the window of the laundry room, as James, the gateman, taught me how to ride my bike. With one hand on the back of my bike, he jogged in his *babban riga*, a flowing caftanlike gown, up and down the long driveway of the compound. The flopping of his leather sandals reminded me that if I toppled someone would be there to catch me. James's job was to sit by the front gate of the compound and allow entry only to visitors or traders, like Friday or Justus. Now each was turned away. I'd wave a small wave, wishing they would still come into the compound. Through the white wrought iron bars of the gate, they would wave back. They knew me because I was always with Madam. If they came in, I thought, laid out their wares in the carport, maybe Mom would come out the front door to haggle.

I may not have understood time, or abandonment, but I knew longing. I didn't have the word for it yet, but I knew *lonely*.

SO CLOSE TO THE EQUATOR, THE SUN SET EARLY IN THE evening. As it got dark, bats flew out of the giant umbrella tree in the front yard. I had to duck when they swooped too close. Alice told me the giant hay-colored fruit bats were good bats. They ate bugs. The disappearing sunlight filtered through the giant bats' translucent, veined wings, the span as big as my own arms'. We watched the bats circumnavigate the tops of the outlined corkwood trees, shrieking and tumbling. I jumped as they rustled inside the banana tree fronds, and Alice hugged me close.

It is a dream, with bats that stays present in my consciousness no matter how old I am. Maybe I should call it a *nightmare* but although frightening and dark, it saves me much grief throughout my life:

I was five years old, and we still lived in Nevada. I had awoken from one of those dreams that seems so real that I felt it might still be going on. When I opened my eyes, my bedroom was dark, but I was trying to listen more than see. The house remained quiet. My sister, Suzanne, lay next to me in our double bed, asleep. I listened for the sounds of any other people in the house, but I heard none.

In my dream giant black bats flew screeching into my mom and dad's bedroom. With their tiny bat feet and clawed thumbs, the bats lifted my parents up and flew off with them. Behind those bats, more bats flew in and replaced Mom and Dad with another set of lookalike parents. A mean version, whom you could not tell apart from the good parents.

Next to me in bed my sister stayed still. I strained my ears for any noises coming from the other side of the wall, the wall shared with our folks' headboard. But, I heard nothing.

A secret was revealed to me, my five-year-old logic concluded: The parents who spanked me when I misbehaved, who left me at home alone when they went to bridge club, who told me they were disappointed in what I did—those were the ones the bats had left behind. The mom who took me to the fabric store with her, who combed my hair into braids and had my picture taken at Olan Mills, who let me eat her chocolate Aids diet candies, that was the good mom, the benevolent overseer of my life. The dream explained why my mother could be so pleased with me and then not have the time of day in one fell swoop.

Easy as that, I explain away any transgressions. Easy as that, I dispel any apprehension about why my family would leave me in Lagos, Nigeria, only three months after we'd arrived with staff I barely knew. Easy as that, she is my beautiful, flawless mother. And to her, I will be as loyal as that dog in the grave, the one curled up under the stone, buried with his master. My subconscious dreamt a new truth: all the hideous people had been lifted and carried off by bats. They made appearances but weren't the real people. My conscious mind directs the traffic of my conscience as though around a wreckage: *Keep going, people. Nothing here to see. Keep going.* When there was plenty to see.

ONE PART OF MY ROUTINE HAD CHANGED.

As the sun disappeared, Alice went home to her family, Philip went back to the quarters, and James changed guard duty with Nicholas, the "watchnight." That's when I crossed the compound to the Griffins' back door, where I would spend my nights.

I slapped at the moths swarming in the back porch light's glow. Alice had told me they were trying to get to the moon. The soft bodies and fluttering wings left gray powder dust on my fingers when I'd cup my palm to catch them. Speckled wings flattened against the surface, they rested, catching their tiny breaths until they were ready to bang themselves against the bulb again, persistent in their determination. Persistent in their determination to get what they wanted, even if it might harm them, like flying into a flame.

It's a phenomenon. A moth is "positively phototactic," meaning they are attracted to fire, even if it means they won't survive. There's no definitive explanation.

No definitive explanation comes to me as to why my mother would leave me alone in Nigeria for so long. Her leaving wasn't negligent, it was like the moths—a phenomenon. An enigma. A mystery with no explanation. No definitive explanation tells me why I keep flying into her light.

Bats and moths, flying, flitting, fleeting.

As my mom said—she didn't leave me alone, she left me with the Griffins.

We had known the Griffins when we lived in the U.S. I had a vague memory of traveling to a trailer park, Mom and I getting out of the car and climbing over the loose toys in the front yard. My mom whispered that this was the *divorced daughter's* place. The toys belonged to Mrs. Griffin's grandkids, *a pitiful slew of them*, my mom reprised.

Mr. and Mrs. Griffin were wrinkled like crumpled brown paper. I considered them nice, except her smile sat crooked on her face like Joker's on *Batman*. Mr. Griffin always looked like he was going to pinch me, like teasing a little girl was his next favorite thing after whiskey and cigarettes. They sat in their dark living room staring out as the fruit bats darted around the trees, the screeching muffled through their glass wall. Swirling whiskey in their glasses, the ice tinkling, Mrs. Griffin said, "You go on up to bed. I'll come up later and kiss you goodnight." Her voice raspy and too happy, she smelled of hairspray and sour mash.

The Griffins' house was identical to ours, down to the same modern Danish teak furnishings, provided by the oil company. The only difference was the color scheme. Their dining room seat cushions were black leather, while ours were white. Our living room couch cushions were aqua blue. Theirs were seaweed green. My same room at their house was the guest room. But the twin bed shoved against the wall by the air conditioner felt the same if I closed my eyes tight. The buzz of the A/C drowned out any noises from downstairs, and deadened Mr. Griffin's phlegmy, emphysemic cough.

When Mrs. Griffin came upstairs to say goodnight the first night, I could hear her thick breathing from the doorway. I pretended I was asleep, afraid she'd come over and kiss me. She didn't, and she never came back any night after.

I crossed the carport to my own house to have Philip fix me breakfast. Every morning he asked the same thing, "Small Sister want pancakes?"

"Can I have kippers instead?" I'd ask.

A row of small brown bottles sat on the lazy Susan in the long table's center. While Philip opened the can of smoked fish, I'd take the prophylactics one by one to keep the various and sundry tropical diseases at bay. I took my pills diligently. The hard, bullet-shaped drugs with the bitter aftertaste always lodged in my throat, choking me before going the rest of the way down. Paludrine and chloroquine we took for malaria. Vaccines: Gamma Globulin for hepatitis, tetanus and typhoid, rabies, polio and yellow fever. I had been told the pills, vaccinations, and boosters protected me.

Who needs parents when you have inoculations?

When Samson honked the horn of the Volkswagen school bus in the driveway, I'd grab my water bottle and run out the door, Philip wishing me a splendid day. Alice would be there when I returned. And this, with a rock in my throat, is how I passed the time Mom stayed away.

What Won't Rub Off

"The world was now peopled with vague, fantastic figures that dissolved under her steady gaze and then formed again in new shapes."

—*Things Fall Apart* by Chinua Achebe

THE FIRST TIME I VENTURED OUTSIDE THE GATES OF THE compound alone, James the gateman had left the white wrought iron gates open, and he was nowhere in sight. Usually he squatted in the compound's front house carport. His pin-striped robes splayed out around his wide feet while he hovered over the tiny tin-can stove. When the Harmattan winds brought a chill, he'd warm his hands over the flame. The dry Harmattan haze made my skin want to peel off like a snake's. I'd heard a tree trunk could break from desiccating during Harmattan season.

Maybe James had gone to run an errand, or maybe he'd gone back to the servants' quarters at the rear of the compound for a pee break. Whatever the reason, the gates were open, wide open, and I was alone and bored with no one to play with. I had been told to never go outside the compound unless someone was with me. Mom had said it with that tone of voice that sounds like she would never want to lose me. So I didn't intend to disobey.

I hadn't gone more than a few feet, maybe to the end of the driveway, maybe across the street. Ladies carrying baskets as big as Land Rover tires, piled high with mangoes or bolts of fabric or even chickens, bustled around me. A cacophony of horns honked. Car engines revved as they sped off the roundabout from the main road on the next block.

I was looking up at the towering skyscraper across the street. The French girl from school lived in the silver-and-blue building. She didn't ride in our oil company vw school bus, so I never saw her except at school. She didn't speak English, and I didn't speak any more French than one to ten, but I wanted to be her friend. I wanted to be her friend for the sole reason that I wanted to listen to the lyrical twill of her words. I wanted to learn how to roll vocabulary around inside my mouth as she did. I wanted to learn how her tongue and lips made all pronunciations soft and lilty, how the simplest sound escaped so gracefully.

With my neck craned upward, I didn't notice what had started. I didn't notice until they started touching me. I had been surrounded by Nigerian children more or less my age. I could tell they also didn't speak English. Their language wasn't so much lyrical like French, but their words seemed to bounce. I liked listening to it too for its excitement and round consonants, letters that sounded nothing like mine. Right then it wasn't the language, it was the crowding. They had encircled me and jabbered so fast, laughing shyly. Their round, uplifted sentences resonated as if they were asking a question. I had no idea what it could be.

They took turns touching my arms, rubbing their hands down my forearm, back and forth, then giggling, then trading places with another kid in the back of the crowd. They'd rub a part of me, then look up into my face and ask the question that I couldn't decipher. If I had the answer, I thought, they'd let me go. It was like when Marty played calf rope with me. He'd hold me down and tickle me until I said "Calf rope!" It's the Texan version of crying uncle. I also imagined they had no idea what a calf rope was. They crammed in closer and closer and closer, until I couldn't budge. Until I couldn't breathe. They held my arms aloft and rubbed them incessantly with their little hands.

I heard James's flip-flops first—flap, flap, flap. Then his voice yelling, again in a language I didn't understand—lots of O's and B's and D's. "Scram," is what he must have said, because the kids surrounding me now scattered. As they dispersed, James touched the tops of their heads and reprimanded them. One smaller boy dodged James and ran up and rubbed my arm quickly before he could get caught then skedaddled off with the others.

"So sorry, Small Sister. So sorry," James said. "They just want to see if it rubs off."

"If *what* rubs off?" I asked, looking down at my arms where I could still feel the gentle, little fingertips.

"The white. They want to see if the white comes off."

The fingers had brushed at me no harder than someone trying to rub off talcum.

"Come back to compound, Small Sister," James said, waving me back nervously. He did not want me outside.

Across the street I saw Philip, our house steward, at the gate. In his white uniform, he was a figure of authority on the street, a man with a House Job. Philip shouted more Nigerian words, words round and thrust from the top of the throat. He didn't acknowledge me, and I knew James was in big trouble. Philip stuck his narrow chest out when he walked, pushing the buttons on his white tailored shirt as he trotted up to James. They shared a few sticky exchanges—I figured there would have been more if I hadn't been there—then Philip turned to me.

"Small Sister, you must not go outside compound." He put his big hand with the pink palm against the back of my arm and steered me ever so gently toward the gate. James rattled off more, and Philip shushed him. No one talked back to Philip.

The gate creaked closed then clanged behind us as James replaced the stick that normally latched the two gates together.

Inside the compound, alone again, I rubbed my arms. The white was there to stay. The Harmattan wind gave me goose bumps.

I will always be white. I will always live in a compound, maybe not physically but metaphorically, whether I want to or not. I will always be American. Does this make me a hideous person? I have my whole life to figure that out, to try not to be, but maybe it's my destiny. Maybe I don't have a choice because of the color that will not rub off.

What I am now in these pages is but a little girl with fingerprints leaving their impressions on my skin.

"Small Sister," called James. He had found me by the hibiscus bush. "Want lesson on bike?" James would teach me how to ride without training wheels.

ONLY A SLIVER OF MOM RETURNED. IT WAS AS IF SHE'D remembered to pack her suitcase but forgotten to pack herself before she left the U.S. She couldn't have known she had contracted malaria before she'd flown home. On the plane ride back to Nigeria, the fever, the chills, the delirium showed up.

The narrow space next to her bed, in my opinion, became too crowded with her friends. They seemed to just want to know what someone with malaria looked like. They worried that they too could end up sleeping the sleep of a thousand deaths. They whispered as if their voices would wake her from her sleep. But they could have shouted, and Mom wouldn't have woken up.

Unlike the other women who came and saw and never came again, Mrs. Betteridge came and sat by Mom's bedside for hours every day. Together we watched Mom sleeping, sweating, shivering. I stared at Mom's mouth hanging open as I hung my body over her big unpacked suitcase. This was the longest nap my mom had ever taken.

MY MOTHER IS PRONE TO NAPPING, SO I QUESTION MY MEMORIES again. I want to confirm that the gaping mouth, death-rattle breathing, and comatose limpness is all true. Her returning only to be wasting away is a twisted course, an unreasonable mash-up of good and evil.

She's like a wet bar of soap—the more I try to tighten my grip, the more she slips out of my hold. I remember her as not even here. Or there. Not with me. But somewhere else. Not in the U.S. at Mommom's funeral, but gone inside her delirium.

According to the Centers for Disease Control and Prevention, the Plasmodium falciparum is the parasite found in the Anopheles mosquito in sub-Saharan Africa. This tiny parasite causes the deadliest form of malaria. The symptoms include severe anemia, fever, chills, shaking, vomiting, and delusions.

This confirms. She was as close to death as I remember.

Near the ceiling above Mom's head, the air conditioner poked out of the wall and rumbled nonstop, pouring cold air into the room. Despite being early October, Africa didn't seem like fall at all. In the tiny spaces between the air conditioner and the wall, geckos slipped through. As I did with the horny toads in Texas, I snatched the long, lithe bodies, transparent with their blue veins visible through the rubbery skin. The geckos were quicker than their Texas cousins though, and I ended up holding many dangling tails between my fingers. I felt I had defiled them. Told again and again that the tails would grow back, I wanted to know how long it would take for the tail to grow back. How long would the lizard have to go about his life without his tail? How long would my mother sleep the sleep of a thousand deaths?

Every day I thought soon Mom would get up, and we could do something: sew, shop, sit in the sun. The things we used to do together. Jankara Market waited. Friday came to the gate with his pattern books and was turned away. Justus sold no thorn carvings at our house. Mrs. Betteridge and I sat side-by-side, waiting.

From my dad's empty side of the bed, I scooched in little increments closer to Mom. I stopped to see if I had disturbed her, then wiggled another inch or so closer. I checked to see whether her breathing changed. Then I zigzagged even nearer, until I was alongside her. Mom's body was so small, so thin that I could line up my body a hair's breadth next to hers. I neatly tucked myself into the crevices of her folds or curves, but we didn't fit together anymore. I had become bigger than she was. Or had she become smaller than I?

She was a sylph, her mass just an apparition in satin. I was seven and solid bone in cotton shorts.

Her breath, the intake and outgo, rattled like quills trying to flitter their way back into place on a wing. As long as I heard the thin whistle of air, I hoped she could still wake up. Since I expected at any moment she would slip away, I kept watch; if I were vigilant, she wouldn't disappear. She shivered. She trembled and shook, and through the covers I sensed she was about to split apart, that her needle bones would crack. I watched and waited, too afraid to touch. Too afraid with my touch her bones would break off into my hands like the lizard tails.

When I returned to our house after school, I ran upstairs, always finding Mrs. Betteridge. I stood at the end of the bed watching the rumpled sheets for movement. The linens puckered, the only clue Mom was there. The curtains drawn, the room felt dank, despite the pumping air conditioner. A dull, pink light cast from the bathroom. Mold grew in the corners of the white concrete walls, like the only living creature in the room. The carved mahogany headboard over her head showed scenes of Nigerian men and women dancing, carrying pots on their heads, strings of kola beads on their ankles, life on the outside portrayed as a still life on the inside.

Her eyes, once sea green now milky gray, opened a slit. They looked at me and said, *You're here.* Of course. I left only because I had to.

AS I AM WRITING THIS VERY SCENE—ABOUT SLIDING ACROSS the sheets to be near her itty-bitty body, about wanting her to wake up, about betraying her—this email from my mom arrives in my inbox:

From: martha wallen
Subject: Re: Hi
Date: August 13, 2013 8:20:57 AM PDT
To: Amy Wallen

Amy, I had such a realistic dream about you, when I woke up I expected you to be there. You were little and I was asleep and you wanted me to get up so you crawled up in bed with me. I woke up and you weren't there.

But I am there. Doesn't she know that? I'm always there. I am right here.

She does that—knows things. Even with her all the way in Texas and me in California. Is this a sixth sense? Is she with me even when she's not with me? Or is it me? Am I with her even when not there physically? Did she hear me banging and rattling the sliding glass doors with my little fist after all? Maybe I am the dream, the apparition. Maybe we are all apparitions. The physical realm is where we come and go. The imagination is where we really reside.

But that is too ethereal an explanation for me. I continue my plundering, my digging, my search to see what is true, what is not. Right now, my mother's absence in Nigeria, both real and esoteric, feels like a curse. But, remember, I don't believe in curses. She does.

It's too early for the Chancay Curse. Maybe it's something we picked up in the ghost towns in Nevada. Or maybe it's just a funeral, a mosquito, and an American child.

She left only because she had to.

THINGS CARRIED ON: DAD CAME AND WENT FROM THE BUSH. I went to school every day. Philip prepared my breakfast of kippers and set my water bottle by the front door to grab on my way out. Samson picked me up in the little blue vw school bus. Alice met me after school. James watched me ride my bike.

And Mom slept.

From Gypsy to Socialite

> When approached by a precocious young girl
> selling Girl Scout cookies, Wednesday Addams
> asks, "Are they made from *real* Girl Scouts?"
>
> —Christina Ricci playing Wednesday Addams in
> *The Addams Family* movie

A MONTH LATER, JUST BEFORE HALLOWEEN, I FOUND MOM sitting at her black Singer sewing machine. With Suzanne gone, my room doubled as Mom's sewing room. Suzanne's bed was covered in fabric swatches, dresses Mom had started before she got sick, and spools of thread and bobbins, her sewing notions spilled from their container.

To see her out of bed, I was electric with both giddiness and fear. Her upright presence, albeit slouched, surprised me. I sat and watched in awe as Mom held the sharp-pointed seam ripper in her hand and snipped the hem of the orange paisley skirt I'd worn for last year's Halloween costume. With rhythmic speed, she slit open each stitch.

"You'll be Mrs. Astor this year," she said to me, holding the orange skirt up to my waist. Her tone as slow as her skin was pallid.

"Mrs. Who?" I looked down at the ruffled hem at my toes. "Isn't this the skirt I wore as a gypsy last year?" I instantly regretted arguing but was disappointed all the same. The air conditioner kicked on, sucking out the humidity.

"*The* Mrs. Astor?" she said.

Doesn't every seven-year-old know about wealthy socialites from the nineteenth century? Aren't all the other seven-year-olds begging their moms, please, oh please, let me be a Vanderbilt, a Roosevelt, or at the very least a Carnegie this Halloween!

"We'll get you better earrings than last year's gold loops. You can borrow some of my faux pearl baubles."

"I don't want to be Mrs. Astor," I said, whoever this lady was. Why couldn't we just go to the grocery store and buy a store-bought costume like in the States?

Outside on the windowsill, an orange-and-purple agama lizard did push-ups, staking claim for his territory.

"I'd love to be Mrs. Astor," my mom said. "She was the richest woman in the United States. She could even turn the Vanderbilts away at a party. She had clout, did what she wanted, and no one disagreed with her." Mom seemed so tired, but worse than that, angry. Right then, she must have felt she could trade herself in to be anybody else. I agonized over how I could be a blessing more than a bother.

"*You* want to be Mrs. Astor?" I asked. If Mom wanted to be Mrs. Astor, whoever she was, then I wanted to be her too. "Okay," I said, still hoping for a better, more recognizable costume. A witch with a pointy hat and a broom would have been nice. But if it pleased Mom, then *The* Mrs. Astor I would be.

Later, I would learn this was the same Mrs. Astor of the Waldorf-Astoria Hotel in New York City. *The* Mrs. Astor who threw elitist parties and considered the Vanderbilts beneath her. Mrs. Astor who the press dubbed *The* Mrs. Astor when the family fought over rightful titles. The same Mrs. Astor whose daughter built her a forty-foot cenotaph at the intersection of Wall Street and Broadway in New York. Cenotaph. What could be a more appropriate tomb for a narcissist than an empty one?

For Halloween the next day I dressed in the long, gypsy-turned-formal skirt, earrings, and a red T-shirt. I couldn't find anything else that matched the orange, and Mom couldn't get out of bed that morning to help me be *The* Mrs. Astor.

Sitting in the v w school bus crammed with goblins and princesses and devils, I endured my earlobes swelling and itching from the clip-on bauble earrings.

"Who are you supposed to be?" Sandra Dodson, my new friend a year older than me, asked. I envied the Raggedy Ann costume complete with red mop hair she wore.

"I'm Mrs. Astor," I said for the first time that day, then I corrected myself. "*The* Mrs. Astor."

"Who?" Sandra showed no recognition.

"A rich lady," I shrugged, wishing for that pointy witch's hat. "High society," I added, although I had no idea what that meant. I figured it had something to do with wearing long dresses and fancy jewelry. "She's famous," I added.

"Really?!" Sandra replied. I wondered whether maybe I did look the part as I scratched at my earlobe.

Our attention switched as we crossed the bridge onto Victoria Island. We drove past the man lying against the green-and-white concrete barrier. He'd been lying there on his side every day that week and hadn't changed positions, so by Wednesday we'd figured him for dead and had started calculating.

"He's even bigger today," Sandra said.

"I bet it's tomorrow," I said, putting my long, straight hair behind my ears.

The dead man had started to bloat. My costume forgotten for the moment, I changed the subject to how many days until the dead man popped.

At school Mrs. Lavigne, the homeroom teacher, asked who I was, and I told her the name of the famous real estate heir's wife. She raised her eyebrows, and asked, "Do you even know who she is?"

I started to explain, but I somehow knew Mrs. Lavigne already knew and only wanted to know whether *I* knew who she was. I did not. So I tried the best way out. "Me?!" I replied. She shook her head and let it go. Mine was an odd duck among the other costumes, but being Mrs. Astor pleased my mom. I would try harder.

When Mrs. Nwoko arrived for Nigerian culture class, she had us make groundnut cookies. I assumed they would be peanut butter cookies as I had made with Suzanne, where we smashed the fork tines crisscross on spoonfuls of dough. When Mrs. Nwoko started to dump chopped onions in the batter to make a special Nigerian cookie, I remembered that Mom had said Mrs. Astor had clout, so I told Mrs. Nwoko *The* Mrs. Astor didn't eat onions. She dumped them in anyway.

SANDRA HAD INVITED ME OVER TO HER HOUSE AFTER SCHOOL. I was conflicted over betraying my mom, leaving her alone or playing with the Dodson's American toys. Mrs. Dodson, a small German mother, fixed us an after-school snack of oxtail soup. I soon forgot my mother was home sleeping.

"Is it really made from oxtails?" I asked.

"No," Mrs. Dodson said in her thick German accent. Her deep voice didn't match her tiny stature, which made me want to watch her as she spoke, as though someone else hid inside her petite body. "It's made from powder." She pulled from the trash the yellow packet that read Knorr in red on the corner. I was pretty sure she was lying as my mom did to get me to eat cream of mushroom soup. Only Mrs. Dodson didn't have to lie, because I liked the blackish-red soup.

Being at Sandra's was almost better than Christmas because she had American toys. At my house, I played Barbies by myself, and mancala, the Nigerian bead game, with Alice. But at Sandra's house, still in our Halloween costumes, we sat cross-legged on the floor of her parents' den and played Monkeys in a Barrel for a while, then pick-up sticks. I had never played these games before, and Sandra patiently showed me how each one worked.

After working our way through Milton Bradley, we ended up outside, me trying to twirl my hips to keep Sandra's hula hoop up. The fun was endless, and I already hoped to get invited back.

Then Sandra took me to the front of the house where a cage took up one whole corner of the porch, from top to bottom and side to side. A monkey, I thought, like the Andersons' in the compound next to ours. But instead, Sandra pointed out a scaly monster the size of Mrs. Dodson's forearm. To me, he looked like a giant version of the Texas horny toads that were supposed to spit blood, although disappointingly, I never did witness the blood spitting.

"A chameleon," Sandra told me. She removed her red mop wig, and now her tangled blonde hair fell to her shoulders.

I rubbed Mrs. Astor's pinching earrings.

"He changes colors." Sandra opened the cage door, and we crawled in. The chameleon's eyes rolled around, keeping tabs on us. His rigid but jerky posture made him appear as if we'd scared him to death.

"What color does he change to?" A big gray-brown sawed-off branch wired to the cage's bars served as the lizard's perch.

"Whatever color he's lying on," Sandra said.

I must not have seemed impressed enough. "Stay here," she said, and she left me with the lizard. After she darted off, I stared at him. He wasn't as fascinating as the blue-and-orange agama lizards in our garden. The chameleon just lay there on the branch. The agama lizards did fast push-ups on the bamboo fence and had fierce hissing fights defending their territory. I rubbed my finger along the chameleon's back. His eyes rolled around toward my finger. I liked the flecked feeling of his skin, how a lizard looks like stone but once touched is soft and squishy like a water balloon. People, dead or alive, could be like that I had discovered.

My touching must have scared him, because his tail curled tight into a coil. When I stepped back, my maxiskirt snagged on a lower limb, tearing my gypsy-turned-socialite skirt across the back of my legs. Mrs. Astor must have rolled over in her grave. I'd have to be the tattered Little Match Girl next year.

Sandra climbed back into the cage, holding a piece of red construction paper.

"What's his name?" I asked.

"Flipper."

I hummed the TV theme song about the rescued dolphin . . . *faster than lightning . . .*

"Watch," she said, and she scooted the red paper under the chameleon. We waited. He turned a darker shade of gray, then kind of brown.

"See," she said. I wasn't sure whether what I saw was a trick of the light or a real change. We waited some more. The chameleon reached this bruised purple stage then shifted to a dull red. Just like the construction paper.

I grabbed a handful of skirt to make sure I didn't trip, and I leaned closer. "How do you get him to do that?" I asked Sandra. This was ten times better than hula hoops.

"I think he just concentrates real hard," she said. "Like when we try to figure out our times tables, and they slowly appear in our brain." I hadn't gotten to times tables yet, so I was still perplexed.

That afternoon, I decided I wanted to live at Sandra's house instead of my own, at least until Sandra's dad came home and yelled at Mrs. Dodson *for no good reason*, as my mom would say. His outburst scared me. My dad never yelled like that, his arms crazy, his chest puffed up.

"Time to go," Mrs. Dodson said. I could tell the fun was over. She drove me back to Omo Osagie Street.

BACK AT MY HOUSE, I DIDN'T GO STRAIGHT TO MOM'S ROOM as usual. Instead, I lay on my bed, still in my Mrs. Astor costume, my earlobes red and pulsing from the clip-on earrings. But I ignored the hurt as I thought about the chameleon. I stayed very still and imagined I was turning into Mrs. Astor. If I thought hard enough it could happen. Maybe, like the chameleon, I could change. In my costume, laid out, concentrating. If I could be Mrs. Astor, then I could be who Mom wanted to be. Who Mom wanted me to be. I wanted it so much, that with my eyes closed I could feel Mrs. Astor from my throbbing earlobes to my flip-flops. I pictured myself turning Friday and Justus away. I pointed my toes like wearing high heels, bending the rubber soles of my flip-flops into C's. I thought hard, harder than I did for spelling. Wanting it enough, willing it—I could make it happen. My fingers fidgeted with the cotton nap of the chenille tendrils, and the air conditioner fluttered the fine hairs on my legs as I thought of nothing else but Mrs. Astor.

When I opened my eyes, I saw it hadn't worked. I was still me. I decided to start smaller. Like the chameleon I'd start by changing color. So I closed my eyes and concentrated on the yellow bedspread. With my eyes clenched, sensed a small presence in the doorway. My mom, silent and wilted.

"What are you doing?" she said.

"Turning yellow," I said. "Have I turned yet?"

"You're close," she said, "but not quite. Why do you want to be yellow?"

I explained about Sandra's chameleon. I didn't explain about how I wanted to be what she wanted to be. I was afraid she'd pooh-pooh my idea. Instead I just told her how the lizard seemed to concentrate, then became red. I pictured my costume, sensed my swollen earlobes, and became dizzy with hope.

She said, "When you're finally yellow, come eat, because Philip said supper is ready."

"How about now?" I asked again, craving her approval.

"Yep, you're practically a lemon." I could sense she cracked a smile. I felt her silhouette turn, and I heard her house slippers shuffle and leave.

I threw open my eyes. My bones ached with disappointment. Looking down at my body, I had already turned back to Amy, the little white girl in a torn dress.

What a stupid idea. I yanked off the bauble earrings, tossed them on my bed and ran downstairs on the heels of my mother.

I could not be her, nor could I ever be what she wanted to be. I would have to settle for being *with* her as often and as much as I could. For being what she wanted *me* to be. My mother was frail. She was all I had. I had to keep her, carefully guard her, ruffle no feathers, or her brittle bones could break. If I caused any trouble, if she deemed me unsuitable as a daughter, she could disappear, she could leave me. And, if something happened to her, well, I didn't want to think of the consequences. I must keep her from leaving me again, I must do what I must to keep her nearby. That was my hope. My delusion.

I TELL MY PARENTS THAT I'M WRITING IT ALL DOWN. THAT I'm telling our stories. "I'm telling about all the dead bodies," I say. My dad laughs. "Did you tell the one about the man in the road that exploded? You and Sandra watched for him every day."

My mother, on her end of the line, makes a sound of disgust, disapproval at our morbid banter. Mrs. Astor, I figure, would not have stood for such activities with her daughter. I am glad I'm not an Astor. Or even a lowly Vanderbilt.

"I did," I say. I am laughing too. My dad remembers how I came home and reported on the man's bloat.

My mother told me once as an adult, "You're just like your father." I don't remember the context, but her comment was meant to be derogatory. I remember feeling shame and pride pommeling each other inside me. I am and I am not like him, just as I am and am not like her.

But which parts of me belong to whom? And which belong to me?

Bees and Bad Men

> The belief in witchcraft and the power to
> change shapes is common in Nigeria.
>
> —BBC News 23 January 2009

MY DAD WAS HOME FROM THE BUSH, AND THAT MEANT I HAD
someone sitting with me at the breakfast table. He read the *Daily Sun*
and didn't say much, but I liked having him home. Outside the dining
room I could hear the bumblebees buzzing over the begonias and
elephant ear bushes that grew beneath the window. The bees made
me nervous. As big as my thumb, covered in black velvet fur, they
flew all over our garden among the hibiscus, begonias, and banana
trees. The dining room sat just under my second-story bedroom, and
each morning I could hear the bees' hum get louder as the sun rose.

"Daddy," I said, when a bee hit the windowpane, tapping per-
sistently to come in.

He looked up, rustled the paper as though shaking off the words
from the page.

"Can bees get inside like the geckos?" The bees hummed outside
the glass, strategizing, planning their invasion, whispering their intentions to the elephant ears.

"They're just bees," my dad said. "They won't hurt you."

"They sting," I reminded him. "Bees sting."

He looked out the window, watching for a moment as the black fur balls bounced, bumbling in the air. "Not these bees," he said.

I watched their clumsy flight, wondering what he meant. "Not these?" I asked.

"These bees don't sting. Not this kind." He returned his gaze to the newspaper, rustling the pages again.

"Why not?" I asked.

"They just aren't the kind that sting. That's the other kind."

I listened to their buzz wondering, Could I ignore them? Could I walk through the garden without having to watch my back? That corner, where the bushes grew lower, I liked to shimmy up the bamboo fence and jump down to the neighbor's garden on the other side. I would try after breakfast, but for now I didn't want Dad to return to his newspaper.

I reminded him we needed to take our malaria pills every day.

"That's right," he said. "You don't want to be sick, like your mom."

"Did Mom not take her pills?" I asked.

"Eat your kippers," he said. My dad liked kippers for breakfast too, and this pleased me to no end. "Stinky, smelly fish," my mother called them. But my dad and I liked the smoky, salty flavor. The stranger the food, the more we liked it.

"Master," Philip came through the kitchen door. "I see you are reading the *Daily Sun*."

"Yes, Philip, what is it?" My father looked up from his paper.

"Then you read about the bad man on the loose. Small Sister should not go out of compound." Philip stood straight as a soldier in his angel-white Nehru jacket and creased pants, his dark, pink-edged bare feet sticking out from underneath. "Too dangerous, Master."

"Philip, all kinds of crooks are out there all the time," my father replied, a little grin on his face.

"Yes, Master, but today the police are chasing a man who attacked a little girl."

"Amy's going to a birthday party today, Philip, so she'll have someone watching her. Thank you for looking out for her."

"Yes, Master." Philip bowed and backed up into the kitchen. He'd said all he could say, but his face drew in with puzzlement. I wish I could have told Philip that I preferred to be confined to the compound with him than go to the birthday party.

"BIRTHDAY PARTIES," MY MOTHER SAID, "ARE *FUN*," AS THOUGH there were no other possibility. The cake, the games, the prizes, the free-wheeling, rambunctious screamfest of it all. As a seven-year-old, other than the momentary stress of wondering whether anyone saw me cheating at pin-the-tail-on-the-donkey, I usually liked going to birthday parties. But not this one. This party was the Italian girl's birthday party. All the sons and daughters of my dad's bosses would be there. And me. Apparently we were the only American family that worked for Agip Oil in Nigeria.

My mom lay in her bed with a saggy-faced look. Dr. Hassan had just visited and said she needed to get out of bed more often, to try to encourage more energy. He said not to overdo it, but she needed some sunshine. Otherwise she was just lying in her grave waiting. I was trying my darnedest to behave, because Mom was angry about Dr. Hassan's diagnosis.

In her suitcase Mom had brought back from the States a collection of birthday gifts. The selection in Nigerian markets for little kids' birthday parties consisted of thorn carvings, elephant hair bracelets. and ivory tusks. Not exactly expat children's first choices.

I watched Mom get out of bed, make her way down the hall, me following, then stop at the closet near my bathroom. When she reached up to the shelf we deemed the Birthday Gift Shelf, a shelf too high for me to reach or see what sat on it, and took down the Miss Polly doll, my awe couldn't contain itself. The Miss Polly doll had golden hair and a tiny comb to keep it tangle free. The Miss Polly doll wore the cutest little green dress with embroidered trim. The Miss Polly doll I coveted for myself.

"Can I have that doll?" I said to my mother. "I think I love her."

In her weakened malarial state, she handed me the doll, mumbled, "It's a birthday gift, Amy. It's selfish to want the gift for your own." Then she headed back to her bed.

"But," I tried to explain. "Couldn't we give another gift?" Even I saw the selfishness in that statement—the gift Mom had picked was too good to give away. But I'd really, truly fallen in love.

My bare feet slapped the cool marble floor behind my mother as her house shoes shuffled back down the hall toward her room. I knew I had only about ten feet to convince her before she'd be back in bed, eyes closed and all communication turned off. "Please!" I whined.

"Amy!" she said in a tone I recognized—subject ended. If she were well she would have added, "Do you want a swat?" But she had no oomph to give a spanking. I watched her slide back into the bed and disappear under the covers. Anymore all she had to do was close her eyes, and her whole body would sag into a limp resemblance of who she used to be. Her eyes fluttered open momentarily as if to say, *you still here?* The air conditioner rumbled on and filled the air, corner to corner, with noisy silence. I held the Miss Polly doll in my hands. Miss Polly was locked away behind a plastic shield with cardboard backing. This was a doll worth keeping. A doll I could have hours of fun with. Although she was small, her body had heft. With her slight smile and the way her big eyes looked up wishfully, she was solid. The other, hollow dolls on the Birthday Gift Shelf had smiles painted on that slipped past the rim of the lips, eyes that stared ahead with a zombielike glaze, and their hair was frizzy.

"Get your dad to help you wrap it," Mom said with a big sigh. Gray and sleepy, she said everything with a big sigh anymore.

Dad! I thought. He would see the Miss Polly doll was too good to give away. I rushed downstairs where he was working on setting up the reel-to-reel tape player to record the new music he'd gotten from his friends. Tom Jones sang, "Why, why, why, Delilah!" and then Neil Diamond, Mom's favorite, sang "Sweet Caroline."

"Daddy," I said from behind him as he knelt on the floor in front of the stereo equipment.

"What is it, Amy?" He didn't turn around at first, fiddling with the knobs and buttons on the big silver Akai machines.

"Look," I said and held up the Miss Polly doll for him to see. He turned around, and I explained that the other toys in the hall closet on that high Birthday Shelf—the faux Barbies with thin, hollow plastic bodies and nappy yellow polyester hair; the pink-and-green plastic jewelry kit with snap-on jewels; the eggs of Silly Putty; and the water pistols—those were all much better gifts to give to the Italian girls.

He smiled. "What's wrong with the Italian girls?"

I was stumped. I had nothing against the Italians exactly. "They speak only Italian, and I speak only English," I said, hoping he'd understand. He nodded. But I wasn't sure he fully comprehended my plight. "They ride a different school bus than I do," I explained further. "I can't go to their house after school to play." Why waste a perfectly good Miss Polly doll, which would fit in quite well with my current Barbie collection, on someone with whom I'd never even get to play with Miss Polly vicariously? He didn't respond to my idea. He just turned around and began fiddling with the knobs again.

"You about ready to go?" he said.

"Yes," I said, wishing I could sound excited. "I gotta pick out something to wear though." My mom usually did that for me. But since she was napping, my dad helped instead.

In my room, I set the Miss Polly doll on the end of Suzanne's bed by the door. Dad and I decided on the red-and-orange plaid overalls and white dress-up blouse that buttoned down the back. While I got dressed, Dad said he'd wrap the gift.

"You know," I said, starting off slow, "there's another doll on the Birthday Shelf that would be just as good and not the Miss Polly doll."

My dad looked at Miss Polly through her plastic shield. "This looks like a pretty good gift to me."

"But there are others," I said, "just look." I struggled to button the blouse in the back, so he helped me and then went to the Birthday

Shelf in the closet just outside my room. Oh, I was so elated to think that just like that he might go for it. He might actually put the Miss Polly doll back and give the Italian girl a faux Barbie instead.

"This looks like the best gift," he said. "We'll give this one. I'll wrap it, you get ready. Hurry up." And he headed down the stairs.

"No!" I said. I had no choice now. I had to resort to whining. "Can't you give her something else? She won't know."

I watched him shake his head no then make his way toward the living room below. "Hurry up," he said, putting his finger to his lips indicating I needed to be quiet because Mom was sleeping.

I pulled up my red-and-orange overalls and put on my red Keds. Then I slumped down the stairs where the package sat wrapped in Donald Duck paper on the table next to the reel-to-reel tape player. My dad sat on the modern Danish couch reading the *Daily Sun*. "Ready?" he asked, lowering the paper, smiling at me.

I tried to smile back, but I just couldn't with the Miss Polly doll all wrapped up, ready for her sacrifice.

He dropped me off at the Italian families' compound. A long gravel driveway led up from the front gate to the five houses. The Marcellis lived in the house at the back of the circle. I rang the bell. A cacophony of little girls and boys echoed all the way out onto the marble front porch. "Buongiorno!" Mrs. Marcelli said to me upon opening the big wooden front doors. Peeking around the front entrance, I could see all the kids gallivanting around the spacious living room decorated in black leather furniture and fur rugs. The mothers all had tall hair and wore tight blouses and hip-hugger pants with high-heeled shoes. The little boys wore suits and ties, and the girls wore frilly dresses like I had never owned in my life. Crinoline and taffeta crinkled and swayed as the girls ran giggling around me. One mother lifted a strap on my plaid overalls and said something in Italian, making all the other mothers laugh. Mrs. Marcelli swiped the gift from my hand, and I knew then it would take all the will I had to keep from crying in the next few hours. Maybe my dad would return early, I hope, hope, hoped.

But he didn't. We, or I should say they, played games as at any birthday party, only not like any birthday party I'd ever been to. No pin-the-tail-on-the-donkey for me to cheat at. Instead there was some game where words were called out, and the fastest kid to raise his or her hand won a prize. I didn't understand any of the Italian words blurted out, so I didn't raise my hand once. I considered raising it randomly just to be the first, as I was a pretty quick draw, but since I wasn't sure what the word was, and I still hadn't recovered fully from the humiliation of my red-and-orange plaid overalls, I changed my mind. A little boy in a pinstriped suit sat next to me at the black lacquered dining room table. He kept kicking at my red Keds.

"Cut it out," I whispered.

He kicked harder.

"Stop it."

He smiled wickedly and hauled off a good wallop into the side of my foot. I moved my feet to the other side of the chair and stuck my tongue out at him. An adult hand, a mother's hand, but thick and burly like a man's, swooped down and slapped the back of my head. I looked up and a tall-haired mother smirked at me. I crossed my little arms so tight I thought they'd pop out of their sockets. If my mother wasn't sick she would have come with me to the party. Make friends, she'd say. That was her answer to everything, and a choice I usually made reluctantly. I looked around the room. I felt none of these kids wanted me as their friend, nor did I really want to be theirs. Not if it meant I had to wear a dress.

Cake! Now that I understood, Italian or English. Cake was being served. The kicking boy got in line behind me, and so I went to the end. I watched as the kids ran by with their cake. For my own birthday, my favorite and first choice was always chocolate. White cake was a waste of time, and any other flavor, that just seemed silly and a missed opportunity for chocolate. But what these kids carried on their plates looked like a slimy mush. Like pudding cake. Not really even cake. "Tiramisu," Mrs. Marcelli said as she grinned at me and handed over my mush-on-a-plate.

I took mine to the leather living room. I liked scooting my

rubber-soled Keds across the fur rugs. The other kids had gone out
to the backyard. They ran around the mango trees, and the kicking
boy, I could see through the sliding glass doors, shook a yellow war-
bler's nest out of the giant red hibiscus. I finally got up the nerve and
tasted my mush cake. Like chalky baby food. Worse than baby food.
Gerber's chocolate pudding baby food that my mom used to buy in
the States in little jars and let me have for snacks after school, that
wasn't so bad. But this pudding was twangy and smelled like Dad's
scotch bottle when opened on a Friday night. I couldn't even swallow
the piece of tiramisu I'd put in my mouth.

While everyone else was in the backyard, I slipped out the front
doors. With my mush cake, I went out to the gravel driveway. The kids
in the backyard could be heard over the roof of the big two-story stone
house. I squatted at the edge of the driveway by the red azalea bushes
and low-lying geraniums. With my spoon I dug a shallow grave in the
gravel, scooped my tiramushu in, then spit out the bit I still hadn't
swallowed as well. Bumblebees flirted with the azaleas. I remembered
what my dad had told me that morning about the bees. They knew
my secret, and they wouldn't tell.

As I shoveled gravel over the cake's grave, I heard, "Emmmmiii!"
Mrs. Marcelli stood at the front doors waving at me to come back.
She was smiling, but so far every Italian I had met smiled when they
kicked or swatted me. She motioned harder. I glanced down the other
end of the driveway to see whether my dad might be coming to get
me. The other families had Nigerian drivers, but my mom and dad
had a Ford Escort with the steering wheel on the right side and no
driver. The white Ford Escort was not coming to get me yet. "Emmi!"
Mrs. Marcelli tried again. "Geefts!" she said in the best English I'd
heard in a few hours. This meant I got to go watch Angela Marcelli
open the Miss Polly doll and claim it as her own. I'd rather be at
home watching my mother die of malaria. But I crunched across the
gravel and handed my now empty plate to Mrs. Marcelli, hoping she
wouldn't notice the slimy skid marks where I'd slid the cake over the
edge into its interment.

Inside I found a place in the back of the circle of kids where I could watch as Angela ripped the paper off the packages. Her black Mary Janes swung under the black lacquered dining room chair as she sat like a queen. She went through each gift with oohs and aahs like the Fourth of July in the States. Then she came to mine, and my nose twitched. This could quite possibly be the moment when I finally cried. Angela ripped the paper off, flinging Donald Duck and his pals to the side, and held up the doll for everyone to see. I blinked. Was I seeing what I thought I saw? It was the faux Barbie. The doll with the smile painted on lopsided. The doll with the red sequined dress who was an inch too tall to fit into Barbie's clothes. I found myself applauding, sitting up on my knees, taking notice of what the next gift might be.

When the party ended, I stood outside at the edge of the gravel driveway while the other kids were picked up. I stood on my tiptoes looking frantically through all the cars for our white Ford Escort. I could hardly wait to tell Daddy what happened. As if he didn't know! But he'd get a kick out of how it all happened, how I was surprised. I would tell him all the details, even about the mushu cake. I pictured us laughing about it. I pictured his big smile.

My dad didn't pick me up.

I spotted the blue Renault in the line of cars. The sting of spitting gravel hit my shins. Pious, the Griffins' driver, waved at me from the driver's seat a few cars away. Pious maneuvered the little blue Renault among the black Mercedes Benzes and green Peugeots and red Fiats driven by other Nigerian chauffeurs. I didn't want it to be Pious. I wanted Dad to pick me up, just as he dropped me off. I wanted to sit in the car and tell him my story. I wanted to laugh with him; after all those hours of wanting to cry at the party, I wanted to laugh with Daddy. Pious pulled up, and I climbed in the front passenger seat and slammed the door behind me.

"Small Sister have good time?" Pious asked. Unlike Philip, Pious dressed in a navy blue suit, pants, and a Nehru jacket. His hands rested with confidence on the steering wheel.

I nodded. "I did," I said. "I had fun." But something was missing.

Something that I wanted more than a doll. I was missing my dad. I was missing my mom. I didn't want to be picked up by a driver. I wanted my family. And I knew Pious would want me to go to church. That's all he ever talked about.

Pious pulled out of the big stone gates behind two Fiats.

I'd gotten what I wanted—Miss Polly didn't go to live in the house with the Italians. I could surmise that she would maybe be mine, probably at Christmas, which was coming up. But sitting in the car with Pious, I didn't feel what had transpired was worth it. I had had a glorious moment of my parent acknowledging me with what I had said I wanted. But what about what I needed? At seven, all I knew was that I'd gotten my doll, but it felt like I'd somehow traded my dad for Miss Polly.

Next to me Pious was talking. "This Sunday, I will take Small Sister to mass at Christ the King?" Every chance he got Pious asked me if I wanted to go to church with him that Sunday. He attended the Catholic Church, but I didn't want to attend any church. We had been Methodists when we lived in the States. All five of us, the whole family, scrambled every Sunday into the Buick to get to church on time. I didn't want to go with just Pious.

"Maybe next week," I told Pious, watching the coconut vendors climb the palm trees as we traversed the side streets.

"Ten thousand people attend mass at my church every Sunday," he told me.

Outside the car, on the main road heading back home, the car horns honked incessantly, passersby walked elbow-to-elbow, and beggars—in handmade sandals, with stained and scarred faces and missing limbs—crammed in with those dressed in both Western and traditional wear. It was the kind of scene where someone could ask, "Where is God in this picture?"

"Ten thousand people who know Jesus Christ as their Savior," Pious continued.

Ten thousand people. One church. Eight million people. One city.

In Ely we had climbed into the Buick on Sundays because that's what we did as good Americans. We went to church on Sundays. That was the only church I knew. We had slipped out of that habit easily. The belief in God was not innate, and we each went our own way. Me, I didn't want ten thousand people. I wanted four. I may have prayed for the Miss Polly doll, if whining counts as prayer. My dad was no savior. So who was I to believe in?

WHEN I REACHED HOME, MORE NEWS HAD COME FROM THE streets about the man who attacked the little girl. Philip stood in the kitchen filtering our drinking water, and my dad stood on the back porch, just outside the screen door. On the concrete chopping block by the door sat the long stalk of bananas that Anthony, our gardener, had just cut from the banana tree. Each banana was no bigger than Dad's thumb but sweeter than pudding. My dad pulled a dark pink banana from the ripe stalk.

"The little girl screamed," Philip continued, "and when the police chased the man around a corner he turned himself into a goat."

"Turned himself into a goat?" my dad asked through a mouthful of soft banana.

"Yes, Master, he turned himself into a goat to escape the police." Philip poured the large heavy kettle of boiling water through the top of the drinking water filtration.

"You don't really believe that, do you, Philip?" My dad swallowed the banana in two bites.

Philip nodded a quick nod. "Oh yes, Master. They have the goat in jail to prove it." Steam curled around Philip's head from the kettle's spout.

"Jail?" My dad's laugh floated out of the compound.

"Yes, Master. The police constable insist the goat turn himself back into a man before they execute him."

I looked in the fridge while they talked. I wanted to tell my dad about the Miss Polly doll, but this discussion, I was certain, meant I wouldn't be able to ride my bike outside the compound, and I had plans to go next door to Lynn Marie Tudge's house.

"Come on, Philip, how could he turn himself into a goat?" My father pulled another banana off the stalk, peeled and popped this one whole into his mouth.

Philip put the kettle down on the stove, his back to my dad. "With the juju, Master." He stood tall in his white suit, very handsome and proud of himself and his position.

Finding nothing in the fridge except the bowl of potato skins soaking in water that Philip would later fry into homemade potato chips, I turned to see what Dad would tell Philip about the juju.

"They should just barbecue the goat."

Grandaddy barbecued goat in Texas. All the cousins gathered at the little house with the big barbecue pit. Cabrito, potato salad, and pinto beans. I'd stuff myself and then stuff myself again when the churned homemade peach ice cream made the rounds. No one in that little house in Texas with the barbecued goat thought of executions or juju or even malaria. I waited for Philip to laugh at the barbecue comment. No one was funnier than my dad, except Marty.

Philip didn't laugh, but he was used to my dad's bad jokes. He lit another fire under the kettle filled with water.

"Madam doesn't want dinner, and I've been invited to the Dels' for a party, so you can have the evening off," my father told Philip. "Keep me updated on the goat." He walked through the kitchen, patting me on the head as he passed through, his sticky fingers on my hair. "And I'll be heading back to the bush tomorrow." Gone as quick as he came.

"Yes, Master," Philip nodded and watched my father walk back into the main house. "Small Sister must not leave compound," he said to me, his voice lowered. I shrugged a disappointed okay.

Because of the Man Turned Goat incident, I figured Philip was keeping an extra eye out and might say something, so I snuck around the back instead of taking my bike. I climbed over the back fence of the compound to get to Lynn Marie's house. How safe was it for me to be out of the compound on my own? I never went far, just in the neighborhood, but I never had anyone ask me where I was going or where I had been. Yet I always had a sense the staff had an eye on me.

THE NEXT WEEK PHILIP ASKED FOR THE DAY OFF SO HE COULD go to the execution of the goat. Because the executions were held on Bar Beach on Victoria Island near our school, and because tens of thousands of people made the trek to view to the public executions, the route became impassable, so we got the day off from school.

Execution days to me, as a kid, were like snow days in Nevada. In Nevada a blizzard arrived overnight and covered the roads with deep white piles of snow. Friends would get together to sled or to build snowmen. In Nigeria we'd get the day off school but couldn't go very far either, so we'd climb the mango trees or chase the neighbor's peacocks, as the case may be. Snow days carried that illicit feeling we were playing hooky, and execution days carried an illicit feeling too, but as you can imagine, what was illicit hung over the day in so many more ways.

A goat sentenced to death meant I got to spend an extra day with Mom. We sat outside on the front patio in the hot sun as Dr. Hassan had ordered. Sitting in her wicker chair, wrapped in a blanket, my mom shivered on this hot afternoon as if we were sitting outside on a snow day. I ate the tiny red bananas and sliced mangoes from our trees. On the table between us sat glasses of iced tea. The ice cubes in our glasses of tea had faded to little white chips. We drank instant iced tea that came in a blue-labeled jar my mother had brought from the States. She told me it was very hard to come by, so I was not to waste it. I sipped my tea, wanting to hurry before all the ice was gone, but not so fast that Mom would think I hadn't tried to save her precious Lipton lemon-flavored tea.

I didn't share my excitement about execution day with my mother because she looked so far away in her head. Her eyes hung in her face, dull green, drowsy and fogged. I didn't tell her that Katherine Grey, two doors up, had invited me to tea. British tea, not instant, with those yummy currant scones her mom made, which I loved to slather with clotted cream. I had said I needed to stay home with my mom. I had to be with her when she was awake. I had to be with her in case, or until, she disappeared again.

When Philip returned home from the goat execution, he told my
mother everyone thought the goat would turn himself back into a
man before they killed him. But he didn't. He stayed a goat, and they
had to shoot him. "That goat is a coward," Philip said.

Nigerian Police Hold 'Magic' Goat Over Attempted Car Theft

Police in Nigeria are holding a goat accused of attempting to steal
a car. The black and white animal was turned in to police by a
vigilante group, which claimed it was an armed car thief who had
used black magic to transform himself into a goat to escape arrest
after trying to steal a Mazda 323.

—*The Telegraph*, 23 January 2009

There is good juju and bad juju. Mom saved the original *Daily Sun*
newspapers from 1971 reporting the story of the Man Turned Goat.
The front page headlines began to abbreviate it to MTG. Mom and
Dad made fun of Philip and the goat story. I wasn't sure what to think.
I wondered about the goat and decided the adults had it all wrong.
The way I saw it was if you're in trouble, if you're going to be executed,
why bother changing yourself back into a man? Mom and Dad said
the fact that he stayed a goat proved there was no juju at work. He was
just a goat. But I figured who was to say if there was or wasn't magic?
What if you could turn yourself into anything you wanted, whenever
you wanted? As I'd tried with my attempt at chameleon wishing. What
if there were another way? That's what I wanted to know. The What
If? The convenience of escaping—more than enough times I had
wished for this: to not be where I was. Presto Change-O.

If a man could turn himself into a goat, a goat that had been a
man who had chased a little girl, shouldn't I be worried? What if that
little girl had been me? What if I had been cornered at the end of the
street by a man? Wouldn't I need to change myself into something
else? I had a whole lot more to worry about than just the bumblebees'
sting. I needed to know how to disappear if necessary. I didn't know
the trickery of juju. I had unsuccessfully tried to imitate the wiles of

FIG.2. Nigerian Christmas with Amy, Marty, Daddy, and Suzanne. Courtesy of the author.

a chameleon. I had even pretended to be Mrs. Astor. If I couldn't be someone else, slip into another skin, I needed to be able to slide out of danger. I needed to be able to go someplace safer. If no one else was around, and that had become highly likely, I needed to know how to disappear.

But not yet—Suzanne and Marty were coming home for Christmas.

Christmas Execution

> Many years later, as he faced the firing squad,
> Colonel Aureliano Buendía was to remember
> that distant afternoon when his father took
> him to discover ice.
>
> —Gabriel Garcia Marquez, *One Hundred Years of*
> *Solitude*

WHILE MOM AND DAD MAY HAVE MADE FUN OF PHILIP AND the other Nigerians believing in the juju, they had no problem prodding my belief in Santa for our own secular Christmas. Not even a Bible in the bookcase, but we celebrated Christmas BIG. In Nevada we would ride in Dad's pickup into the White Pine Forest in the Sierras, find a suitable tree that would reach the ceiling of our tiny house, chop it down, and haul it home. We encircled it with strands and strands of red and green lights. We tossed silver tinsel on the pine needles. And we hung homemade ornaments collected from the years of projects and family hand-me-downs. Boxes and bags with toys and gifts filled the deep space under the tree. On Christmas Eve, with the help of my siblings, I wrote a note and placed it on a plate with cookies Suzanne and I had baked, then once in bed, I squeezed my eyes tight trying hard to go to sleep, otherwise Santa would not arrive. How easy to believe.

In Nigeria Christmas believing took some effort. Not even so much as a pine needle existed, and all our decorations, handmade over the years by all of us, had disappeared in our shipment.

Another American family transferred to Norway gave us their silver tinsel tree. The red, green, and blue rotating bulbs placed behind the tree lit up a disco halo overhead, catching on the reflection of the foil needles and branches.

I loved that tree. Everyone else despised it and called it contrived. I think the Schreibers even apologized when they brought it over. But that bright and shiny silver mesmerized me. The disco lights flashed at night, and during the day the sunlight pouring in the sliding glass doors glistened on the tinsel. Bright and shiny was what Christmas was supposed to be.

My dad joked that Santa might not know we were celebrating Christmas with a tree like that. "How's he going to know where we live?" he said while he and I stuck the tinseled limbs into the plug holes in the broom-handle tree trunk. "We don't even have a chimney."

I thought about my father's question. It was true, I'd never seen a Christmas special on TV where Santa didn't land on a snow-covered, sloped roof like we'd had in Nevada. Here in Nigeria we had flat roofs covered in black mold. But I had seen on these same TV shows Santa flying in the sky from the pulled-back camera lens as he traversed the entire globe. "Do you think he might not find us?" I asked. This news was disconcerting.

"It's a long way from Ely," my father said. "I guess we won't know until tomorrow."

Everything had to happen on Christmas night, or it didn't happen at all. There was an order to things. The story was that Santa could find me anywhere in the world. But if the story, the way it had been told all seven years of my life, now had holes, then what had always been the happiest day of the year could falter. This, along with everything else I was losing my grip on, could mean I would have nothing to believe in. "Santa knows things we don't know," I said.

"Does he?" Daddy asked. We were hanging the green balls on the tree now. The tree came with only one decoration, green glass balls.

"How does he get everything done so fast in one night?" My dad hung the green globes at the top of the tree, and I skirted around the bottom.

"He just does," I said, getting irritated that my dad was messing around with the believing part of the deal I had with Santa.

"And doesn't he get jet lag?"

I couldn't worry about things like that. Santa had it figured out, and we had to trust that he would show up.

"I don't know," I said, frustrated. "It's just for one night." Then I stopped and looked at my dad, the hook of the glass ball in between my fingers. One slip and the ball would shatter on the marble floor. I knew the fragility. "Do you really think he might not come?"

Dad laughed. I'd learn later those laughs at the end of a good tease were for his own sake—he'd got me. "Are you leaving him cookies?"

"Yes!" I said. "Suzanne and I made cookies yesterday."

"Then he'll come."

We stood back and admired the tree. Brightly colored lights like precious jewels in alabaster marble splashed against the wall. Santa might even come to our house first, I thought, just because he'd want to see our special tree up close. Maybe Africa was his first stop.

BETTER THAN SANTA, CHRISTMAS MEANT SUZANNE AND Marty coming home for holiday from Switzerland. And, they brought green apples. While we had plenty of mangoes and citrus and bananas, we had no apples in Nigeria. The clean white flesh snapped in my mouth, and the Toblerone chocolate bars with the tiny pieces of nougat tapped against my teeth like bits of gold foil. But my family together in one place, that was another delicacy. It was almost as though I could breathe again. Like I'd held my breath until this moment. Maybe I had.

Christmas morning I woke up as I did every year—electric. I strained my ears to hear whether anyone else was up yet. I heard nothing. Open-eyed, I stared at the ceiling.

Over my bed, a fat-tailed gecko skittered. They ate mosquitoes, Alice had told me, and I liked anything that ate mosquitoes. Mosquitoes and their whiny buzz around my ears, mosquitoes and their helicopter trajectory to our landing-pad flesh, mosquitoes that brought malaria into our house. Mosquitoes, my mother's foe, therefore my foe. Geckos came and went as they pleased, their translucent bodies making them evanescent. But this one above my bed hovered, hesitated, lifted its head and looked at me. A second one came along. This one I must have encountered before because he was missing his tail. Both geckos paused and rolled their eyes in my direction. Apparently I passed muster because they went on their way, slithering down the wall, then slipping through the sliver between the air conditioner and the sill.

I crawled out of bed, careful to be as quiet as the geckos. Across the room I recognized Suzanne's quiet snore from when we shared a bedroom in the States. I tiptoed past Mom's sewing machine, now covered with fabrics from the bed, then past Suzanne and the piles of clothes spilling from her suitcase. I made it out the door to the staircase. From here I could make a straight shot down the stairs. I liked to arrive at the gift-laden tree first.

Halfway down the floating staircase, sparkles scattered across my toes, then across the wall. A few more steps, the whole living room was sparkling as dots of jade, lapis, and bloodstone light danced in circles, rotating around themselves and over me. Maybe Santa was still in the living room. I leaned down to look through the banister to the tree.

Oh, how I loved that tree. Why did no one else appreciate the jubilant spectacle it created? The spinning lights had been left on and rotated the red, green, and blue dreamy sequence over the silver tinsel in the otherwise dark room. The colors splashed on the wall, and tiny reflections of white light danced on the ceiling. Rubies, sapphires, emeralds, and diamonds flickered in the air. I wanted to reach up to grab the bits of light, but I knew they'd escape before I could open my hand.

A red plastic blow-up reindeer sat at the edge of the pile of gifts. That reindeer had not been there when I'd gone to bed. Santa never wrapped his gifts like everyone else did. I had believed, and he had made it to Nigeria. I knew it—if I just believed hard enough, anything could come true.

And then I spied her. Right there, leaning against the wrapped gifts, still inside her clear plastic box, stood the Miss Polly doll. Her long hair and the tiny comb next to her, the little green dress with the embroidered edges. Santa knew!

I heard Suzanne behind me, "Don't open anything until we are all down there." Everyone followed down the stairs. Even Mom. She wore her peach satin pajamas and robe. Her house slippers reminded me of genie shoes: metallic gold mules with curlicue toes. The soft shuffle then sharp flap of the shoe against the wooden stair marked each step she took.

We propped up a pillow on the couch next to the tree. This would be Mom's spot while we unwrapped gifts. Our Christmas tradition had always been that we opened gifts first thing, before breakfast, before anything else. A brilliant tradition, in my opinion, to make the gifts a priority. Dad handed the gifts out one at a time, dragging out the whole routine as long as possible—anticipation boiling over.

We did one full round until the gift giving got back to me. My anticipation was doused only by the continuous glitter from the metallic tree. Daddy dillydallied over the gifts, hamming up his decision-making on which package to hand out next.

He handed me a smaller package wrapped in green tissue paper. Inside I found a Hummel "Happy Wanderer" music box. Suzanne had brought it from Lugano. The little boy in lederhosen painted on the lid carried a red umbrella and wore what looked like snow boots. I opened the lid and in tiny tinkles the "Wanderer" song drifted out. My sister started to sing along with the music. The only other music box I had ever encountered had been my cousin's in Texas—a pink, satin-covered jewelry box that, when opened, displayed a miniature ballerina in pink tulle twirling in a plastic circle while music played from somewhere inside the velveteen interior—at least until my cousin popped the ballerina off her spring to see how the whole thing worked.

Inside *my* music box, a piece of glass enclosed a two-inch metal contraption—a spinning cylinder covered in spikes. As it turned, an itty-bitty row of metal fingers grabbed hold of the spikes, lifting then dropping one at a different interval coinciding with each note. It was like the teensiest player piano. How the music came out of the spinning wheel, with what at first seemed random markings, enthralled me.

". . . with my knapsack on my back," Suzanne sang.

Then we were all singing. The von Trapps we were not, but the glittering sparkles that jumped across every surface in the room transported the moment to another time and place.

"Valderi! Valdera!" my dad chimed in on the chorus.

"Can we turn off those annoying lights?" my mother asked. We all stopped singing. I turned to face her on the couch. I sat on the floor and looked at her sallow face. How could she think the lights were annoying—the colors that flickered in the air like tiny red, blue, and green fireflies?

"Yeah," Suzanne said, "that tacky tree is making me nauseous."

"Me too," I said, not wanting anyone to know I liked the tree and not wanting to be outside the family circle.

As my dad unplugged the light from behind the tree, I watched the sparkles drift down the walls, then disappear. Suzanne opened the curtains to let the sunlight in, and the room had a new shimmer from the silver of the tree. Mom readjusted her pillow several times. She had put on a smile, a put-on smile. I wouldn't let myself think she didn't want to be there. But soon she asked if we could close the curtains too, the bright light hurt her eyes. She wants to be in her bed, I thought. Not down here with us.

"Do you want to go back upstairs, Mart?" my father asked. The air conditioner kicked on, vibrating the wall, making the Christmas tree shudder.

"I will take a nap," she said, "then I will help make Christmas dinner."

Everyone got up and made themselves busy with new tasks.

"Just for a little bit, Amy," Mom told me when I asked how long she'd be napping. I wanted a promise, a moment to watch for, a specific time that she would reappear.

As the family dispersed, Dean Martin belted out of our reel-to-reel, "It's Beginning to Look a Lot Like Christmas." Marty slipped off to the kitchen to make our traditional Christmas chocolate pies. Suzanne took a shower, and my dad disappeared across the room behind Robert Ruark's thick *Uhuru*.

I danced Miss Polly doll's stiff plastic legs on the coffee table, but I kept my voice to a whisper knowing Mom slept overhead in her bedroom. I sang to Miss Polly and to the tree with its silver shadow, and I sang to the geckos that now slithered through the knee-high piles of wrapping paper.

When I heard the spoken words I recognized, I perked up. "A little girl, of five or six or seven . . ." Maurice Chevalier sang. I hopped Miss Polly across the couch, her blond hair flying as we danced. "Thank Heaven for Little Girls," I sang along with Mr. Chevalier. Maybe, I thought, he was singing it to me. Maybe I was one of the little girls he was glad for, and I was a little bit in love with Maurice Chevalier for that. I'd heard the song so many times over my seven Christmases and knew the words. I imitated his guttural French accent as I repeated the chorus, "Thaank Haaaaven . . ." I'd had a good Christmas, as good as any spoiled little girl could have. But could I ask for one more thing? That we, the Wallens, could all stay together like this? That Christmas would never come to an end? That we could all stay in the same house making noise, making messes, teasing, singing, and being our fivesome?

With no one in the room except my dad, I plugged the rotating tree lights back in. The reel-to-reel tape could be heard flap-flapping around as it reached its end. Muted sounds of traffic from the circle on Awolowo Road, the whir of the bulbuls sitting on eggs in their dense cup-shaped nest high atop the hibiscus bushes, and the patter of feet in the driveway came through the glass. I didn't look up until I heard the drumbeats, then I peeked through the curtains Suzanne had closed when Mom asked. My dad turned off the flapping tape player and followed me. The drumbeats with the clatter of kola beads brought Marty and Suzanne to the living room. Suzanne pulled the cord to draw open the curtains again, since Mom had disappeared upstairs.

In the front yard, just beyond the wicker patio furniture, the troupe, in full headdresses that flowed from their head to their toes, danced the Igbo dance. Their kola bead and shell ankle bracelets and waistbands rattled and jangled to the African rhythm. The swish and sway of the straw skirts and rattles and headdresses had us spellbound, as the Igbo dancers squatted, kicked, and shuffled traditional steps across our garden's moist green grass. The drummer slapped the tight dried animal-skin head of the drum, his head bobbing with the tempo. We ran out the front door and stood on the patio's edge to watch. As the Nigerian boys gamboled on the grass, I felt the kola beads and deeper bum bum of the drum inside me making my own little body rock back and forth. The revelry ricocheted off the bamboo fence and the banana trees. Echoed off the plate glass across the front of our two-story white house. And reverberated through our bodies.

The dancers finished their dance, and we all applauded. I could hear a tiny clap clap behind us. My mother stood on her balcony outside her room watching. Just as quickly she vanished back inside.

AFTER CHRISTMAS DAY TIME WAS RUNNING OUT BEFORE Suzanne and Marty had to return to Switzerland. I was still out of school. Gifts had been packed or put away, and we were settling into being an ordinary family. I didn't like to think about anyone leaving, and I don't know if at seven I even had a time frame for it yet. But I knew the departure was inevitable.

On their last day no one was home but Marty and me. Dad had gone to the office, and Mrs. Betteridge had taken Suzanne and Mom to lunch at the Federal Palace hotel. Mom was getting up more, trying to be her old self, while I watched with bated breath.

While they were all out, I followed Marty onto the rooftop of the carport. He showed me how to shimmy over the railing of Mom's balcony then hoist myself, with his help, to the flat black-tarred roof.

We'd ended up here because I'd shown Marty how I could climb up the Griffins' back porch pole. He hadn't seemed as impressed as I had hoped. Maybe it needed to be night with moths fluttering around. "I got a better idea," he said, and I followed him to the balcony then onto the rooftop. We were trying to find stuff to do while we waited for Mom and Suzanne to get home, when he had plans to go to Bar Beach. He'd heard there was to be another public execution, and he wanted to go. He'd asked Philip which buses to take, so he didn't have to tell the folks he was going.

I wanted to go, but he said it wouldn't work. He'd get in worse trouble if I went. Like the time in Ely when his friend invited him to go flying in his Cessna, and Marty was babysitting me, so I got to tag along. Mom and Dad banished him to his room for eternity when they got home and heard the plane buzzing around the house. I remember they kept saying, "Do you have any idea what kind of danger you put Amy in?" I didn't think that was fair. I had just had one of the best adventures looking out the plane window. He'd learned his lesson, he said.

I wanted to go with him, not so much for the execution, but because I wanted to be wherever he went. He would be home only one more day. I had to squeeze out every little moment.

"I can ask," I said. "If we get permission this time, we won't get in trouble."

He stood at the edge of the carport roof, looking down at the lush green lawn that Anthony, our gardener, cut with the machete. Anthony would squat-walk across the spacious yard, all around the umbrella tree, and up against the banana trees on one side and bamboo fence on the other, as though he himself were a lawnmower. With the whack-whack back-and-forth motion of the machete in his arm, his blade so sharp that each swing of the long knife whistled in the air, he would shave the top inch off the blades of grass.

"If you ask permission, they'll just say no," Marty said. "I'll tell you about it when I get back." Then he swung his arms back and sprang off the carport roof. He landed with a big thud then rolled across the lush floor of the garden. He shot up onto his feet. "Bend your knees when you land," he said, rubbing his shins, looking up at me. "Now you try."

I stood where he had just stood. I remembered when we lived in Nevada, and Marty had jumped from the top of the gymnasium staircase in the high school basement. He hadn't estimated the bend in the convex ceiling, and his skull met the sharp corner that protruded from it, cracking his head open. I was already out of kindergarten for the day, so Mom took me along when the school nurse called. I sat in the red plastic chair in Dr. Christensen's office as he stitched Marty's head closed.

Now as I leaned over the edge of the carport roof, he smiled up at me, his chipped tooth front and center. "Come on," he encouraged. "It's not that far down."

"It's not as far for you because you're taller," I explained. I didn't want him to think I was chicken.

Black mold crept over the roof's edge and down the white plaster like a spill. The mold felt dry and scaly, so I never touched it. I was tempted to jump, Marty standing on the soft garden of grass, the flower border of pink four o'clocks blooming at his feet, his arms outstretched. But I *was* chicken. It took a few moments to weigh being a scaredy-cat over disappointing him. He would be gone soon, and I needed him to remember being proud of me. I needed him to want to come back. A namby-pamby little sister? Who wants to hang out with her?

"I'll catch you," he said. But he looked so far away, how could I be sure?

In the distance I heard the creak of the compound's front gates and a car engine. From my roof vantage point, I could see James swinging open one side of the big white gate, then running to the gate's other half.

"They're home!" I said. "Mommy's here."

"Jump!" he said. "Or it'll be too late."

This was a tough decision. I didn't get to be with Mom much anymore. But hanging out with Marty was even more rare and more fun. If I didn't jump I would disappoint him. He might not ask me again. We could get in trouble for this as well. I didn't want Mom to be mad at me. And that cinched the deal. "I'll do it later," I said.

I turned around, scrambled back up the balcony railing and into the house. Already I regretted my decision. It was a no-win. Mom would hold it against me if I misbehaved. It exhausted her, she'd say. Marty reeked of fun. But I didn't get to live with Marty.

Once inside, I could find my brother nowhere. I thought he'd come in the front door with Mom and Suzanne, but he hadn't. Getting away was simple in our house. You just left. Odds were no one would notice. That's what Marty must have done.

"Hey, Lamb Chop," Mrs. Betteridge said, running her hand down my long hair.

"Mommy!" I said, wanting her attention more than anyone else's.

"Not now, Amy," she said, as she made her way into the kitchen to ask Philip to make them tea.

Once the ladies were all seated in the living room, knees crossed, tea served, all proper, I concluded I had made the wrong choice. This was boring. I'd tell on Marty, I thought, and then Mom would pay attention to me. "Marty went to the execution," I blurted out.

Mom's energy slowed her reactions. She sighed and shook her head. Turning to Mrs. Betteridge, she said, "That must have been why we had that horrible traffic jam. The execution on Victoria Island."

"That's disgusting," Suzanne said. "Why would he want to see something like that?"

"I wanted to go see it," I announced.

"Amy, ew!" Mom said.

"Lamb Chop," Mrs. Betteridge said, "An execution is ugly. It's just a big crowd of people." She sounded like she'd seen one.

None of them understood, I thought. None of them realized the opportunity missed. Or maybe I didn't. Maybe I imagined it was nothing to be scared of. It's just a little death. Hadn't I seen plenty of that?

The opportunity missed was to be with Marty. I wanted to see what he saw. I wanted to be grown up so these things didn't bother me. Firing squad, schmiring squad.

I sat with my legs crossed like the ladies, their shimmering knees in panty hose, and waited for Marty to return.

When he did return from Bar Beach, I asked him what he saw. I wanted to know the gory details. I knew the soldiers carried their heavy machine guns and marched on the beach along the barbed wire fence along my schoolyard.

"I saw nothing," he told me. "Masses of people, I couldn't even get close enough to see anything." But, I thought, I could have been with him. I could have been on that beach walking alongside him. We could have elbowed through the crowd together. That's all I wanted.

The next day, suitcases sat at the top of the stairs. We woke up earlier than usual to make the trip to the airport.

At the chain-link fence next to the runway, I stood with Mom and Dad as the SwissAir flight lifted off then ascended over my head. The jet engine's roar rushed in my ears. My ears absorbed the sound, holding it inside my drums, inside my body cavity, the vibration, keeping us connected until the roar dissipated. The plane now silent, I watched the bold red cross on the jet's belly get smaller and smaller until it was swallowed by the sky.

The only thing back at the house to remind me of Suzanne and Marty was my music box and the shriveled brown apple core I kept in the drawer of my nightstand until it disappeared.

Arriving home, Mom headed upstairs. Dad would be returning to the bush. I grabbed my water bottle from the kitchen counter, as Samson would be tooting his horn in the driveway soon. On the dining room table, I spied the *Daily Sun* where Dad had left it. I climbed into his chair and gawked at the front page. A series of photos. The first shot: a man tied to a post, the green and white oil barrels behind him. He faced the camera. The second shot: his head flung back, his eyes wide open, and his shirt ripped apart at his chest. The third shot: the man's head dangling forward, his body limp, his eyes still open. Like Mom's, I thought, when she lay in bed sleeping the sleep of the dead.

That was the final shot. In black and white. Just like that, from light to dark.

What did this mean? What did this horrific violence signify? How did it relate to me? Who was next? Anybody's life could be taken at any time. Not just through an execution, but by falling in a sewer, getting malaria, turning into a goat.

I may not have thought this at seven, but I felt it in my bones. I sensed anything could happen at any moment, and I had no way of knowing when, or who, or how. The not knowing, the piles of possibilities like bodies stacking up in my imagination. Stacking up around me, blocking my view. I was being smothered by the closeness of death and musty emptiness unless I could figure out how to climb over to the other side.

Valderi, Valderahahahahahaha.

EXECUTION ON THE BEACH IN NIGERIA OR IN A GAS CHAMBER in San Quentin, one public, one private. Is one more heinous than the other? Fewer than forty countries in the world still practice corporal punishment, and America and Nigeria are two of them. Sharia law dictates public execution, and states in the United States await a new drug that won't botch the lethal injection.

This is my heritage but not my inheritance. Instead the effect of the physicality of death presented me with a cryptic understanding. I left Nigeria with the feeling that we all have a death sentence. Only I wasn't awaiting mine so much as everyone else's, wondering like the dream I'd had years ago if maybe everyone was already dead. When we died, were we merely an empty body in or on top of the ground? Did a spirit float up and away? I contemplate this too. Do these spirits visit Earth? Do we have souls? And by "we" I mean my family. Because that's what spirits do, and that's what my family did—visit me.

Pine-Solo

. . . gloom crowding in on me, a sense of dread
and alienation and, above all, stifling anxiety.

—William Styron, *Darkness Visible:
A Memoir of Madness*

THE LUNCH HUT AT THE AMERICAN INTERNATIONAL SCHOOL
in Lagos, Nigeria, always smelled of pine-scented disinfectant. Buckets of the diluted Pine-Sol's sloshy gray-brown water sat at the end of each picnic table. The open-air thatched roof hut housed rows and rows of tables crammed full of students and sheltered us from the beating midday African sun. The occasional teacher, two heads taller, wandered the rows with that supervisory meandering gaze. The rule was whoever finished lunch last had to clean the table. I lingered because I wanted to wring out the dingy rag pulled from the bucket, sniff the Pine-Sol, then wipe down the sticky table. How I liked the smell of disinfectant—how it made my head spin a little. I also liked being the good kid, the one that made the wandering teacher smile. I wanted to make the teachers happy. I wanted to wash away the sticky residue leftover from mangoes and bananas and have the teachers say I had done a good job. Good girl. Thank Heaven for Little Girls.

An ingredient in the cleanser both burned and smelled metallically sweet, like the Magic Marker or the glue pots in Nigerian culture class. I lingered over the pungency, took extra care to bring the rag to my face, to inhale. The piquancy reminded me of touching the chile pequin jar on my grandmother's table. The tiny red peppers, no bigger than a bead, wallowed in a shaker of vinegar used to season every dish. Under the metal screw top, the rippled rim was caked in oily capsaicin. In South Texas chile pequin vinegar always stood between the salt and pepper shakers. My brother pointed, then poked me in the ribs. "Rub your fingers on the rim," he said, "then rub it on your eyes. See what happens." He wiggled his eyebrows.

"No, you," I told him. We both knew if the spicy oils got near the eyes, hot zings would seethe around the rim of our lids. I came close to doing it just to please him.

I liked being alone as I cleaned the lunch hut tables. Alone in my head. Alone with my thoughts. My memories. I could remember Christmas arrival, not departure. My family made appearances then just as quickly disappeared. How they did it, how they came and went on airplanes and through illness, I got, but when and where they would reappear, I didn't know. I had to wait. Waiting was the hardest part. When they did appear, the joy, the feeling of sanctuary hovered as temporary, because I had started to realize it would inevitably come to an end. What makes ghosts scary is not knowing when they will appear or disappear.

The pine-scented cleanser made me both light-headed and singed my eyes. The sting burned, causing me to blink. I slowed down my breathing and looked beyond my periphery, out beyond the horizon. My gaze so far off in the distance that it became unfocused and rested inside me.

The other kids had rushed out to the playground after lunch, and I usually joined them after I'd wiped down the tables and breathed in the piney scent. But on this particular day, I stood in the lunch hut doorway, staring across the playground. The painted four-square lines on the asphalt had faded, making the boundaries indeterminate. The playground looked washed out, the fun dulled.

A teeter-totter banged loudly as one end slammed to the ground. Dwayne Dalton had jumped off his end while Eddie McDaniel was still midair. The plywood board laid across a fulcrum needed two weights, one on either end, to maintain the cant of balance. Someone had done that to me before—jumped off midteeter, and now I knew to never play on the teeter-totter for fear of my own weight dropped hard on the ground. I still recalled how my teeth had pounded together in my head with the force of hitting the concrete after someone abandoned me midair. I watched from a secure distance now.

With my pine-scented hands kept close to my sides, I waited. I had this darkness in my peripheral vision that wouldn't fade. And like when my mom drug me through the grocery store parking lot, away from the hands-out, palms-upturned, mutilated beggars, the gruesomeness of their sores made me want to look, the curiosity a seduction. Like the astringent odor of the cleanser: I knew it would burn, but I couldn't resist the head-spinning aroma. This periphery of darkness, too, intrigued me.

All the kids playing: the screeches of jubilee, the swing set's metal chains creaking, a kid pushed higher in the air laughing, the rubber four-square ball ringing on each bounce, stomping feet vibrating the ground, dirt devils swirling, and the bright, bright sun scaring out most shadows, all the sounds became muffled inside my mind. I was intoxicated by my own darkness.

On the playground and outside the gates of AIS, beyond Victoria Island, across the bridge to Ikoyi, to Omo Osagie Street, inside my compound's gates, I was seduced by my own muddled psyche.

A shadow leaned over me. A teacher asked, "Amy, are you okay?"

I only nodded. I couldn't speak. I didn't want to be disturbed in the place I had found to inhabit. Inside myself where no one could disappear.

I REMEMBER MY SECRET—MY OWN SPECIAL JUJU, MY OWN dedicated chameleon act, or maybe a way to not think about how at any moment—poof, everyone could be gone. It became my way of not being left behind or forgotten; it was how I disappeared myself. It was a secret because it was a way to be alone that *I* chose. A little dissociation is good for the soul.

My family could have been magicians, their specialty the disappearing act.

Two New Knees

WE WERE TRANSFERRED AGAIN. THE ONLY THING I REMEMBER
about leaving Nigeria was Mom having all the household staff line up
in the front garden so she could take a Polaroid. "Stand in front of
the four o'clocks," she directed. "I loved those flowers."

I thought they were too frilly, too pink; I never liked pink anything.
But I didn't want Mom to think I disagreed, so I just observed.

Philip posed with his wives on either side of him, Okinaya holding
a baby in her arms, and Ayo's little boy standing at Philip's feet. Pious,
shorter than the others, stood an arm's length out at the far end.
Alice smiled at the other end by Ayo. James, taller and two shoulder
widths wider, would have filled the space in back, but he wasn't there.

The night before, just after dinner, James had knocked on our
door. Dressed in a fancy ocher *baban riga* with gold embroidery, he

asked my dad, "Please, Master, can I borrow twenty pound to get my father out of fridge?"

My dad gave James a hard time about how we were leaving the country the next day, so "borrowing" the money was probably a misnomer, while I tried to wrap my mind around the father in the fridge. Dad pushed James almost to begging, then handed him twenty pounds, and sent him off to have the funeral for his father, a funeral that needed to happen as soon as possible, according to Muslim custom.

After he was gone, my father explained the concept of dead bodies on ice: the morgue. "Their bodies start to stink," my dad said, "even more than they do alive." He thought he was funny. I couldn't quit picturing how to fold a body to fit in something like the frost-free freezer we had in Ely. I also couldn't quit thinking about how James would have to take him out, how James would have to put his father in the ground. How James would have to go on without his father.

MY EIGHTY-TWO-YEAR-OLD DAD HAS TWO BRAND-NEW KNEES. When he passes through the metal detectors at the airport security, he must show a special card from his doctor, because the stainless steel and titanium that replaced his joints and kneecaps will set off the security alarms. He loves his new knees.

We, he and I, are walking around the one-mile track at the Kroc Center, a senior center gymnasium near his home in Texas. He can make it around the track one time, at a slow amble. Better than the last few years before his new knees, when he could barely make it up a curb. It pains me to watch him now, when in his much younger days he used to chop wide swaths through the jungles as he explored the geography and topography, searching for oil. My liberal politics make me cringe when I think of his career, but it's not the job listed on his business cards, Geophysical Field Operations, that I am most curious about.

As we walk, he's telling me about his friends, the men who worked with him in the bush of Nigeria and jungles of Peru and Bolivia. He tells me about Bob, a chemist who worked for the same oil company selling fertilizer, who worked for the CIA on the side.

This is how my dad tells the story:

"In his office he had big bags of fertilizer piled against the walls. 'Bob,' I'd say, 'you even know how that fertilizer is applied?' and Bob would say, 'I think there are instructions on the side of the package.' And we would have a good laugh about it." My dad's laughing now as he tells the story. So am I because I know Bob, a longtime family friend. His wife was my mom's good friend. Jan had been Miss Jan on Romper Room.

But I didn't know Bob was a CIA operative. I didn't know his job was just a front for his real job. Until now I have pictured my dad and Bob drinking scotch and waters on the deck of a boat on the Niger Delta while they talk. Bob is large and jovial; he likes to sing the Nigerian National Anthem when he's tipsy. He and my dad cook chili together and drink beer in the garage. I wonder if my dad worked with Bob and the CIA. I've wondered this most of my adult life. I think my dad's about to tell me.

He often repeats the same stories. I could tell them just as well as he does I've heard them so many times. But today's stories are new. He's confiding something.

I asked once years ago whether he worked for the CIA. Although a consistent jokester, he answered my question with a terse negative. But on this walk, the retirement community's pool and outdoor exercise facility in the background along with the giant McDonald's PlayPlace in primary colors, my dad reveals his past to me. Now at eighty-two years of age, he begins to give me the story.

Before we had left the house to go on this walk, my dad and I and his two new knees, I had asked him to tell me about his first days arriving in the bush in Nigeria. He regaled me with many stories about the bush, the Brits, and the bugs. Again stories I'd heard him repeat at dinner parties and among gatherings of old friends. He added a new detail this time—how he always carried, in a small case the size of a short cigar, his own personal radio crystal in his shirt pocket, the diode necessary for direct transatlantic communication. My dad told me he could switch out the diode in a two-way radio and call headquarters. This is how they communicated from the jungles to the United States. My radio frequency engineer husband explained to me later that this crystal diode is for direct private communication into which no other radio transmitter or operator can break. James Bond, I imagine, has a radio crystal such as this one, in its own protective case that he carries in his shirt pocket as my dad did.

We are coming near the end of the track. Dad finishes another round of stories about more of his friends, the men in collusion with the secret spies. So I ask again, "Were you in the CIA?"

"Nope," he says, and then he responds with a quiet comment, "I don't know why they never asked me to work for them."

Do I really feel sad? My reaction surprises me. I think it's not fair, he's always been a hard worker. We come from blue collar stock and believe hard work deserves a reward. I'm feeling sorry for my dad not being in the CIA?

His friends, he tells me, had four to five thousand dollars transferred to special deposit accounts each month. "In addition to the regular salary we all received," he adds. My dad likes to earn a decent paycheck, so I know this hurts him. He also hates to be left out, just as I do. But I wonder why his friends would tell him the dollar amount. Just plain bragging? If it's so undercover, why would they reveal it to him? Four thousand dollars in 1972 was a lot of money.

My father retired early on full pension. So he's not revealing all, I tell myself. He's telling me about the others, but not telling me about himself. He's still covering up the truth. I don't want him to have been left behind.

Do I want him to be a secret stealth spy on dangerous missions so badly that I add to the stories in my head? Do I like the mystery surrounding the possibilities? Wouldn't it be so much more romantic to know that my father had a job in special intelligence—a spy rather than a man reading maps and rocks and pillaging the earth for fossil fuels?

As my father with his new knees huffs along the gravel track, he doesn't so much walk as shuffle. A young woman jogs toward us and passes. "We'll catch you on the next round," he teases her. She laughs in the cold air, puffing out warmth in a cloud. He's always one to get a smile. I also know that we both extend this joviality because we want people to like us. We want to make others happy, so they won't leave us. Won't leave us behind. This is why I know it would be hard for my dad not to be included in the collusions with the special agencies. That and the money.

WE HAVE FINISHED THE ONE-MILE LOOP. "I MADE IT THE whole way without even being out of breath," my dad says. I praise him, "You're doing great." Inside he gives me a tour of the facilities. He knows everyone on the staff. "Hey, Jim," they all wave and smile as we pass. Except the seventeen-year-old barista at the coffee shop—she's new. "This here's my daughter," he tells her. "She lives in California but came out to visit me." She's shy and waits with pencil in hand for our orders. He looks at the tag on her uniform's lapel, "Trainee" it reads, only he pronounces it, "Tra-nay" like Renee. "Great name," he says. She giggles, and I know he will make her laugh every morning, and soon she too will know him by his name.

We get our coffees and sit at a table by the window, looking out at the giant gerbil tunnels in red and yellow, the oversized blue slide into the Olympic-sized swimming pool. "I never use that stuff out there," he tells me. "I just walk the track and do some weights."

I have one more question I want to ask. Over the years and suspicions, I actually came to believe it was not the CIA he was involved in, but the Drug Enforcement Agency. Based on the locales we lived in and The Butcher story.

"What about the DEA?"

"What about them?" He glances out the floor-to-ceiling windows, sipping from his cup of hot coffee.

"Weren't they also involved?"

"No." He's returned to his negative, abrupt stance. The curtain has been dropped again. Our stroll has ended, and soon we will be back in his pickup driving to the house. I know he won't talk about this in front of my mother. We don't have much time left.

"What about The Butcher?" I ask. This was my best evidence of all.

He loves this story and nods with a smile. "He told me I'd never see him again, and I never did."

"Wasn't he DEA?" I ask again.

"No," he responds. No expression other than pursed lips blowing on his hot drink.

That's odd, I think, the DEA would be prominent in drug countries like Peru and Bolivia where coca grew thick like the black jack oaks in Oklahoma.

My dad flexes his newest knee, the left one, to show me how it clicks. "Hear that?" he asks. I don't hear anything the first time, so he bends the joint again. Through his khakis I hear a grating noise, like when brake pads have worn down and rub against the disk, metal on metal. He smiles when he sees I'm a little queasy. "A loose screw," he says. "They left it in there." I laugh, and this pleases him. I want to ask whether he's joking or not, whether there really is a screw tumbling around on the other side of his kneecap, but I don't. One way or another, his story is true.

The Vestibule

> "As my wise friend Didi has more than once
> observed about life's passages, every depar-
> ture entails an arrival elsewhere, every arrival
> implies a departure from afar."
>
> —Claire Messud, *The Emperor's Children*

WE WERE LONDON-BOUND, OUR EUROPEAN STOPOVER ON OUR
way to the States to visit family and get more inoculations. Then we
were off to our new country, new continent, new hemisphere.

The next thing I remember was waking up in a dreamy sweat.
Everything was white. And soft. I couldn't untangle myself from the
cloud I roiled around inside.

"Amy," my mom said, holding me still. "You need to wake up."

When I opened my eyes, the only thing I recognized was her.

"You have jet lag," she said. "You need to wake up." But I only felt
like sleeping. The air outside this big blanket cloud was bitter cold.

"Where am I?"

"We're at the Betteridges'," she said. "In Swindon. England."

"What is this blanket?" I tugged at the white, airy cloud tangled
around me that kept me so warm.

"It's a down comforter," Mom said.

"Can we get one?"

"We won't need them where we are moving to," she said. "It's warm in Peru. Not hot like Lagos. But warm. Now get dressed. We're going into London for the day."

She left and I lay very still trying to keep my eyes open and feeling the fluff of the comforter floating on top of my body. I could hear voices in the distance. The kitchen maybe? I heard dishes clinking and smelled eggs.

Who would watch me in Peru? Nobody gave hugs like Alice's soft, pillowy ones. I already missed Alice. And Philip, Pious, and James.

My head out of the covers, I let myself cry, but just a little in case someone came in the room and caught me. When Mom caught me crying she would say I didn't have a good enough reason to cry. And maybe she was right. In comparison to so many, I had a good life.

WE'D BEEN TO LONDON BEFORE, ON THE WAY *TO* LAGOS, A YEAR before. We'd shopped in stores where long strings of beads hung in the doorways, and the clerks wore miniskirts. We had still been a family of five then. We were rarely five all at once anymore.

We were like an unsolvable addition problem that had a quadratic equation stuck in the middle of it. $5a^2 - 2(2 - 3b)^2 = c$ where c equals 1.

This second trip to London was different. This trip we already knew about tea and Nice biscuits and the funny black taxicabs with the doors that opened backward. A year before on our first trip to London at the Kensington Hotel, we had learned about bidets and ate curry for the first time. This trip we stayed outside London with our friends, the Betteridges. This time it was just me with Mom and Dad.

Today I would go into London with the adults. I thought of myself as one of them. I was often told I "behaved so adult." I couldn't wait to grow up, to be a true grown-up doing grown-up things on my own. Hanging out with grown-ups. I was tired of being a little girl who had no say. I just didn't know what to say.

The typical London, drizzly and gray; I shivered in the frigid air with no African sun radiating my skin. An adult's borrowed heavy wool coat hung on my shoulders as we meandered the sidewalks. Our feet were weary. We all complained. We all wanted to relax.

We tried to go inside the pub together, but the man behind the bar pointed at me and shook his head. So we backed through the swinging doors into the vestibule.

"What should we do?"

"A beer sure sounds good."

"Too good to pass up."

"Think it's okay to leave her?"

"We'll just have one."

"Wait here," I was told. "We won't be long."

"We'll just have one," someone else said. "Come on. It'll be just a minute."

"Look, there's a bench. You can sit there, Lamb."

All of it delivered with smiles. I suppose that relieved them, to be able to say it with smiles. Being appeased was something I was good at, and so I smiled back and watched them go. Not a whimper or a whine from me. No one would ever say I was a bad kid. I would guilt them into coming back sooner, that was my strategy. A lousy strategy, but all I knew. Maybe if I had shown how upset I was, how sad to be left alone, they would have come back sooner? Doubtful.

A tiny tornado could have been created from the hot and cold colliding in that vestibule. This passage between the rain and the beer was where folks slipped out of the cold and into the warmth on the other side of the swinging doors. The wooden bench felt sticky; above my head hung fuzzy wool coats and about my feet large adult galoshes sat in puddles.

When someone came through either set of doors, to the inside or the outside, I had to scooch over to let them find their galoshes or hang up their coat. As the groups of patrons came from the outside, groups of friends, they'd sometimes take notice of me: nod, smile, then pass on through. I smiled back.

Sometimes someone would ask, "Does anyone know you're here?" And I would nod, smile, and say, "They'll just be a minute. They're just having one." The person would nod again then hesitate before going either in or out. The dark wood paneling became darker, and the air around the wooden bench felt too thick to breathe.

Who noticed me coming, who noticed me going, and who didn't notice me at all? Who came in alone, then left coupled? I watched their faces, their moods. Everyone's breath was warmer when they left. The air in the antechamber filled with cold, anxious coming-in breath and warm, relaxed going-out breath.

If a group of friends too big to fit in the vestibule at one time came through, they'd hold open the outside and inside doors simultaneously, letting the drizzling cold from one direction and the boisterous noise and yeasty smells from the other collide right where I sat among all their laughter. Sometimes if the doors were held open long enough, I could get a good long glimpse of the crowded interior of the pub. I had a direct shot at the grouchy bartender, but he quickly disappeared behind all the customers bellied up at the bar. Standing on the other side of the vestibule, I could see the tables. Once, I thought I saw my mom's frosted head of hair and Mrs. Betteridge's reddish bob. But too many people walked back and forth, blocking a clear shot, and then the doors shut, so I went back to my bench.

A man leaving sat next to me, reached down and grabbed his rubber shoes to put on. "You waiting for someone?" he asked me. His white beard had yellow-tinged edges like the snow in Nevada where our dog had peed.

"My mom and dad," I said.

"It's busy. It might be awhile. Especially if they're having fun." I wasn't sure whether he told me this to reassure me that time would continue to pass slowly, but they would return eventually, or whether he was warning me. I tried to recall that glimpse I had caught of my parents—did they look as if they were having fun? I got up and stood on the other side of the entry, pushing against the wall with my back. The next person to come through, when they opened the door to the inside, would allow me a good long glance inside. Then I could confirm whether it was my folks and whether or not they were having a good time. This would give me some estimation of how long I'd have to wait. But when someone did open the door, I didn't see a woman with frosted hair. I didn't see anyone I knew anywhere in that room. I scoured wall to wall. When the door swung closed, I hopped down and pushed it open to peek. Just strange bodies in wool. Had they gone out? Had I missed them? I couldn't think of what to do. I started to panic.

Should I go outside to look? But if I weren't in the vestibule when they came through, they might forget about me altogether and walk off. No, I needed to stay so they'd see me. I wanted to smell their yeasty breath and see their eyes glittery like the other patrons. My little heart raced. What if it became closing time, and I still hadn't found them? What if they had completely forgotten they brought me? What if they were having fun somewhere else and didn't think about me until tomorrow? Or ever!

I hid inside the wet coat bottoms, peeking out just enough to see whether anyone I knew passed by, but not so that I had to engage with any of the strangers who were coming and going, going and coming, bringing the outside in, and taking the inside out. I didn't want to have to explain anymore why I sat there. I didn't want to have to say, "They'll be out in a minute. They're just having one." I wasn't very good at lying.

I disappeared.

I stood up on the bench, tucked myself behind the woolliest coats, the rough wool scratching my face. The dim overhead light was blocked by the coats, and only the light from inside the pub flashed when the door opened and closed. The dark felt safer. No one could see my shoes, no one knew I was there. I remained invisible to anyone coming into the vestibule. I pretended I was somewhere else. Somewhere warm, like the downy cloud blanket, where the cotton smelled of eggs and in the distance breakfast dishes clanked. The pub noises matched the breakfast noise, and I was in Swindon, Mom and Dad just downstairs.

But I could pop back in the pub when I needed to. I never went so far in disappearing that I would close both my ears and all my senses to the world. I always had one foot in the real world. I was always ready to return if someone wanted me. If someone called my name, for that's all I wanted. Always waiting for someone to want me.

When they walked through the doors, I appeared from behind the row of cloaks. I already had on my coat, as the vestibule wasn't heated.

"Lambie, there you are!" Mrs. Betteridge said, as though they had been waiting for me, not the other way around.

"See, that wasn't long, was it?" Mom said.

I shook my head no. How could I disagree? I had no idea how long it had really been, and if I was difficult then I might not be invited along next time. I waited silently for them to put on their coats, but what I really wanted to do was tug at their arms and get them out onto the sidewalk.

"I wish we didn't have to go back out there," Mom said. "It's so cold." But I wanted to get back out to wherever we were going next. I didn't want to be waiting. I didn't know what the next stop was, but I just wanted to be with them, not waiting for them, no matter how cold. But I didn't want them to leave me again, so I thought I should say something.

"I was ascared!" I said.

"You were *afraid*," my mother corrected.

"Yes, afraid," I said.

"That's better."

I WAS AFRAID OF MANY THINGS, OF BEING LEFT BEHIND, OF being forgotten, of my mother dying, of everyone dying. I knew complete world annihilation was coming, and I would be left entirely alone on this earth.

Any day now.

PART 2

PERU

We own the country we grow up in, or we
are aliens and invaders.

—Michael Ondaatje, *Running in the Family*

FIG. 3. Summer holiday in Texas, 1973: Marty, Daddy, Amy, Mom, and Suzanne. Courtesy of the author.

Deer in the Headlights

MY FATHER ONCE EXPLAINED TO ME WHY DEER GET HIT SO often on the highway. They have poor vision, he explained, but their eyes have a photographic lens. It's why they appear skittish. When she hears a bush rustle, a hunter unlock the safety, or a car engine approaching, the white tail deer's big ears twitch, she looks, snaps the shot, looks away, then looks again. The first image must match the second image; the two images must overlap without any shifts. If she detects an alteration in what she saw on the first take, she intuits change and possible danger. That's when she takes off running in the opposite direction. When the same deer, standing on the side of the rural highway at dusk, hears a car engine approaching, she looks, then looks again, but the headlights blind her—the photographic image filed first in her brain has been overexposed. She knows the image has changed, but she doesn't know what is a true image and what is not, and she runs directly in front of the image she can't make out: the car.

That is how I remember Peru. I know we were in Peru the longest, but it is the place where I have the fewest memories. I stare into the past, trying to replicate it. It is where we dug up the grave. I telephone my parents to see whether my remnants overlap with their remembrances. Like the deer, I know something moved when I learned my brother was not in the graveyard with me. Like a white light, the memories overtake me. Peru is where I run straight into those damn headlights. Or maybe it's too late, and my memories have already been overexposed. The figments of my imagination confused by the high beams, the overlapping image just a splotch of white.

The way a ghost appears in a photograph.

Arriving at Midnight

All things truly wicked start from innocence.

—Ernest Hemingway

THE ROSE BUSHES WERE MY FIRST MEMORY OF LIMA, THORNY bushes taller than I.

Mr. and Mrs. Riley greeted us at the airport. Mom was so impressed that complete strangers would come to welcome us. Mrs. Riley said it just sounded so awful to have to arrive in this horrible country in the middle of the night. "Horrible country!" my mother said, letting the bellman take her suitcase. "Just look at these roses. They are the size of footballs." All I could see were the silhouettes. But I could smell their pungent sweetness. I was relieved to know the malodorous air of Lagos had not permeated the lining of my nostrils.

My arms loaded down with my Barbie doll carry-on, my head felt drippy from jet lag. I always perspired when I had jet lag. Even my eyelids seemed to sweat. I slogged up the rose-lined walkway to the Hotel Country Club's palatial entry—our new home for six months while my mother tried to find us "suitable housing."

The wide staircase to our hotel suite curved up and around to a long hallway. The wooden floor creaked under the plush runner carpet. The hallway was wide enough to carry a casket with pallbearers side-to-side. The high ceiling arched with thick, dark, carved wooden beams. Crystal wall sconces scattered shadows. At the end of the hallway a set of French doors had a small brass plaque that read "Presidential Suite." Our room was just to the right of those doors.

No president was ever in residence while we were. The hotel was more like a mausoleum than a hotel. The economic crisis in Peru meant we pretty much had the entire hotel to ourselves. Like the Torrance family in *The Shining*.

The long hallway created the perfect spot to kick the soccer ball Mom bought me at the downtown Sears. No more Jankara Market, now it was Sears. I had no one to kick the ball back to me, so I whacked it against the Presidential Suite doors. It would ricochet back to me. This was how I was certain no president stayed there during our tenure. My adroit soccer skills can be credited to this hallway. But soccer would be the only thing I got right at my new school.

Every student in Peru was required to wear the same uniform. The only difference was male or female. Girls wore a white blouse, dark gray wool sweater, and dark gray skirt of a polyester fabric that pilled badly, with a hem no higher than the middle of your knees. Fashionistas we were not, with thin gray kneesocks that ran like my mother's hosiery. The whole ensemble was finished off with basic black round-toed shoes. Boys wore slacks instead of skirts, and in the coldest months girls donned a lumpy red wool poncho, and boys wore blue. Pinned over our hearts, a plastic badge with the school crest distinguished us. All I remember of ours was red, white, and blue. I would venture to guess the badge had stripes and an eagle, since it was an American school.

Other than Samson's little blue-and-white vw microbus, I had never ridden a school bus before. My new big yellow school bus had "Colegio Franklin Delano Roosevelt" painted in black letters along the side. At first I relished the idea of riding a REAL school bus, yellow and all. When it pulled up along the hotel drive, and the glass folding doors creaked open, the bus driver at the wheel was no Samson. I never learned his name, but it easily could have been "Lurch" from the Addams Family. His scowl made me feel he was always pissed off.

This first morning Mom stood curbside waiting with me. Since she spoke no Spanish, she hoped for the best and spoke to everyone in English.

"We are new to Lima," she told Señor Lurch through the bus doors. "This is Amy." Her hands on my shoulders, she positioned me in direct line with his angry puss. She nudged me up the two steps into the rumbling, diesel-smelling vehicle. She tried to initiate a response. "Will you be the driver who brings her home too?" Her Southern wiles in this Spanish-speaking metropolis didn't work. Nor did anyone say, "Yes, Madam," put their hands in prayer and bow.

I don't know if my mom got it, but I could tell the driver didn't understand a word, nor did he care. And once I was on that bus, I was certain I would never return to my mother.

The glass folding doors creaked shut, and I nabbed the front row seat, afraid to glance to the back. The inside of the bus had gone silent—all the other kids busy staring at the new kid. I didn't even have to witness it. I could feel it. I felt their eyes on my skin like creepy crawlies. In my hair like spiders. My ears picked up low-level whispers. I had never been a shy kid until now. I had never been afraid. I had never been so afraid of the new and unknown. I learned over and over in Nigeria that we were all clearly mortal. Now all I had to do was wait for mortality to arrive, to pick any of my people.

Philip, Alice, Samson, Pious, and James, none of them were here. Anyone I became attached to never stayed for long. I was solidifying my fear of attachments to people or relatives. I had also garnered that it wasn't just Death that took people, but Fate. Everyone eventually left. All I could do was try to prolong their presence.

In my peripheral vision, my mom waved goodbye on the curb. I focused straight ahead. I would not be a crybaby on my first day of school. Mom's image became just a blur of a wave, then disappeared completely. If eight-year-olds can have panic attacks, I was having one. My heart raced, my breathing became shallow and echoed in my ears.

My focus dimmed and didn't want to see what might be coming at
me. I just looked where I was going, not at what was possibly following
me. Like a racehorse wearing blinkers, I limited my distractions to
where I had to go.

THE SCHOOL CAMPUS SAT ON TWENTY-FIVE ACRES OF LUSH
green grass. Once at the school, the yellow bus disgorged me, and I
had to find my classroom. The day before Mrs. Riley had driven my
mom and me to the school in her station wagon. A woman from the
office had given us a tour of the auditorium/gymnasium with Olympic-
sized swimming pool, the high school buildings, the elementary school
buildings, the sports field, and the administrative offices. Clusters of
palm trees swished above us as we walked around the green campus.
We had walked past the music room, and I recognized "Marching
to Pretoria."

Introduced to my third-grade class and my teacher, Miss Hamlin, I
thought she had to be the most beautiful blond American woman after
my mom. She acted perturbed her class had been interrupted, but
shook my hand and pointed to my cubbyhole along the wall of cubbies
to store my book bag. She turned in a circle for a moment, then she
waved toward an empty desk in the middle of the classroom. "You
can have that seat," she said, disenchanted. I stared at the abandoned
seat, while the roomful of kids stared at me. Miss Hamlin seemed to
be waiting to get back to what she was doing. So we left.

Today would be different though. Meaning today would be even
worse. Today I was alone, other than the three thousand other students
getting off the line of buses simultaneously. And today I would have
to stay the whole day. My heart pummeled my chest as I stepped into
the melee of gray uniform–clad students. The sidewalks heading off
toward all the buildings we'd been shown the day before were now a
sea of gray-and-white uniforms.

I did find my classroom on the first building's second floor.
The modern architects hired to build Franklin Delano Roosevelt
School had created an open floor plan of hallways and three-walled

classrooms. I put my book bag in the cubicle that now had my name written on masking tape above it. In Ely we had cubbyholes where we kept our blankets for naptime. In Nigeria, we just had water bottles, and we kept those slung across our chests. Here in Lima, I placed my new leather book satchel into my cubby. It didn't matter that the satchel was empty, I liked the buckles and soft feel of the leather. Mom had bought it for me at Sears when we'd gone to get my uniform with Mrs. Riley the day before.

A couple of girls behind me giggled as they walked toward their desks. I heard the word "gordita" exchanged in whispers. Why couldn't I have the seat in the back of the classroom, a nice out-of-the-way invisible seat in the corner?

Before lunch, one of the junior high kids whom I had seen in the office the day before delivered a note to Miss Hamlin. Miss Hamlin didn't even read it. She just walked over to my desk and handed it to me. "You've been called to the office," she said. "The vice principal wants to see you now." Miss Hamlin was so beautiful with her thick blond hair and svelte figure like Samantha Stephens on *Bewitched*. I admired her natty clothes and chic high-heeled pumps like my mom's, but she found me instantly disagreeable. She never smiled. Not once. At least not at me. Not even to wiggle her nose to cast a spell. A spell would have at least been interesting, something her plain, cold-blooded meanness was not.

I had never been sent to the office before. Not in all eight years of my life. Getting sent to the office meant Big Trouble. Getting sent to the office was a great sin for a kid like me with an overdeveloped superego. I could think of nothing I had done wrong other than just existing. I walked slowly, hoping I'd get lost and never find my way. But I made it down the staircases and through the twenty-five acres to the administrative offices. The cool wind blew, as I would learn it always did. I'd left my gray pullover on my classroom chair, and my thin cotton blouse did nothing to absorb what little sunshine leaked out from the overcast sky. I shivered from the cold. And impending doom.

Up another set of stairs and inside the principal's offices, I handed the note to the secretary. She opened it, read it, looked at me from head to toe, then opened the swinging gatelike door to allow me behind the counter. Down the sterile hall we went, and then she handed the vice principal the ominous note. The VP opened it, read it, then looked at me from head to toe. What could it possibly say?!

"Have a seat, Amy. We're going to have your mother come and pick you up."

Not my mom! That meant even bigger trouble. Oh, to have my mother by my side was what I wanted more than anything, but not under these circumstances. She didn't have a car, and she didn't have any way of coming to get me. She didn't want her day interrupted. She had a hair appointment in the hotel's basement beauty shop.

I was seated on the cold plastic potato chip chair just outside Vice Principal Macintosh's glass office. I was too afraid to ask why I was there, what I had done wrong. Obviously I had done something too heinous to mention. Something so awful that it was unspeakable. I would wait a long time for my mother to arrive. I was too scared even to cry.

Why couldn't I have stayed in Nigeria? I had just started Mrs. Mbanefo's third-grade class. She'd even thrown a Bon Voyage party for me. I didn't know what "Bon Voyage" meant, but to have someone throw a party for you, well, who doesn't want that? We had just started learning cursive and the times tables. And in the afternoons I had gone to a Quonset hut classroom across the dusty courtyard where I took French lessons. Now I'd have to learn Spanish instead. The Spanish class took place in yet another building. I hadn't even figured out where it was yet. Someone said it was on the "west side," but where was west?

When my mother did finally arrive she looked nervous and harried, but she often looked like that, so I didn't know whether it had to do with my predicament.

"What happened? What did you do?" my mom asked, grabbing my hand tight inside her hard knuckles. I shrugged. The secretary escorted us both to Mrs. Macintosh's desk.

The vice principal sat across her big desk. She held the folded note in her fingers. "Your daughter's shoes are patent leather."

I loved my black patent leather shoes. Square-toed, black-and-white striped laces, and silver eyelets. I loved anything patent leather and shiny.

"Yes," my mother replied. She was no idiot; she could see they were patent leather. In fact, she had bought them in the States specifically for me to wear with my school uniform. "Black patent leather," my mother pointed out to the VP, in case she was the idiot. I looked down at my feet, at the shoes everyone else was already staring at.

"And the laces are striped," the VP said, making another obvious point.

"Are you saying something is wrong with that?" my mother asked.

"Yes, all laces must be plain black to match the plain black leather shoes. The regulation shoes are for sale at the Sears in Miraflores."

"I see. Well, I bought these shoes for Amy in the States." My mother sounded like she still needed to catch her breath from the trip to the school. Her hair hung limp from being shampooed but not styled. The cab waited at the curb where the long line of buses had rumbled earlier. "Surely you didn't call me here just because of her shoes?"

"She cannot have something that the other kids don't have or can't have. It's the Peruvian government. If you disagree, you'll have to take it up with the president and Congress of Peru." Now Mrs. Macintosh's voice turned surly.

"Can't she at least wait until we get a chance to get to the store?" my mom pleaded.

Mrs. Macintosh wasn't a mean person, just a rule follower, as Peru's Nationalist government was wont to insist. "Sorry, it's not allowed. Amy will have to stay home from school until she has the proper uniform."

"Stay home?!" My mom's surprise sounded a bit more like the idea of me being home was more of a bother than the ludicrousness of the order. "You expect me to go *now* and get her new shoes?"

"It's the law," Mrs. Macintosh said.

The law! I had broken the law!

"Yes, I understand." My mother had been sitting, but now stood, pulling me up. "We will go buy the plain black leather shoes with the plain black laces."

"Thank you," replied the VP.

I knew my mother was mad, the thing I feared almost as much as her death. I never wanted her to be upset. "I'm not mad," she always said when I asked, "I'm just disappointed." Heavy sigh. My disappointing her seemed to take so much energy, energy she needed to live. Still there was an upside—now I got to spend the day with her, and I didn't have to go back to my classroom. I would get to go shopping at Sears, even if it was to dig in a big barrel of cheap Communist-era black leather shoes looking for the right size, in both a right and a left.

Everything about Peru seemed disgruntled. My memories, the few I have, the ones that get washed out by headlights, they are all angry and in black and white. It's a mood, not a fact. A Truth, not a truth.

I wonder if this time, under this anti-American government, is when we started to become entitled. Or did I pick up a juju curse from the streets in Lagos?

Seeds Don't Grow in a Hotel

> Ambition. Thoroughly immoral and foolishly
> mortal.
>
> —Endora, played by Agnes Moorehead, on
> *Bewitched*

IN PERU THERE WERE NO MORE DEAD BODIES TO STEP OVER,
and even the beggars were less dismembered and infected. From all
appearances things on the surface improved. But my anxiety had
wound itself around me like a thread pulled tight, pinching my skin.
I recall the incongruity of the beggars on the steps of the Catholic
churches, which rose in grandeur at the throne of every plaza. The
beggars' hands were cupped upward and their eyes cast downward
as the congregants came and went from the solid gold encrusted
interiors. But it wasn't just the outside world. At night I dreamed I
showed up at FDR in my white summer culottes—the PE uniform.
I dreamed I stepped off the school bus in my gym outfit instead of
my gray school skirt and then realized my mistake as the school bus
pulled away. I spent every day thinking I was going to get in trouble.
That I would break the law without knowing I had. That I could get
sent away on another school bus even farther away. Or worse, just not
get off at the right bus stop and end up forever far away.

After a few weeks, my seed chart would be due. Miss Hamlin told the class that we would make seed charts. I had no idea how I would collect seeds, since we lived in a hotel and ate in a restaurant for every meal. In the fruit basket delivered to our room each week we got oranges. That was one seed for my seed chart. I'd asked the hotel waiters, Mario and Xavier, whether they would help me collect some seeds from the kitchen, but it was never clear if they understood me. My Spanish class had covered only animal sounds so far. "Pio, pio, dice el pollito." Peep, peep, says the baby chick.

Every day I fretted about the seed chart, but the restaurant waiters had assured me they'd save what they found in the kitchen, and my mom told me to quit worrying, we'd get some seeds over time.

A week later, I would break the law again and be sent to the office for wearing a blouse that buttoned down the back instead of the regulation white Oxford button-down. Who was it that was reporting me to the office every time? Did Miss Hamlin despise me that much? I didn't have the insight then to think someone might be intentionally hateful.

Recalling Miss Hamlin now, I am certain she had an issue with me. What it could have been is hard to say; maybe a pudgy girl was a disappointment to her? In Lagos, though it was a huge metropolis too, I had an element I didn't have in Lima: staff watching out for Small Sister. There was no one keeping an eye on me from the back of the compound, no one making sure I didn't get nabbed by the Man Turned Goat, no one idly waiting to catch me if I fell off my bike. No one to say, "So sorry, Small Sister" if I took a misstep. No lunch hut. I had a spread-wide-open school campus and strict-rule environment, a disgruntled teacher, hordes of students all dressed identically, and nary a friend.

The seed chart was due, and I still hadn't collected any seeds. My mom had taken me to Sears to buy a piece of poster board, and that was as far as I had gotten with the assignment. I wanted the fuchsia poster board, but Mom insisted white would be more appropriate for a class project. "Your seeds will display better," she said.

"What seeds?" I asked, wondering how I would ever get this assignment done properly with no access to seeds in my near future.

"You'll figure something out," she said. Then, seeing my face, she added, "I'll help."

The day before the project due date, I neatly wrote SEED CHART across the white poster board in block letters with a black Magic Marker. To one corner, I Scotch-taped a crisscrossed cellophane patch and wrote "ORANGE SEEDS." I stared at my blank chart. How was it possible that I had no seeds? The weekly fruit basket delivery to our suite contained oranges and bananas.

Bananas, I learned from this assignment, didn't have seeds. I peeled back the yellow skins, broke the perfect white concave meat in half. The tiniest of black spots, a total of maybe five specs circled the center. Not really a seed to speak of, at least not one that could be taped to a poster board. A fruit with no seeds. A conundrum that worried me. How would more bananas grow? I would be an adult before I knew anything about banana republics and the first genetically modified food. But I had a homework assignment, and I did not want to wreck Miss Hamlin's day. So, to show I had higher expectations, I wrote "BANANA SEEDS," and I smeared a little banana goo where the seed packet would go. Now I had two seeds.

I groused to Mom, but she would have her Spanish lesson with Señora Albon on the balcony shortly. So we made a quick trip down the street from the hotel to a bodega. No fresh fruit or vegetables were available at the small, dark market. "This will do," Mom said, and she bought a bag of rice.

While she had her Spanish lesson I glued a few grains of rice to the poster board. I stared at my pitiful substandard chart propped up on my bed. The banana looked like I'd blown my nose on it, and the tiny packet of orange seeds next to the similar packet of rice looked like I'd not successfully made it past kindergarten coloring books and paste. If I could tell how bad it was, I didn't want to know Miss Hamlin's opinion.

The next day I waited for the bus at the end of the rose bush–lined walkway, the Southern Hemisphere's late October summer air damp and cold. Mom had told me the night before, "Just explain to Miss

Hamlin that you live in a hotel and have no access to seeds." She went on to explain that it in no way meant I knew nothing about seeds. I wanted her to come to school to explain, but I knew that would never happen. As I stood at the circular drive's curb, I held my poster board tightly to my chest to hide the disastrous results from the public. I fought the wind that wanted to rip the board from my grip. This, I knew, would be a sad, sad day. Sadder than usual.

When I stood in front of the class to give my presentation, I decided to do exactly as Mom had suggested. My poster board lettering slanted slightly, but I reassured myself that otherwise the board was tidy.

I was the only third-grader with white poster board. Shelly, the mean girl at school, had the fuchsia one I had wanted. But again I reassured myself that didn't matter; I had done plenty, considering my hotel handicap.

"My seed chart has three seeds," I began my talk. "I collected the orange seeds from our fruit basket delivered every week to our hotel room." With my forefinger, I pointed at the dried out and sickly look-ing orange seeds. My gaping audience waited for me to explain further. They stared at the banana snot. I moved my finger over to the rice.

"This is rice." I smiled. No one seemed to see the humor in this.

"Rice is not a seed," Miss Hamlin said from the child-sized school chair she sat in. Shiny panty hose strained and shimmered across her knees that poked up practically to her chin.

I went right to relinquishing blame. "My mother thought it would be a good idea."

"You were supposed to make the chart yourself," Miss Hamlin derided. The giggles among the other students had started their slow creep to the surface.

"I live in a hotel," I started to explain again, "so we don't have any seeds."

Miss Hamlin stretched out her legs and said, "Keep going. What else do you have?"

My voice got quieter. That tiny moment of confidence—poof—gone.

"This would be banana seeds," I said, willing my hand to point to the smudge spot on the poster, but I couldn't look up nor raise my hand I was so humiliated. "But bananas don't have seeds."

We had formed a circle with our chairs. Miss Hamlin stood up from her diminutive chair in the back of the circle "Why would a banana not have a seed? How would it grow if it didn't have a seed?" She sounded frustrated. This had turned out so much worse than I had expected. It wasn't just a bad chart, I was also pitiful.

"I don't know," I explained. "I looked for the seeds, but they didn't have any." That sounded so lame. This poster board was lame. My seed chart was lame. I was lame.

"Living in a hotel is no excuse." Miss Hamlin reached across and lifted my chart into the air above my head. "You're wasting our time. Sit down."

Yes, I was a waste of time.

Mom had said it would be okay, but it was not. Living in a hotel was not an excuse, just as Miss Hamlin said. Why couldn't we live in a house like other people?

I REMEMBER MOM TELLING STORIES ABOUT HOUSE-HUNTING while she and I ate dinner in the restaurant of the hotel. We'd be the only two people in the whole dining room, except the waiters. She'd talk about her day while I was at school, about the crazy, good-looking real estate agent who sped down the Panamerican Highway in his Jaguar showing her houses like mansions with wine cellars and swimming pools. "Not us at all," she'd say. And I'd want to say a swimming pool wouldn't be so bad.

Rapt, I listened to her tell the stories, she a little bug-eyed as she tried to find her way in this city the size of Los Angeles. We were together again. When we sat together over dinner in the wood-paneled dining room or ate sandwiches on the patio on the weekends, I felt like I was Mom's best friend. Who needed a house if we could just be together, ladies lunching.

My head swims with memories of the adults referring to President Velasco's Land Reform. I google the seventies Velasco Nationalist government to find out why we had only mansions to choose from. So many articles pop up about the popular new economic strategy in Latin America—rarely put into use—that aimed to find a "third way" between capitalism and communism.

When I was eight, it sounded so fair. *We are all created equal* floated in my little brain—who knows where I learned it, as I don't recall ever reading the Declaration of Independence. But I know I didn't learn it from listening to the adults—unless they were bashing the expression.

As I read the articles, this expression, correctly quoted, "All Men are created equal," is ever present. The Peruvian Land Reform declared country houses would go to the peasants who worked the property unless the owners lived on the land. This law created a mad dash to the country house among all the wealthy Peruvians. To save their deeds meant moving to the country to their weekend homes and renting out their homes in Lima. But my family didn't need a lavish house, especially since it was just Mom and me most of the time. Unfortunately in a country where there is no middle class, the smaller house selections were thin. Yet the big fancy houses were plentiful.

Maybe I was socialist at an early age, but I remember asking an adult, or someone taller than me, why we didn't all have the same things if we were truly created equal. Whoever it was I asked replied that we were born equal, but after that it all fell apart.

THE LAND REFORM WASN'T SUCCESSFUL, BUT THAT WOULD be later, after the government also nationalized the oil and drilling companies. Later when we would be asked to leave. Later when Americans were no longer welcome. Except Sears and RC Cola.

Buche de Noel

Come in,—come in! and know me better,
man! I am the Ghost of Christmas Present.
Look upon me! You have never seen the like
of me before!

—Charles Dickens, *A Christmas Carol*

MOM PUT THE HOUSE HUNT ON HOLD. SUZANNE AND MARTY
were coming home for Christmas soon, so for the time being Mom
reserved the adjoining room to our suite for them. We would have
Christmas in the hotel. Christmas in a hotel was not Christmas. No
homemade chocolate pies, no swirling disco lights, no tinsel tree, not
even Maurice Chevalier. And this time, not even Santa.

Along with our weekly fruit basket, a *buche de Noel* had arrived.
And along with Suzanne and Marty came a friend. The Yule Log, a
symbol of coming spring, a tradition to ward off evil spirits, sat on
the coffee table. The friend slept on the living room sleeper sofa,
his feet next to the *buche de Noel* on its foil-lined tray. The *buche* was
not doing its job.

Stephen had been Suzanne's boyfriend in high school when we'd
lived in Louisiana. His father had become governor, and he had
money to travel. In my opinion, he had no reason to visit her now.

But despite my opinion, the three of them went off to climb the Inca Trail, to tour the gold-walled colonial cathedrals, and to visit the city's underground catacombs, all without me.

It was as if Suzanne and Marty weren't even visiting. They showed up then were gone again. Who could tell if they had even been there? Their apparitions didn't even leave a warm, lingering air pocket I could walk through.

For one tiny moment, I had their attention. It was Christmas Eve. The *buche de Noel* sat on the coffee table imploding, everyone having prodded a sampling. In the adjoining room the teenagers hung out, and I sat on the floor among them.

"Let's go do something," Stephen said.

"You bored?" Marty asked. He flipped through the travel guide.

I sat Indian-style, pulling on the bedspread fringe. "It's never boring at Christmas time," I said. Please don't go, is what I really wanted to say.

"What's Santa going to bring you, Amy?" Suzanne asked.

Stephen swung his head around to face me. "You still believe in Santa?" Incredulity unraveled from his tongue.

Time slowed, all sound became deep and hollow. I tried to read his face. He must be teasing me. He must not mean what I think he means.

Suzanne tried to rescue the situation. "She believes more than anything, so don't ruin it for her."

At this point my head buzzed. I recall Stephen's head flopping back, his laughter bellowing, and how it made me lose my breath. My rib cage squeezed together as all the air was sucked out. His awful guffaws reverberated off the wallpapered walls. Suzanne and Marty eyed each other, and that's when I knew I'd been made a fool. I could die from this, I thought. I could suffocate, and no one would care.

"How do all those presents appear during the night?" I asked, trying to get my grip on the concept.

"It's Mommy and Daddy," Suzanne said. She was always the logical thinker, the truth teller, the one who wanted to get the facts straight. She was studying psychology at college. Marty shrugged, but nodded his head in confirmation. My gut tightened while I pulled in all my muscles to keep from crying.

"Come on, let's go check out the San Francisco Monastery," Stephen said, the guidebook now in his hands.

"What's there?" Suzanne asked, sitting on her twin bed.

"Catacombs," Marty replied. Piles and piles of dead bones. Once again, they took off without me. Gone to the graves under the city. I sat on the couch, alone in the hotel suite. I thought about Santa. I had heard rumors before. Other kids said he didn't exist, but I considered that a foolish consideration. Who wouldn't want to believe in Santa? But now I was the foolish one.

My face scrunched, trying to hold back a cry. Why hold back when there was no one to see me cry? No one to say, "What's the matter?" To hold me, to rock me in their arms like Alice would. No one to say it would be okay. No one was there to even say I didn't have anything to cry about. No one was there.

I went into my bathroom. I looked in the medicine cabinet mirror. I didn't want to cry. I didn't want to be caught crying. I watched the tears well up then spill over. I didn't want to feel all those achy feelings, those racking sobs like my lungs have been sucked of all their air. I hated that familiar crush of ribs. I watched my face turn pink and swell up into a mess of tears and snot. A face that made me look like the blubbery fool I was. In the blur of spilling tears, I said to myself, "There is no one." I watched myself bawl, how it all poured out. I watched through swollen eyes, I watched my cheeks and eyelids puff. I watched with fascination, not tenderness. I watched because no one else was there to see me cry. I had become a crier.

If I had known how to comfort myself, maybe my reflection could have relayed solace. Maybe watching proved I existed. Maybe on the other side of the aluminum coated float glass, there was somebody there.

After I examined the details of my breakdown, I cleaned my face, removed all traces of my cry, and returned to the living room sofa to

wait. I poked my finger into the uneaten, but beaten *buche de Noel.*
Poke, poke, poke. At first it looked like a fat-beaked woodpecker had
attacked the chocolate icing bark.

Eventually the *buche* turned into a pile of gooey crumbs.

EVEN WITH THE EXTRA PERSON, CHRISTMAS MORNING FELT
ten times smaller with the most important spirit gone. At breakfast,
the waiter in the restaurant had even tried to tease me about Papa
Noel, but I didn't respond.

Around the tiny tree in our room, we, the whole family and Stephen, opened our gifts in our usual tradition. My father took turns
giving us each a wrapped present, but I felt the presence of bad juju.

Didn't Stephen have his own family to spend Christmas with in
Louisiana? His own family Christmas to ruin?

As my dad passed a tiny maroon satin-covered box to my mom,
all our eyes shot open. Inside the box lay a 24-karat gold sole coin
in a gold mounting. My mom held the brooch up by the thick gold
setting. "Oh my, Stephen," my mother said. "This is too expensive."

"Yeah, incredible," my dad said. "You don't need to buy us with—."
Mom shot him a look, so he stopped.

The yellow metal twisted into filigree to impress my mother. Gold,
gold, gold. The treasure of pirates. Stephen had already stolen my
brother and sister, had swiped Santa right out from under me. Did he
really think he could get away with my mom too? I wished he would
leave even before his scheduled departure time the next day. Braniff
couldn't get him out of Lima fast enough.

Everything in Peru was about gold—the jewelry, the Inca, even
the interior walls and icons of all the Catholic churches were made
of solid gold, while those bedraggled beggars sat on the front steps.
How, I wondered, did the priests justify the discrepancy? Didn't they
know *all men are created equal?* Everything seemed so unfair.

SUZANNE AND MARTY RETURNED TO THEIR SCHOOLS. MY
family now existed on three separate continents, in two different

hemispheres. My father returned to the piranha-infested waters of the Amazon jungle.

Sometimes my siblings' absence made their earlier presence feel like a slipped memory, a memory so recent the sounds of their voices and laughter still echoed off the walls. The wadded wrapping paper, demolished *buche de Noel,* and rearranged furniture were all remnants of their having been there. But the sealed and locked doors to the adjoining room and missing suitcases left no signs it was true. Each visit we seemed less like a family and more like visitors. Out-of-town guests. If I were lucky, perfume or a soap smell might linger, a wrinkle on a pillowcase—where an invisible specter's head lay.

But as soon as the maids came the next day, every scent, every wrinkle, and every crumb would be gone.

GOLD. WE KEPT UPGRADING OUR COLLECTION OF TREASURES. Greed? We were wealthy compared to what we were in Nevada. American expatriates. Mom tried to find a smaller house. The Peruvian government tried to share the land. The priests still try to feed the poor while their churches are lined with gold. Maybe a curse was left with that gold Peruvian *sole* coin framed in filigree, bought by the American who was later indicted and sent to federal prison along with his father, then gifted to my mom. Expatriates. Ex-patriots.

The Lima Welcome Wagon

> There shall we three meet again in thunder,
>   lightning, or in rain?
> When the hurlyburly's done, when the battle's
>   lost and won.
>
> —Shakespeare, *Macbeth*

WE FINALLY MOVED INTO A HOUSE IN JANUARY 1973. I WAS about to turn nine. I remember well because my birthday present was in our shipment from Miami. Who doesn't remember their first Big Girl Bike?

I stood on the flat roof of our new home. Up from busy Avenida del Prado rose a cacophony of horns honking and tires skidding. Across the street sat a doughnut shop wafting the fried pastry scent, next to that a Peruvian public school where the kids' laughter and screams comingled.

Waiting for the moving van, I watched the fog roll in from the ocean. "A blanket of fog," my mom said. I leaned against the cold, waist-high concrete wall bordering the roof. The fog unfurled like the blue-paper-wrapped cotton I'd seen in Mom's sewing room. A dark dampness mantled our house, stifling the clatter from the street.

With little precipitation in Lima, the roofs could be flat. Flat-roofed houses used the extra space for laundry rooms, maids' quarters, and growling dogs. Everyone had a dog on their roof—the Peruvian alarm system. We didn't have a dog. Instead of flesh-tearing guard dogs, we had Juana.

Juana lived upstairs, essentially the third story, in a set of flimsy, wooden buildings connected to the laundry room, all built on the roof. A set of stairs led up from the family room to the top of the house. To Juana's den.

The day we moved in, Juana showed up on our stoop. The movers were hauling in the beige couch, squeezing it through the front door. Mom inside made sure they didn't get their greasy black paw prints on her new sofa. I stood outside, tearing open the cardboard container my bike had come in. This skinny Peruvian lady, almost my height, walked up beside me.

Mom kept barking, "¡Por favor!" and "¡Cuidado!" as the movers tried different angles to get the couch through the door.

"Is that your mother?" the tiny dark brown lady in a pink cotton dress asked me. She smelled of toilet bowl cleaner.

"On the other side of the couch," I said. Mom wasn't visible. She could only be heard.

"She need maid."

I wasn't sure if it was a question or a statement. I knew Mom was interviewing housekeepers, as several had already come by, flummoxed by Mom's Uvalde, Texas, Class of 1950 high school Spanish.

Juana said she could speak nine languages, didn't like to cook, and wanted Mondays off. Mom hired her on the spot. Mom said it was like Mary Poppins the way she arrived. I had started to get a pretty good sense of people, and I was pretty sure she was more like Maleficent. Or Juanabane.

Godzilla, the Witch, and the Wardrobe

> "My darling," she said at last, are you sure
> you don't mind being a mouse for the rest
> of your life?"
> "I don't mind at all," I said. "It doesn't
> matter who you are or what you look like as
> long as somebody loves you."
>
> —Roald Dahl, *The Witches*

SCHOOL DIDN'T START AGAIN UNTIL LATE FEBRUARY IN PERU. South of the equator, it was summer vacation and Christmas break. Once we moved in, Mom and Dad hosted parties on the weekends he was home, or they attended parties that other expats and diplomats threw.

The house didn't end up being a mansion like the fast-driving real estate agent wanted my mom to rent, but it was bigger than any house we had lived in before. And it had a pool. A pool the size of a billiards table, but still a pool!

School soon started again, and I had the stress of Miss Hamlin and the third grade gnawing at me. "Make friends," Mom said, which sounded to me like she wanted me to find someone else to hang out with. I really didn't see the need if I had Mom all to myself again. But that wasn't going so well either.

Mom had gone to the parent/teacher conference, and Miss Hamlin must have filled her in on what a dullard of a child she had. She came home furious and said I was grounded for life. She thumbtacked a calendar on the front of my new bedroom door and crossed out every day forward, saying that's how long I'd be in my room. I didn't even bother to count the days. I just closed my bedroom door, letting the calendar hang on the outside, visible to everyone but me.

Every day forward I came home and went straight to my room, which wasn't really any different than what I would do prior to being grounded.

Attached to my bedroom, a smaller room my mom deemed my "study" became my retreat, with a yellow desk and chair and a small chalkboard bought at Sears. The muted beige and browns, and even the soft blues and grays of my furnishings were too dim for my tastes. I needed brightness. I liked flashy things. One day at the market, I begged my mom to buy a gregariously orange alpaca rug with a giant daisy centerpiece, each petal a different bright color—fuchsia, azure, purple, yolk, and emerald with a polka dot pistil. The rug covered the middle of my study's floor.

The week before Christmas, I came home and as usual went straight to my room. I hadn't seen Mom or Juana when I'd come in the front door, but now, standing at the end of my bed, I could hear the TV in Mom and Dad's bedroom. My parents' walk-in closet joined my room to theirs. Sliding doors allowed entry from either side. I peeked through the narrow space where two doors came together. Mom and Juana sat side by side, the television's glow on their faces as they stared aghast at the dubbed Spanish over Japanese destruction of Toyko. I had watched Godzilla so many times that I knew from the growls and screams what images were flashing on the TV screen. Often Mom and Juana watched *telenovelas* together, something Mom never would have done before. And now Godzilla. Until Juana, Mom never liked those sorts of movies, dubbed over with fake effects. Juana had that kind of sway over her. I didn't understand why, just that it took away from my time with Mom. Looking back, I think my mother needed companionship. That she may have been even lonelier than I was, at least for adult friendship. She didn't see Juana the way I did, as conniving and manipulative. Mom didn't know I needed her as much as she needed someone.

"Juana just knows things," Mom had said to me once. The three of us stood on the roof, hanging clothes on the clothesline just outside the laundry room.

"I have the eye," Juana said.

"You are prescient," Mom said.

"I know things before they happen," Juana said.

She made things happen.

"AMY," MOM SAID WHEN SHE CAUGHT ME STARING BETWEEN the closet doors into her bedroom.

"I'm just listening," I said quietly because I didn't want Juana to hear. But Juana snickered because she liked it when I was in trouble.

"You know you're grounded from television," Mom said.

I turned and went back through my mom's closet/dressing room, through the other set of sliding doors to my bedroom.

Godzilla roared on low volume in the background while I tromped with my arms splayed overhead and my claws clenched, growling as I entered my study.

Since there wasn't really anything to ground me from, except hanging out with my mom, I did the same thing I'd do after school anyway.

I played School. Mr. Pinky, a pink stuffed monkey and my favorite, although I wouldn't let the others know because I didn't want to have teacher's pets, sat next to Catsby. Catsby, a flimsy black cat, couldn't sit up, but only flounced around, his soft furry bean-bag body slumped either forward or backward, no matter how I folded or rearranged him. I decided lying back would be more comfortable and a position more open to learning, although I preferred more order in my classroom. He wouldn't be able to see the blackboard from that angle, but no matter, he would learn what he could. Velvet, my doll with the broken hair growth contraption, bent easily into a spread-eagle sitting position. My relationship with Velvet had gone awry when my sister broke the hair growth mechanism. I had never been that interested in baby dolls anyway; I preferred Barbie—grown up and steady in what I perceived to be the adult world. WOL, named after the owl in Winnie-the-Pooh, because he was an owl, a tubby owl at that, completed that row of students. The back row consisted of a few smaller animals, my plastic Polly Doll, and metal llamas lined up, posed, and staring at me with their plastic eyes. I lined them up in rows because that's how classrooms worked. We would have story hour later, I told them, and then we would sit in a circle.

WOL was distracted by the sound of the whoosh crash of Godzilla's tail wiping out a small fake village. He was sensitive to sounds and peculiarities. Sometimes he picked on Mr. Pinky about his skin/fur rash. The rash was acquired after going through the washing machine when I'd thrown up on Pinky one night. I didn't have favorites in class, but Pinky was my overall favorite stuffed animal. I slept with him, his little monkey arms and legs wrapped around my bicep, his bulbous face tucked in, fitting perfectly snug under my chin.

I heard the Japanese ladies scream as I told my classroom what our lesson would be. I vowed that I would be a more benevolent teacher than Miss Hamlin and that my school would be safer than Franklin Delano Roosevelt American School. My seed chart had been returned with a large C– scratched in red Magic Marker across the upper-right corner.

The crackling of flame and panicked Japanese fleeing filtered through the double layer of closet doors. I stood up at the small blackboard hung over my desk. I would teach my stuffed animals the times tables. Times tables were what got me grounded in the first place. Miss Hamlin had told Mom at the parent/teacher conference that I knew only up to eight times. It wasn't true. My cousin had taught me the secret to nine times when we visited last summer. He said you took one less than the number you're times-ing, and then you add what it took to make nine. I also knew ten and eleven, which were so easy Pinky could do them. Ten you just added a zero to the multiplier, and eleven times was just the same number twice. Like 11 × 2 was 22. The multiplication got trickier at 10 × 11. And I still couldn't get twelve times, so that was what my class sitting on my study floor would learn.

Pinky and WOL stared at me. Catsby was still lying on his back, so I had no idea what passed through his mind of fluff. Velvet stared at the closet doors, where now a screeching roar could be heard, as Godzilla was zapped by the giant electrical tower in Tokyo. I couldn't teach the 12 times tables because no one was paying attention to me. I feared I would never learn my times tables, that I would be in this room forever. Alone.

Like Godzilla, I wanted to roar in agony, I wanted to growl and shriek. I wanted to, but I couldn't. I had to be good. Like Godzilla, that giant electrical tower shock buzzed through my body. Only mine said everyone has left you! Everyone is gone! No one wants you! But no one would hear me over the TV.

I made my class recite the twelve times I wrote on the board. I tried to memorize them too as we kind of sang the list. "12 × 1 equals 12, 12 × 2 equals 24, 12 × 3 equals 36," and I started to see a pattern. The first number was equal to the multiplier and the second was its double. Then my mind started to wander, and though I came close to figuring it out, I got to 5 × 12 = 60, and it was not so easy again.

Godzilla had stopped. The monster was quiet now. Outside my window the screech and whoosh of the traffic on Avenida del Prado sounded like ocean waves. Mom and Juana's voices faded off down the stairs. I decided Catsby had the right idea, so I went to my bed to lie down.

I fiddled with the music box Suzanne had brought me from Switzerland when we were in Nigeria. I'd already broken the plunker that drummed out the notes with the teensy brass cylinder pins. I just had to touch the levers; I had to know what it felt like to make music. So now instead of soft, pianolike plinks, the box thunked out a flat "The

Wanderer." I still liked the music box because Suzanne had picked it out for me, so I listened carefully to the slow, flat notes.

I began to think I might really be grounded for life because it didn't seem like I would ever learn my times tables. My tears had begun to wet the bedspread around my temples, so I climbed off my bed and snatched Pinky from the classroom setup. Just once I needed to show favoritism. Supine on the bed, with him wrapped around my arm monkey-style, we stared at the ceiling until it was time for dinner.

My stomach growled like Godzilla. Mom had said I was always hungry, and I needed to ignore it. I considered sneaking downstairs. Who would know? Juana would. She would hear me. She would tattle.

I could smell the top of Pinky's smooth, silky, pink-washed-to-gray fur on his round monkey head. Like cheap, starchy laundry detergent and polyester, that's what he smelled like. Like Juana's cotton dresses when she walked past me. I rubbed my hand over his noggin to erase the smell.

Each day that I was grounded, I was not to leave my room until Mom came to get me for supper. But I wondered whether she might forget about me. I didn't hear anybody at home right then. Avenida del Prado whooshed, but no voices murmured, no floors creaked, no monsters roared. I wished Godzilla was still on, so I'd know where my mom was.

High on the wall, close to the ceiling across from my bed hung a black box the size of a transistor radio. On the face of the box clicky numbers flicked over if the doorbell button on the wall next to my bed was pushed. It connected to the bigger main black box in the kitchen. All the rooms had a clicky numbers box. Originally, the system was created so the maid of the house could be "rung for," and she'd know which room to tend to. Mom told me I was NEVER EVER allowed to ring it.

"We don't want Juana to think she's a maid."

"Then what is she?" I asked. I got a swat on my behind for that. I thought, *Juana is a witch*, but didn't want another swat, so I didn't say it out loud. But now as I lay on my bed with Pinky, I thought, *What if*

I ring it so the family knows where I am? Not Juana. I couldn't care less if she knew where I was. So it wouldn't be for the same snobby reasons that Mom said I wasn't allowed to ring the bell. But I didn't have the guts. I didn't want Mom to be mad at me.

I heard my father come home first. Then other voices traveled up from downstairs. Suzanne and Marty had come home excited from wherever they went for the day. They were home from boarding school. Juana must have gone out or back up to the roof to her chambers. From the sound of the voices I could tell my family was all in the den at the bottom of the stairs. The bamboo bar my dad bought in Nigeria had been set up in that front room, the bamboo half-circle with red upholstered stools. He'd be mixing drinks. Suzanne and Marty were drinking with Mom and Dad. My brother and sister were grown-ups now. They were all having fun.

I decided to open my door a crack and call out. Just a reminder.

I left Pinky on the bed. When I opened the door, voices and laughter became louder and clearer. My father and Marty recounted their day, and their stories were always ribcage-smarting funny. I heard Marty's laugh—a big guffaw. My dad had told a joke with a straight face. I couldn't see it, but I knew in my mind's eye. "No, no, wait," Marty said, as he did when he had something to say that was even funnier.

"Mom?" I called out. Quiet, too quiet at first. Then again louder. "Mommmmy?" I waited. They kept talking and laughing. Maybe they were too far away to hear me from my bedroom upstairs across the vestibule. Now I could hear Marty tell another story. He'd gone to the market. He said something about live chickens.

"Mom!" I called louder. "Mom!" My family talked all at the same time. Then Marty stopped midsentence. "Wait," he said. "Shh." I heard a soft mumble of Mom's, probably telling him I was grounded. A pang of shame from her to me. "Oh, oh," Marty said as he was taking it in. Then Suzanne's smart voice. She was always serious. They were talking about me. Discussing the situation.

"Mom!" I yelled quick, so they wouldn't forget I was waiting.

Marty didn't wait, he yelled out up the stairs, "Amy, come join us. Amy, what are you doing up there?" Like he didn't know, like he thought I was innocent.

Mom said something else I could barely hear from my doorway where I still stood. Where I strained my ears to catch everything each person said. Then I heard Marty's deep voice: "Oh let her, it'll be okay."

I escaped. I ran out before someone said I couldn't. I left behind my room, my toppled classroom, my crumpled bed. At the top of the stairs I paused. I waited to hear if they were still talking about me, but my dad had started telling another anecdote, and Suzanne was arguing. But Marty was at the bottom of the stairs looking up. He called to me, "Amy!" He smiled. I smiled back at the broken front tooth. "What are you doing up there when we're all down here?" he said.

"I was grounded," I said.

"Grounded? What for?"

"I don't know my twelve times."

"Aww, nobody does. Get on down here."

I slip-slided down the big staircase, rounding the corners like a race car on just one wheel. At the bottom, he squeezed me tight and let me stand next to him at the bar.

A loneliness permeates my memories of Peru. My drafty family who was neither here nor there. They were lost to me not just in the physical sense but in an even harder to understand way. They were gone, but not forgotten. They were there, then they weren't. We were not the people we once were. None of us knew our way, so we made it up as we went along. Like the deer in the headlights, when I thought I saw something move I'd run right toward it.

IN AUGUST 2016 I'M ATTRACTED BY A HEADLINE IN THE *NEW Yorker*, "An Isolated Tribe Emerges from the Rain Forest." In the first paragraph it references where my dad worked, "Madre de Dios—a vast jungle surrounded by an even vaster wilderness, frequented by illegal loggers, miners, narco-traffickers and a few adventurers." The article mentions other minerals, not oil, but I know it's part of the referenced desecration. But the piece is about the mysterious people called the Mashco Pico who live in this jungle, one of about one hundred isolated indigenous peoples. When a farmer and river guide was tending his vegetable patch and a bamboo arrow flew out of the forest and pierced his heart, "the incident generated lurid news stories about savage natives attacking peaceable settlers." This happened in 2015.

I pick up the phone and call my dad. It's happening all over again—a story I know from the seventies revisiting me in the here and now.

"Do you remember the guy who was shot with an arrow in the Amazon?" I ask.

"Oh yeah," my dad veers off. "Those natives hunted naked. There were four or five tribes who had never had contact with civilization before. They couldn't swim, so they never crossed the river." His details are repeated in the article. I want him to tell me the story he's told so many times before about his oil company crew member shot by an arrow, a barbed arrow, so that where it pierced the man in the shoulder the only way to remove it was to pull it the rest of the way through. They cut both ends off the arrow, carried the man miles back to where they'd left the "chopper," and helicoptered him back to get medical attention. Probably to Puerto Maldonado, also mentioned in the article as the town founded in 1902 by Carlos Fermín Fitzcarrald, immortalized as the Rubber King made famous by Werner Herzog's film, *Fitzcarraldo*. "[T]he rubber barons [were] the equivalent . . . of modern-day narco-traffickers."

"Puerto Maldonado," my dad says, "was a little village, but the locals were finding gold in the river, panning at the water's edge. I met a fellow in a saloon who had nuggets the size of my knuckles. I told him, go up the mountain, find sandstone, you'll find a vein, and you can mine it and have all the gold you want." My dad, the geologist.

Jon Lee Anderson, the *New Yorker* author, writes, "Eight decades after Fitzcarrald's rampage, I took another trip, on the Madre de Dios, where a gold boom had recently begun." This would have been 1974, which was when my dad would have been there too.

I struggle to reconcile the stories, the adventures, the tales I both witnessed firsthand and was also so close to—am a direct descendant of—with the reality of why we were even there. I read, "Opening up the jungle has made Peru one of the world's largest exporters of gold (as well as the second-largest producer of cocaine)" and "Alan Garcia, [Peruvian] President from 2006 to 2011, insisted the isolated tribes were a fantasy devised by environmentalists to stop development; an official in the state oil company compared them to the Loch Ness monster."

The Loch Ness monster, I think, that's what I feel is the response when I tell our stories. But it's the reconciling with why we were there that makes me hesitate to believe my own memories. Or want to believe. Or is it? I hold back because I feel a sense of this, "I have this great story to tell you, so incredible you won't believe it." But the response from my listeners is not one of disbelief, but instead, "Why were you even there?" Because we were hideous people, is what I want to say. As though we killed the Loch Ness monster and are proudly displaying her scaly skin on our wall, her head mounted and hanging in our entry.

"Did you find oil?" I ask my dad.

"It wouldn't have been worth it," my dad replies. "The Peruvian government wanted us to partner with a communist oil company. So we left."

Mr. Anderson finishes his article with a description of flying out of Puerto Maldonado. "As the airplane banked over the jungle, I could see the great river, looping like liquid silver below. Then, for several long minutes, the jungle disappeared, replaced by an expanse of giant craters. The scale of destruction was breathtaking: it was reminiscent of aerial photographs of North Vietnam after it was carpet-bombed by B-52s. I realized that I was looking at the goldfields of Madre de Dios."

And another memory pops into my head of watching a *National Geographic* documentary on TV with my dad a few years ago. As an aerial view of the Nazca Lines, geoglyphs from 500 BC to 500 AD in southern Peru, came on the screen, the narrator mentioned how the narco-traffickers had caused destruction in certain areas where they had driven their vehicles across the UNESCO World Heritage site. From his recliner, my dad proclaimed, "It wasn't the drug dealers, it was our crews."

I have Loch Ness monster blood on my hands.

IT WAS DURING THIS TIME THAT THE TRIP TO ANCON, THE pre-Colombian necropolis grave digging occurred. Our house on Avenida del Prado filled with the pots and *telas*, when the curse was brought home. And in our pantry, our very large pantry, sat the prince's skull eye level with me.

Black Magic and a Guitar Solo

Three chords and the truth. . . .

—Harlan Howard, musician

THE SEED CHART FIASCO OVER, I NOW HAD TO WORRY ABOUT the new assignment: building a musical instrument. When Miss Hamlin had described the assignment, she said we could either build and invent our own instrument or bring something from home if we couldn't create our own. I didn't trust that and knew I had to make up for the seed chart. She said we'd have a band made up of our classmates, and we'd play our instruments. This, I knew, would be when I'd be made a fool again, and I was determined not to let it happen. Hope!

Dad was home from the jungle and sat at the head of the table, Mom and I on either side of him. When he was gone, which was most of the time, we ate at the booth in the kitchen, and Juana ate with us. I much preferred it when Dad was home. We would spend the whole evening filling Dad in on all the latest goings-on in our lives.

"I have to make an instrument for school," I said, cutting into the boiled potatoes and smearing the smoky *papas ala huancaina* sauce around my plate.

"What kind of instrument?" he asked, serving up a big dollop on his fork. We both loved that creamy sauce on starchy potatoes.

"Her teacher is always giving these impossible assignments," Mom said. That felt like Mom was on my side, that Miss Hamlin really was as mean as I thought.

"I want to make a really good instrument, something better than everybody else's," I said to my father. This time, Miss Hamlin be damned, I would get it right.

He looked at the ceiling for a moment, exaggeratedly thinking, teasing me. "Name any musical instrument you want, and we'll make it."

That seemed ludicrous. You can't just make anything at all. But I went for it. "A piano!" When we had lived in Nevada, my mom refinished an old piano, and it sat on our front porch. Suzanne had taken lessons, and I wished I could have too, but we moved before I was old enough.

"Maybe something a little more portable," my father said. He put another forkful of the yellow potato in his mouth. I had to pause to think of another instrument I loved as much as the piano.

That's when my mother took the opportunity to bring up what she wanted to talk about.

"Do you know how intelligent Juana is?" my mother said. We both looked at her wondering where this was going. "She knows nine languages. She says she's learned them all just from the families she's worked with. She picks them up that easily. German; Italian; Spanish, of course; English; Quechua, her native tongue; and even some Arabic."

That was only seven languages. I wanted to point out Juana was lying. But it wouldn't do me any good. To say anything derogatory or against Juana meant I would get the evil eye from Mom, an indication she was disappointed in my attitude.

"I'm going to help her get to the nine states," Mom was telling Dad.

I had been hearing about Juana's desire to move to the United States for months. Everyone wanted to move to the United States.

What made her any different? It's not that great, I wanted to tell her. Everything's expensive. And everyone's arrogant.

Dad listened, at least partly, but I could tell he was confused. He looked at me and raised his eyebrows as though we were in cahoots. I was trying to come up with a more portable instrument.

"Nine states?" Dad ate the eggplant served with the *aji de gallina*. I hated eggplant. Mushy and seedy and stringy. Mom cooked. Juana didn't cook. It was never clear what Juana did.

"That's what she calls it," Mom said, "The United States. The Nine States. Isn't that cute?"

"Maybe she needs to learn how to say it before she can go there." Dad turned his gaze to his plate.

He and I laughed a little, but not so much that Mom would do any more than look at me sideways. She ate slower than any of us and still had her whole first serving left on her plate, while Dad and I had almost finished.

"She wants to go so badly. She almost had a visa with the last family she worked for, but it didn't go through at the last minute, and they had to move so she was left behind. I'm going to help her." Mom spoke fast now. Maybe she didn't want the story's holes to be too visible. Her tone said she would be going through with this, even if my father wouldn't agree to it.

My dad, like me, didn't ever want to cross Mom, but he would try. "Mart, do you know how hard it is to get a Peruvian to the United States? The paperwork involved? She has to have a sponsor."

This was when her speech turned prepared, as though she had anticipated my dad's retort. "We can sponsor her," Mom said.

My father took another big bite of the chicken. "We can't sponsor her; we don't live in the States."

On the other hand, I thought, if she found a way to the States, then she'd leave and go live with another family. I'd like that.

"I'll find someone who will be her sponsor, then we can adopt her when we move back." Mom was whispering now.

Adopt her! Like, as in, her photo would hang on the staircase wall in line with Suzanne and Marty and me?

"Why are you whispering?" Dad asked Mom.

"I don't want her feelings to be hurt." Mom motioned toward the swinging door between the kitchen and the dining room. No doubt Juana had her ear to the other side of the door listening to every word.

"Who would you get to sponsor her?" Dad asked. I was rooting for him to win, although he rarely did in conversations like this.

"I'll find someone. I was thinking maybe the Conrads in Nevada." She cut into her slice of eggplant with the side of her fork, struggling with the tough skin.

"No one in Ely is going to want a maid."

"She's smarter than a maid," Mom said. "She could settle in with maybe a nice Mormon family in Salt Lake."

"She's not that smart," my dad said.

I was keeping score and my father just got a point, at least on my scoreboard.

Mom chewed her eggplant slowly, staring at her plate, thinking of what she could say that would convince my father. I tried to conceal the smile on my face.

"Fine," Mom declared, her fork clattering against the china plate. "I'll do it myself. I'll go to the embassy." And she rose from the table and took her full plate into the kitchen to eat with Juana.

"I think we made her mad," my father said. I knew whose side I needed to take. Dad would go back to the jungle, but I'd still be here with Mom and Juana. I would be better off not disagreeing with Mom. So I changed the subject back to me.

"How about a guitar?" I asked. Guitar was my second favorite instrument after piano. Mom kept buying me reed pan flutes at the market, but I didn't have the lung capacity.

"That sounds like it could work." He seemed happy to change the subject.

"How can we make a guitar?" I said. Strips of *aji de gallina*, spicy hen, hung from my fork. I didn't want to get my hopes up until I knew for certain that I could have an instrument as cool as a guitar.

"Come on," Dad said. "Let's get started."

As we passed through the warm kitchen, Juana stood next to the sink with a dishtowel in her hand pretending to wash the dishes. Mom stood next to her, a dishrag in her hand, scrubbing her plate in the sink. They had been talking but went silent the moment we appeared.

The big old houses in Lima had two kitchens. The warm kitchen was just off the atrium, and sun came in and kept the space warm. The oven sat here, across from the kitchenette sitting area. The second kitchen, really just an extension of the warm one, had a separate set of water faucets, no windows, and led to the shaded patio and into a dark series of rooms. We headed past the cold kitchen to the farthermost back pantry, like a dungeon.

Mom didn't look at us, but after my dad passed, Juana gave me a glare that sent a chill through me, a chill colder than the cold kitchen. I hurried to catch up to Dad.

As we entered the first section of pantry we had to pass the prince's skull. The same skull that had been tossed out of the grave. He sat eye level to me, so I rarely went back there alone. He'd been stuck in the way back, practically forgotten except by me. The patina silver band encrusted around his forehead, his long hair wrapped around his jawbone, and his big, empty-socket stare resembled Juana's gaunt face, which sent me lockstep in behind my dad.

We walked past the canned goods, farther into the depths of the pantry, to a second and darker, danker room, the room inside the room that stayed cold all year. Before refrigeration this pantry system kept perishables fresh. Now Dad kept his tools back there, out of sight. I never ventured into the farthest rooms alone because there was only one line of escape, and it was past the skull. My father yanked the string to turn on the overhead bulb, casting a dull yellow light.

"How do we make a guitar?" I asked again. Bewildered, I thought he might be teasing me that he wasn't really going to make a guitar, but something of a lesser quality, and then I'd have to play it so I didn't hurt his feelings and endure further abasement from my classmates and Mrs. Hamlin. Please, I wished silently, don't let this be the seed chart all over again.

My dad filled my arms with a few pieces of plywood, a hammer, and his reel of fishing line. He grabbed a few more items off the top shelf, and we headed back out. As we passed the skull again, I ran ahead so I wouldn't be behind my father and out of his sight. Back in the daylight of the main kitchen, we piled the supplies on the cold kitchen's round table. The skull sat just around the corner, one empty eye socket still on us. I scooted around the table out of its sight.

I watched my father pull out a one-foot scrap of a two-by-four. With wood glue he attached a small, thin shim as a fret, then another at the other end. Then with tiny nails hammered into the flat top end of the wood, he tied the fishing line into tiny slipknots. He spun a helix around his finger, then with a slip and a twist of the transparent line, he slid the viniculum over each nail head. He nailed in an equal number of tiny nails on the opposite end of the wood, then stretched the fishing line tight across the plank, letting it rest on each shim, and tied another braided slipknot.

"How do you know how to do that?" I asked. I'd never seen complicated ties like that.

"Learned all my knots from being an Eagle Scout," my father said as I knelt in the chair next to him and leaned over to watch every braid being stitched. Maybe I should have stayed in Brownies, I thought. "Here." He showed me how to wrap my finger, then contort the ligament into a yoke.

I started to see a guitar of sorts come to life. Now that I knew how to tie a slipknot, I could much more easily get it over the nail head with my smaller fingers, but I couldn't pull the rosette as tight as he could, so he would do the final tug, then trim the excess fishing line. Together we strung the guitar with four strings.

Juana stepped out and watched what we were doing, then pretended she wasn't interested. I ignored her. The skull watched with pity at our mortal tasks.

"As soon as the glue dries, you have a guitar." He handed me the two-by-four. "What colors are you going to paint it?"

Paint it? I hadn't thought that far. I held it in one hand and plunked at the strings, but the positioning was awkward, and I couldn't get a good grasp with my little hand. "It's not working," I said. "I can't hold it." The verge of a whine eked its way up from my throat.

"It's a steel guitar," he said, taking it. "You hold it in your lap like this." And he placed the board across his knees, plunked at the strings. He plunked out a few more notes, closed his eyes and had "Twinkle Twinkle Little Star" or some semblance of its rhythm floating in the air.

"I want to do it!" I took it back and tried. But all I got was dead notes.

"Think about the song, sing it in your head, and thrum the strings along with the words."

I was intimidated knowing Juana was watching over my shoulder. I tried. I even closed my eyes and swayed as he was doing. Like the hippies in the airport in Rome did when they sat against the wall and played their real guitars. When I got only plonk plonks, I opened my eyes and looked up at my dad.

"You'll get it," he said. "You just have to practice. Now go get your paints, so we can finish."

With my watercolors, I painted the wood red and the frets green. A little too Christmassy, I realized, after the paint had dried. Watercolors left the hues muted and more of a stain. But Dad smiled and nodded his head with approval.

I picked up my new guitar and headed to bed. As I passed through the warm kitchen, Dad headed back past the glaring prince's skull to put away his tools.

Juana stepped out in front of me. We were alone. I clutched my guitar to my chest.

"I was listening to you at dinner," she said, stepping closer, then looking toward the pantry. I knew she'd been hovering behind the kitchen door.

"Your mama is going to get me to the nine states." She pulled the plywood guitar away from my chest.

"No, she isn't," I said. I yanked on my instrument, the fishing line taut with two hands pressing. I worried the glue wasn't dry enough, that she'd ruin my guitar.

"She said she will do it herself." Juana had the blackest eyes I had ever seen, before or since. Her whites were dirty yellow as though the black was dried blood seeping into the rest of her eyeball.

"I don't have anything to do with that," I said. "Daddy said you can't go."

"You need to help me." She gripped the guitar harder. I used the kitchen counter to give myself some heft. "I know magic," she said, "I know black magic. Do you know of this?"

I stopped tugging. She dropped her end of the guitar.

"I am witch," she said, and I held the plywood against my chest again, fret side toward me, trying to protect the strings. She leaned closer. "I will be watching you," she whispered. Then she smiled. If I'd seen fangs at that moment, I would not have been the least bit surprised. It was not the first time she had told me she was a witch.

That night I fought sleep. I lay awake staring at the ceiling, my stuffed monkey, Pinky, wrapped around my arm, staring at me. Both of us were afraid to close our eyes. Eventually exhaustion took over, and I fell asleep. I slept so hard that nothing could have woken me up. I dreamed I had to pee. That I couldn't find a place to go. I wandered about a dark forest. Fallen logs blocked my path. I finally crouched behind a big log, pulled down my panties and let go. Something warm woke me up, and I realized I was peeing in the bed.

I cleaned myself up and went downstairs for breakfast. While we ate our papaya and eggs, Juana made the beds. I thought maybe she just wouldn't notice, that she'd yank the sheets off the bed, wad them up and stick them in the washer, and no one would be the wiser. Instead, as Mom and Dad and I sat on the patio by the pool eating breakfast, I heard her call, "¡Señora!" Juana was hanging over the railing of the upstairs landing when we ran inside to see what was wrong. "Amy wet bed!" She held up the wet sheets as proof.

"Amy!" Mom turned to me, disappointed. Everyone had a talent, Mom always told me, and I now realized I had a talent for disappointing her.

"Go help her clean up the mess," Mom said.

Upstairs, Juana held up the sheet. "Ruint," she said.

"Why did you have to tell her?" I asked.

"You must grow up," Juana said, her rose-colored dress swishing around her knees. "You are not good daughter."

She would be a better daughter, I knew she wanted to say. And so far, she was winning.

She eyed the muted red-and-green guitar on the dresser. "You go to school now?" she asked, but I didn't answer. I slipped the guitar into my book bag and out of her sight. "I will be watching you even there," she said.

I got to the bus stop much earlier than usual and watched over my shoulder for any signs of Juana.

WHEN I GOT TO SCHOOL, I COULD TELL MY GUITAR SURPRISED Miss Hamlin. That made me puff up even prouder. My instrument was clearly the best in the class, among the drums made from baskets covered in paper sacking, Tupperware filled with dried beans as maracas, and castanets made from walnut shells. When our band went out onto the playground to begin rehearsals, Miss Hamlin let me sit cross-legged up front, my instrument in my lap, like the steel guitar players I'd seen at my grandma's Wheel Inn Café in Texas.

Since our homemade instruments didn't have particular notes to play, we worked on a rhythm. We had learned "Streets of Laredo" in music class, so we tapped out the rhythm and did our best to replicate it. The day was sunny, and for the first time I felt warm in the spot under the flowering pink pepper tree. But I should have known better than to trust that feeling.

On the last day of the semester, an assembly was held in the gymnasium. As the crowd of kids made their ways to the row upon row of yellow school buses parked at the curb in front of the school entrance, I wove in and out of the sea of gray-clad students, wending my way back to my classroom to collect my guitar. The halls were quiet since the gymnasium was across the campus. I didn't have to worry about missing my bus, because my mom and Mrs. Riley were giving me a ride home when they finished cleaning up the PTA mothers' sloppy joes final day celebration.

When I got to my classroom, the lights were dim, but Miss Hamlin sat at her desk. She glanced up as I approached the three steps down into our classroom. She never had a smile for me, and today was no different.

"You need something?" she asked, never ceasing to intimidate me.

"I just came to pick up my guitar." A simple task, the instruments had been kept in the basket under the craft table. When I noticed the basket was empty, I turned around. "It's not here." I expected to see it sitting on her desk or maybe on the windowsill along the hallway windows where we had set the white mice or the seedlings we grew in paper cups.

"I threw it away," she said. "You were supposed to take it with you yesterday."

"You threw it away?" I looked at her face, at her blond hair like a movie star's. No matter how much I wanted her to like me, it would not ever be. My chest tightened. She glared at me with the same disgust she'd had on my first day of school. I thought I might cry.

"Did you want it?" she asked.

Want it? Of course I wanted my guitar. Had she forgotten? "It was the best instrument in the band," I reminded her.

She cocked her head. "The best? Is that how you think of your-self?" She was right, why would I want the guitar? It surely wasn't as cool as I thought it was. How silly of me to figure I could have created something worthwhile.

"No," I said, trying one last time to please her, to show her I could be good. I slumped out of the room, down the hall, and then downstairs, careful to walk on the edge near the wall in case there was an earthquake. The previous weekend I had gone to see the movie *Bedknobs and Broomsticks,* and I'd heard about the movie theatre stampedes. How an earthquake could strike at any moment in Peru, and the floor would open up, how everyone would push and shove and charge out the doors. A particular story told of a staircase that cracked open to reveal the core of the earth. Two kids fell in. When the crack closed back up the kids were gone forever. No one could retrieve them.

Miss Hamlin had made it clear I wasn't center of the universe, and I certainly didn't want to fall to the center of the earth. While I was certain no one would notice if I disappeared, I walked on the extreme sides of the staircase. I worried the shaking could still toss me into the chasm, so I held tight to the banister, convinced I would end up in the fiery core.

Once I made it safely down, I ran out the door. Across the campus at the gymnasium doors, I tumbled into my mother.

"What's the matter?" she asked. I'd tried to stifle my tears, but this time they turned into a gusher.

"She threw my guitar away," I said, and flung myself against her again. She rubbed my back with her free hand. In the other, I could smell she carried a bucket of leftover sloppy joe sauce.

"You can make another guitar," she said.

"Not the same," I said. The guitar had eight slipknots that weren't just any ole entanglement.

Mrs. Riley came out of the doors then too. I was embarrassed to cry in front of her, so I tried to snuff my snot back inside my nose.

"What happened?" she asked. "Are you okay?"

"Oh, Miss Hamlin threw away Amy's instrument. The one she and Jaime made."

"That's mean," Mrs. Riley said. "Let's go talk to her."

I liked this. I liked that I had backup, that we were going to find Miss Hamlin and give her some of her own back.

When we got to the classroom, the lights were out and the room dark. The only light came from the windows where we had kept the white mice that had given birth to squirming, pink babies with no eyes.

When we got home, I stood in the kitchen emptying my book bag of my weeks' of stale lunch trash.

Juana stepped out of the cold kitchen, her borax smell warning me she was nearby. "You finish school?"

"For now," I said, not looking at her. The skull was behind her, keeping its eyes fixed. "Just half-days for parent/teacher conference the rest of the week."

She riffled through the empty sandwich wrappers and school announcements on the counter. "You not bring guitar home?" She held up a plastic bag smeared with peanut butter.

"No—" I started to explain it to her, to tell her the awful story of Miss Hamlin. But when I looked up she was staring at me with her black eyes, her grin saying she already knew. How could she? But I knew.

Black magic.

I AM EMAILING WITH MY MOTHER ABOUT A MEMORY OF PERU, Granja Azul, a restaurant with a play area for kids we used to frequent. *Juana used to take you on the ponies,* she writes. *Juana told me I was too fat to ride the ponies,* I tell her. *I'm sorry if she was mean to you,* Mom writes, *I wasn't aware.* I explain that I believe none of us was aware of so many things in those days. I always include myself as though I was in collusion with the adults. As though. I describe the messed up deceit and mistreatment that Juana delivered. *She told me she was a witch,* I write back to my mom. *Yes, she used to say she was a witch,* Mom writes. *But I thought she was joking. That teacher you had, she was a witch, or that thing that rhymes with witch.*

Phantom Limb

One is the loneliest number that
you'll ever do . . .

—Harry Nilsson, songwriter

"MAKE FRIENDS," MY MOTHER KEPT NUDGING ME. HOW TO GO
about this when I had become a recluse, a solitary introvert, was
beyond me. But I got desperate, and desperation will make a person,
especially a chubby nine-year-old, do completely irrational and dangerous things like try to make conversation.

My fourth grade teacher, Mr. Wilson, was a fresh start.

At FDR we ate lunch outside on picnic tables, similar to the lunch
hut in Lagos, only here there was no hut, and the sun didn't come
out from behind the clouds. And no janitor and cook chased each
other with knives. In other words, uninteresting.

I sat alone, as usual, waiting for lunch hour to be over so I could go
back to desks that all faced forward and not have to make eye contact
with anyone. I'd wandered off inside my head, making up scenarios
much more interesting and certainly humorous than the current
one in which I picked at my lunch sack's brown paper wrapping. The
backdrop of sound was the girls' voices at the table next to mine.

Before I could think about which way to run, a group of girls dressed in their Bluebird uniforms sat down at my picnic table. The pocked concrete bench pinched the backs of my knees. The girls ignored me as they opened their lunches. I'd never heard of Bluebirds, but the bright cerulean skirts caught my attention. The only time you could get away with not wearing your gray school uniform was when you had Girl Scouts or some other club requiring a uniform.

"What's Bluebirds?" I asked. They seemed friendly enough.

The group of girls looked at one another, giggled, and one finally said, "Like Girl Scouts only better."

"We're like Brownies," another girl answered. "We'll be Camp Fire Girls in two years."

I'd been a Brownie in Nigeria for about twenty minutes. I made a potholder with the word "Mom" embroidered at a diagonal across the square of quilted fabric, which Philip used and eventually singed, leaving crackly, black edges. Our Brownie troop made beads from some sort of plaster concoction. While the other girls all ended up with strands of colorful plaster gems around their necks, I never got the chemistry down right, and mine crumbled into powder when I tried to paint them. I asked my mother if I had to keep going. She had gone to so much trouble to get that size 7 brown uniform from another American family, but she figured that if I really hated it that much I didn't have to go. That would be the beginning of my inability to participate in anything that involved groups.

I scooted over to the very edge of the bench to allow another Bluebird in. Shelly, the meanest girl in my class and the palest girl I had ever met, said, "Do you want to be a Bluebird?"

"Sure," I said, not believing that I might become part of this popular clique, even though I didn't know what popular clique meant yet, and never really would. I tingled thinking maybe, just maybe—

"Well, you can't," Shelly said, "because only pretty girls can be Bluebirds, and you're a *gordita*." They all howled in laughter. In truth, I probably didn't give a damn about those lousy Bluebirds, but when she called me *gordita* to my face the hurt was both physical—a tug at my binding waistband—and in my heart, because for one tiny moment I thought I'd made a friend.

Silly, silly fool.

I knew Shelly was mean, but I carried with me always an inordinate amount of trust. Her reputation inspired both popularity and fear among the other girls in my class. Then one day, all that changed. For reasons unbeknownst to me, she'd been ostracized from the regular kids. I surmised they'd grown tired of her cutting ways, but all I really knew was she started making gestures at being my friend.

"Wanna play jacks?" she asked when no one else would play with her. She sat next to me at the lunch table when no one else did. "They're stupid," she said when the other girls looked in our direction and laughed. Maybe she figured I was better than no friend.

When she invited me over to spend the night, I so badly wanted her to like me, anyone to like me, that I said yes, even though I was afraid to spend the night someplace that wasn't my own home and was also afraid of *her*. I'll be friends with anyone—a good and bad trait.

My mom dropped me off at Shelly's house in our pretty new tangerine-colored Toyota Corona. Shelly lived in Miraflores in a one-story with two front windows, curtains drawn. I stood on the curb with the same overnight bag that had carried Barbie around the globe. Something didn't feel right to me. The house's exterior was a dull gray like the Lima sky. From the street it looked quiet, as though no one was home.

My mom leaned over to the passenger side window and said, "What are you waiting for? Go on." As I walked up to the front door, she drove off—that orange car the last spot of color in my vision. I wondered what I would do if no one was home. That would be the kind of trick that Shelly would pull—invite me over and then not be there to answer the door. My mom, as far as I knew, didn't know Shelly's parents. I heard the putter of our Toyota in the distance, and I wanted to run after it and wave my mom back. I hated the idea of spending the night away from her but was torn. "Make friends," Mom was always saying, but I sensed I didn't know how.

When the door opened, Shelly grabbed my hand and pulled me inside quickly. "Shhh," she said. I hadn't even uttered a word yet. The interior was dark with the curtains closed, but I could see an outline of a couch on one side of the room and a wingback chair on the other. A beam of dim light came from what I gathered from the linoleum to be a kitchen. "Wanna come see my baby sisters?" she asked. I didn't really have much choice as she dragged me by the arm. My other arm still hugged my overnight bag.

We stopped in the dark hallway before her baby sisters' closed bedroom door. "Shhh," she said again. "They are sleeping. We have to be quiet."

I nodded, afraid to make a sound.

"Don't wake them," she said, blond eyebrows curved in. She sounded as though she were imitating her parents. Opening the door, she leaned in closer to me. Her bologna breath warm on my face, she said, "They are Siamese."

My Aunt Gene in Houston had a Siamese cat. And my mom and I had watched *The King and I*, the movie with Yul Brenner and Deborah Kerr. That's all I knew of Siamese. I must have shrugged, because Shelly sighed like I was ignorant.

"They're stuck together. See." Then she yanked me inside the nursery. A tiny line of light peeked out from around the shades above the baby girls' crib. The hall's dim light cast a small amount of yellow light so I could see two babies lying like a tent, not on their backs and not on their sides, but with rear ends caressing and supporting one another.

Shelly still held my hand and pulled me closer. I feared we'd wake them. Although I couldn't see where they were attached, Shelly explained that "Siamese" meant conjoined. I noticed how dark brown they were, unlike Shelly who was so blond and fair. They didn't look like they were part of her missionary family.

Shelly watched me watching the babies. I'd never been around babies much, and whenever I was I had no concept of what you were supposed to do.

"What do you think?" she said, and I detected she really wanted to know but was a little afraid to ask.

"I think it'd be cool to be Siamese," I said.

"Come on, let's go play," she said and wrenched my arm in the other direction, dragging me and my overnight bag out of the room. "We're friends now," she announced, as though I had passed the test.

Had she had other friends over and not had as good a reaction to her sisters? My curiosity and lack of affect seemed to please her, but only to an extent. Maybe I didn't make fun of her, but pulling me out of the room, it was clear she didn't want me to give her twin sisters too much attention either.

"The doctors say they will separate them, then they will be normal," she told me in the kitchen while her maid set out *empanadas* on paper napkins for us. "They're just attached at the butt, so it's easy to saw them apart." One would get one kidney, and one would get the other two.

I didn't want the doctor to separate them. Something inside me longed for them to stay together. I wanted to know what would happen instead if they grew up attached and had to get around as one. I wondered what it would be like to have someone who was always there. To never be alone. To have another me. I pictured the two of them making decisions on which direction to walk, and how did they sit in a chair? And I wondered about eating and who sat facing the table while the other one had to look at the person sitting next to them? Could they take turns? Or could they even sit? How did it all work and how did they work together? Was it hard being a Siamese twin? I wondered what was it like having someone you had to always consider who considered you at the same time. Was it more of a bother, would we always be craving to be alone? I wanted to be a Siamese twin! I wanted never to be alone.

But I was painfully aware that was never going to happen. I would always be alone. I was an Igbo twin whose other twin had been thrown into the bush. I had no attachments.

Then I wondered what their butts would look like when the doctor had shaved them apart. Would they have a scar? Would one butt cheek be flat and the other round? Would the spot where the other twin had been feel numb, the exposure to the world not natural to them?

Would they ache for one another like a phantom limb? Would they feel each other's pain even when absent?

THE NEXT MONDAY AT SCHOOL SHELLY PRETENDED SHE didn't know me. My feelings were hurt, but I sat on the edge of the cold concrete picnic bench and didn't hear the Bluebirds call me names.

I had questions I would never have the answers to. I worried how the separation went. Did it hurt physically as much as I knew it did inside their hearts? One twin got only one kidney. Would she be weaker? Could one survive without the other? What if one survived, but the other one died? It seemed there was always a sacrifice.

I STILL WONDER ABOUT SHELLY AND HER ADOPTED TWIN sisters. American missionaries were prevalent in South America. Adopting the deformed, Shelly's parents were doing God's work. I also had a sense they were neglecting Shelly. She wasn't friend material. I would have to find another friend.

When I said I make friends with anyone, good or bad, I believe this is true. These experiences, these moves we made, new schools, new adults, new people showing up constantly, forced an extroverted persona to come out. But attachments, being truly attached to someone, to let them inside me—like the twins who shared that butt cheek and kidney—that has been the hardest lesson. A lesson I am still working on. A curse that I may never be able to break.

Christmas Bird

He continues to smile expectantly. I take a
step back. I don't want to catch whatever he
has. He is a disturbing out-of-uniform Santa.

—Augusten Burroughs, *You Better Not Cry: Stories
for Christmas*

THE DOOR TO MOM'S SEWING ROOM HAD STAYED LOCKED FOR
what seemed like months. I could hear her in there, the Singer
machine's shu, shu, shu. But under no circumstances was I allowed
in. That meant the only way into the family room was through my
bedroom. When Juana went up to the roof to her own apartment,
when Marty was home for Christmas, or when anyone wanted to sit
in the family room to listen to music or go down the back staircase to
the swimming pool, they had to go through my bedroom.

I didn't mind it, as I liked having people in the house. When home
for Christmas, Suzanne shared my room and my double bed as we
did in the States. Christmas was my favorite time, not just for Christmas's sake, but because everyone was home. All family members were
present. For the time being.

On Christmas Eve I was lying in my bed with my eyes staring into
pitch black. The house was silent after we had all returned home

noisily from the Mickeys' Christmas party. A good expat party flowed with alcohol, and afterward everyone had fallen into their respective beds and passed out. Except me. I was only nine, so my alcohol consumption hadn't reached their levels yet. I lay in my bed hoping beyond hope that I wouldn't pee in the bed while Suzanne was in it and that this second Christmas without Santa would be worthwhile.

Suzanne's snore made a tiny whistle as she inhaled. Then I heard a scuffling sound, like something heavy being shoved across the family room's Berber carpeting. The sound would stop then start again, as though the shover didn't have the strength to push as far as they wanted.

"Suzanne!" I whispered, then nudged her.

As tipsy as she was, I knew my attempts were futile. Still I had to try. Someone was moving furniture in the next room. "Suzanne, someone's out there."

"Who?" she mumbled.

"I don't know," I said. "They're scooting something." I thought of the neighbor's house that had been stripped clean to its baseboards by burglars. I'd heard about burglars who sprayed something in people's rooms that made them sleep so soundly they didn't even know they were being robbed. It didn't matter that we were all here at the house.

I had it all figured out: the thief could come up the back spiral staircase from the garden and in through the back family room door. The stereo equipment, speakers, books, sleeper sofa, our Christmas tree, and all the gifts under it, all of it could be being swiped right now as we lay sleeping. Or as *everyone else* did.

I heard it again. Somebody, or something, was out there.

"Suzanne!" I tried again.

"It's Santa, Amy." She rolled over.

Santa? I'd pretty much put that fantasy away. But what if it was Santa? Wouldn't it be important to believe? Everyone was definitely asleep except me, and that would be when he'd come. He could be in there placing gifts under the tree, or it could be the burglar snatching every ribbon-tied box. Or a spook. Whoever it was, I reasoned, Santa bringing gifts or a thief stealing them, or a banshee, it wouldn't be prudent to surprise him.

I lay there with my eyes wide open, holding my breath so that if it was the thief or banshee, he wouldn't know there was a little girl in the next room. The scooch, scooch continued.

I must have fallen asleep, because light crept in from the windows that faced the side street, and I heard the whirring of the mourning doves that perched outside my window now. The strangest sound of all was the silence from Avenida del Prado. Christmas morning in this Catholic country, and everyone was at home, not on the road.

It must have been Santa, after all, because the sun doesn't shine after a house has been burglarized. I confirmed I hadn't wet the bed and stayed still for a moment listening. When I heard no scooching, I crawled out of bed, not caring whether I woke Suzanne now. As my feet hit the teal shag carpet, I noticed the door between my room and the family room sat ajar. It had been closed tight before we climbed in bed.

I peeked through the crack in the doorway. The family room looked untouched. If there had been a thief, he didn't take the big furniture. Then I pushed the door open wider. The dollhouse had been positioned so that when I opened the door I could see straight into the four-room house. A Barbie house. A perfect Barbie house. Was it for me? It had to be for me. I was the only one who played with Barbie.

I couldn't catch my breath. I knelt down, peered around the inside of the house. The front wall and roof were open, the house cross-sectioned for easy access. Every single thing Barbie could want was inside that house. Barbie's dream home. Two bedrooms upstairs and a kitchen and living room downstairs.

Across our family room from where I had planted myself in front of the dollhouse, Juana stepped out through the rooftop door. She was dressed in another starched-stiff red cotton dress with tiny white forget-me-nots scattered across it.

"We do Christmas in our pajamas," I told her.

Juana wore black communist shoes like I wore with my school

uniform. She walked through the prohibited sewing room and out of my face.

I went to get my Barbie and Ken to see how they fit in their new home. I could hear Marty coughing in the tiny room off the family room where his twin bed had been shoved up against the wall. He'd started meditating since he'd been going to TASIS, and he didn't like to be bothered in the morning, so I didn't call out to him as I wanted.

Back in my room, as I dug inside my closet for my favorite Ken and Barbie, Suzanne stretched across the bed. "Are we getting up?"

"I am," I said, excited. "You should see what I got." And I ran back to the family room. Juana had gone downstairs to make the coffee, and sounds came from the bathroom revealing that Mom and Dad were up and about.

Back in the family room, I let Barbie and her beau examine their new home. The bedrooms each had a twin bed the perfect length for Barbie and long enough so Ken's feet didn't have to hang off the end. Mattresses and pillows came with slip-on pillowcases to match the sheets and bedspreads. The trim on the pillowcases was identical to the yellow polka dot trim on the sheet. The yellow bedspread was the same sunny yellow polyester as the sundress Mom had made herself the summer before last. I recognized her details—her intricate piecing together and stitching with colored thread, the straightest of lines from her black Singer sewing machine. So this was why the sewing room had been off limits.

"Do you like it?" Mom said as she came into the family room wearing her peach-colored satin robe, carrying her coffee in one hand, her gold slip-on genie slippers on her feet.

"I love it!" I said. "Look how they fit." I placed Barbie on her bed and Ken on his. On the bedspreads Mom had incorporated pleats and quilting to make it custom-fit Barbie's bed.

All four rooms had been wallpapered. Barbie's resembled the yellow contact paper in our kitchen drawers. Ken's ruby-and-navy plaid wallpaper pattern matched his crimson bedspread and teal sheets and pillowcases.

Suzanne stood behind me now. "You know Ken's not anatomically correct," she said.

My dad came in behind her. "That's why they have separate bedrooms."

I didn't know what "anatomically" meant, and I didn't care. I had the world's greatest dollhouse ever. Built just for me and Barbie and Ken.

The Barbie living room had a long couch, the square throw pillows reminiscent of the aquamarine polyester dress that no longer fit me. "That couch is long enough for Ken to nap on," my dad said. "Santa made sure he could fit." My father still wanted me to believe in Santa. He would have been happy if I believed in Santa for the rest of my life. But I knew it was Mom and Dad who had built this house for me. Mom doing all the hours of sewing.

Each of us found a place to sit in a semicircle around the tree. As I shoved the dollhouse closer to where I wanted to sit, the familiar scooch, scooch reminded me of what I had heard the night before. I situated myself next to the house and next to Mom, but then Juana came and sat between us. Trying to be good since it was Christmas morning and wanting Mom to know how much I appreciated my gift, I didn't say anything and left Juana and her smell of borax alone.

Our elaborate gift giving went on and on. I kept track of how many gifts Juana got. Only a couple. Mom bought her a new hair comb with engraved silver across the bow. "You have such beautiful hair," Mom said. "I thought the silver would look nice against the black." I thought her hair looked like black plastic straws and that the comb should have come to me instead. I had an awful feeling inside, as though I were the worst daughter ever, a selfish child. How could I be so selfish when the dollhouse was a thousand times better than a silver hair comb?

My father went around the room giving out gifts, and the floor filled with wrapping paper. When it appeared all the gifts had been distributed, Juana said, "There's one more gift." Yet under the tree was nothing but piles of torn, flashy, metallic red and green paper.

"It's for you," Juana said, poking me in the shoulder. "Behind the speaker," she said, pointing to the oak Akai box. I expected some cheap trinket from the market.

Behind the speaker, under all the tossed wrapping paper, I found a red plastic net bag tied with a twist tie. Inside was a green ball, but it shuddered and wiggled. My father reached over with his Swiss Army knife and quickly snapped open the springy cross-hatching.

The green ball oozed out, and Suzanne screamed, "A parrot!"

A green *lorito*. When I squeezed him out of the plastic netting he scurried to a safe place behind the sofa. A place so out of reach no one could get to him. With my face on the floor peering under our yellow-and-black plaid sleeper sofa, I spotted one tiny round black eye blinking at me. Marty and my dad pulled the heavy sofa away from the wall. Up against the baseboard, the soft, olive green feathered parrot shivered and looked up at me as if to say, "Is this it? Is this the end?"

"Juana wanted to get you something," Mom said. "She wanted you to know she likes you." Sure, she wanted me to like her so I'd back Mom on getting her a visa.

I crawled after the bird as fast as I could. I scooped him up, afraid I'd scare him more, but held him next to my chest. I rubbed the top of his silky head with my fingertip and slowly his shuddering subsided. The two of us stayed like that.

"Can't you say thank you?" Mom said.

I looked at Juana, and her yellow-toothed smile crept open. The bird trembled in my hands. I couldn't bring myself to say it. I erased the idea that this little green fellow could come from her.

Pretty Bird remained my parrot's moniker until I could think of something more clever, which I never did. Marty claimed my new parrot said *Pretty Bird* when he chirped, and if Marty said it was a good name, then I would leave it. We didn't have a cage to put him in, so I used the atrium off the warm kitchen. Pretty Bird was free to move around. His wings were clipped, something I didn't quite understand. Over time, he got to know me. If I moved slowly, I could reach my finger out while he would gently pinch the flesh of my finger between his beak. Then, gradually, if nothing spooked him, he'd step one claw, then the other, onto my finger and let me bring him up to my face where we would kiss, beak to lips.

I AM GOING TO PUT THAT ON RECORD AS MY BEST CHRISTMAS ever. And it didn't even include Santa. Or at least I realized Mom and Dad were the best Santa ever. The gift didn't make me trust Juana any more, and I kept my eye out for more of her bedevilment, but now I had my own small companion.

FIG.4. Amy handing out candy at Yagua Village in the Amazon. Courtesy of the author.

Our Best Imitation of Gringos

See You Later, Alligator. After 'While,
Crocodile.

—Bill Haley, songwriter

WE HAD FLOWN TO IQUITOS. IQUITOS, PERU, IS THE WORLD'S
largest city not accessible by road, the most isolated city in the world.
I identify with Iquitos, with its ability to grow without the normal
method of influx. Isolation I understand.

We were taking a family trip, all five of us, to the Amazon. As usual,
I can't recall all the details, so I call my mom and dad.

"It was a package group deal," my mom says.

"We took a boat downriver to the small native village, and we met
the people there. I made a deal with them," my father says.

"You didn't have it planned?" I ask. Did we just wing it, like the
time we tried to go to the Galapagos? The closest we got to any blue-
footed boobies was spending the weekend on the beach in Ecuador
watching fishermen fight off flocks of seagulls and their guano. I had
forgotten to bring my bathing suit and had to swim in the ocean in
my underwear.

"He's making that up," my mom says. They are talking to me on
the speakerphone. Both at the same time.

"We stayed at that Dutch couples' lodge," my mom says.

The trip was a package, complete with an organized visit to a native tribe, organized crocodile hunt, organized trail blazing, and all meals included. Opportunities to see the Amazonian wildlife up close and personal, the brochure probably read.

The lodge is clear in my mind—a long hut complete with thatched roof and a veranda encircling it. Straight out of Mutual of Omaha's Wild Kingdom or Disney's Jungle Adventure ride. Or Grey Gardens after its demise.

"Was I the only kid?" I ask my mom, because in my mind I am alone in my bunk for much of the trip.

"Marty was with us," my dad says.

"He wasn't a kid," I say. He was headed to a small liberal arts college in Oregon.

"Suzanne and Marty and Stephen," Mom says. "It was a holiday trip. They were home on vacation."

"Stephen wasn't with us, I am sure of that." I am adamant.

Mom pauses. "We were living in the hotel. Weren't we?"

"No, we went when we were living in the house." Our timetables are set by location, by hotel versus house within each country, each hemisphere.

"Our second year of living in Peru, then," she concurs. I feel a bit of relief in confirming Stephen had not been on this trip.

"Stephen is who told me there was no Santa Claus," I remind my mother.

"Who?" my father asks. "Stephen told you there was no who?"

"Santa Claus," I say a little louder to compensate for hearing loss.

"He's a felon, you know," Mom says. "Went to prison."

"Serves him right," I reply.

"His dad has his own reality show now. I heard him on the radio," Mom says, referring to Stephen's dad, the governor.

Today's American wildlife.

AT THE END OF 1973, I WOBBLED BETWEEN BOAT AND LAND. Greeting us at the bottom of the steps to the veranda stood a rotund animal the size of hogs I'd seen in Texas. This hog wielded a proboscis, like an elephant, but smaller like the size of my nine-year-old forearm. His snout lifted as though waving hello, otherwise he didn't budge. He seemed fat and slow, and I wanted to wrap my arms around him when his little rhinoceros ears flickered and he wiggled his prehensile snout.

"That's a tapir," the Lodge Lady told me. She could tell I was as puzzled as probably most gringos were by this tubbo the color of a chestnut horse, his fur wiry and not really fur at all, but more like balding steel wool. I had never heard of a *tapir* before.

A few feet away the anteater was much more focused on the ground as he vacuumed with his own long snout. Resembling a hunched over Cousin Itt from the Addams Family, he waddled off away from us. This was like a zoo without bars. Although I had never been to a zoo.

Three macaws sat on the banister of the veranda, each one nudging to see if I held anything in my hand, each one a new palette from an acrylic paint box of brilliant jewel tones. A scarlet, a hyacinth, and a blue-and-gold macaw. Pretty Bird was not a parakeet, nor was he a macaw, which can grow to three feet in length. None of these fowl were so green, so deep green as my bird at home.

Marty broke off and handed me a piece of banana the Lodge Lady had given him. The Lodge Lady also handed me a big leather gauntlet to wear. In the same way Pretty Bird stepped onto my finger, the macaws situated their big claws on my forearm now protected by the stiff, heavy leather.

I was a little bit skittish with the thick-taloned parrot on my arm, so when Marty tapped me on the shoulder I jumped. Then I turned to where Marty pointed.

"It's Toucan Sam."

Only it wasn't Toucan Sam at all. In fact, it took me a few moments to even understand what he referred to. The Toucan Sam I knew, the bird on the front of the Froot Loops cereal box, had a bright, multistriped beak like a rainbow, a cartoon character with large, floppy orange feet. And Toucan Sam spoke with a slight British accent or the affected fowl version of Alistair Cooke. The bird Marty pointed toward was black with a clean white neck. His beak appeared awkward and too big for his head, as though someone had read the measurements wrong.

He opened his sandy yellow, cumbersome nozzle wide, and his long sliver of silver tongue, like a thin piece of metal, flopped in and out of the side of his beak.

"Did you see that?" No cartoon character had that kind of tongue. When he closed his mouth, his oversized beak clacked together. When he opened it again, as if showing off that dipstick tongue, and then closed it once more—clack, clack—the misplaced beak situated itself on his face.

"He looks out of place," Marty said, and I understood that he didn't mean because the toucan wasn't on a cereal box, but because he was like the geeky kid on the playground that didn't know how to fit in, his feathers pristine and his beak plastic-esque.

"Let me show you to the bunkhouse." Lodge Lady gestured for us to follow her around the veranda.

Two rows of small beds lined up against each long wall. Each bunk was draped in flowing, white mosquito netting, each cot like a miniature canopy bed. Each bunk, covered in its own shroud.

I flounced the fabric surrounding my bed out and let it flutter down. "I want a bed with mosquito netting," I announced. I had always wanted a canopy bed, but full-on down-to-the-ground mosquito netting would be better.

"Why didn't we have mosquito netting in Nigeria?" Mom asked.

"The net doesn't really keep the mosquitoes out," Daddy replied. "There is no complete protection from anything." Complete protection from what? I thought. Does he mean just mosquitos? He worked in the jungle most of the time we lived in South America. He'd slept under these mosquito nets most of his nights in the bush in Nigeria. "You can still get malaria with a mosquito net."

It might not keep out mosquitoes, but I couldn't wait to sleep inside my elegant netting like a grown-up lady. Like Katharine Hepburn in *The African Queen*. I climbed onto my bunk, closed myself inside the web of thin gauze and watched everyone around me, pretending they couldn't see me.

"Mom?" She stood just a couple of feet away, changing from her airplane outfit of cropped Eisenhower jacket to a tank top for the jungle heat. The average humidity in the Amazon jungle was 115 percent. "Mom, is malaria like the mumps?"

"The mumps?" She kept folding her blouse like she didn't know where to put it. "Good gosh, no, why would you ever think that?"

"Once you have it, is it gone, or does it come back?" I had closed the mosquito netting neatly all around me, leaving no visible openings for lurking mosquitoes. I was stretched out on my bunk, as though ready to go to bed now, in the middle of the day. I could see everyone around me but felt I was invisible to them.

"Yes, malaria comes back," Mom said. "But it's not contagious, if that's what you mean. It's just between you and the mosquito and your blood. Now put on your shorts." She stacked her blouse on top of the makeup bag at the foot of her bed. I watched her netting flow around her as she traveled the circumference of her bed. All around us the white, opaque sheets fluttered as other folks arranged their tiny territories. Like a family of eidolons.

I worried about Mom, whether her malaria would come back again. I watched her thin net float up and down. Dad said there was no complete protection. What did that mean? Here I had all five family members together, so wasn't that complete protection? But he said mosquitoes could still get in, and Mom said malaria can come back. No, she said it "comes back." Like it would, we just don't know when. When it came back, would I be all alone again? There was no Philip, Alice, Samson, James, or Pious. Would I be left with Juana? I got a chill in my bones even in the jungle heat.

"Are you ready, Amy?" my mother asked. "Did you get the candy?"

"You have it," I said.

In Lima, Juana had followed us around the house as we packed, instructing us on what to bring. I thought she was working on getting herself invited. If Mom could have, if my father hadn't only bought five Aeroperu tickets, Juana would have been sleeping next to me under her own mosquito net. As we were leaving the house, suitcases in hand, Juana told us we'd be visiting a native tribe, and we would need candy to give out. She handed me a big bag of the cheapest candy you could buy in Peru.

"You always know the little important things like that," Mom had told her and motioned for me to take the bag from Juana.

I was relieved Juana was left behind, and that it was just me and the grown-ups. That was when I remembered I had stuffed the candy in my carry-on that sat at the end of my bed.

As I crawled out of my white, encased sanctuary, I heard the flapping of wings, big wings, much bigger than a mosquito. I jerked my head up, frightened.

"Look, a swallow!" Suzanne said.

I watched the blue-and-white, sleek-feathered flier flap from one end of the ceiling to the next and out the other end's tented opening. Anything that wanted to get in our bunkhouse could. From mosquitoes on up. How big? I didn't know yet. I dug out my duckling yellow stretch-knit shorts and matching Charlie Brown shirt with the unflattering black zigzag across my protruding stomach.

The Lodge Lady announced to my family as well as a couple of other groups of tourists who gathered on the veranda again, "We're going to visit the Yagua Tribe."

We took a harrowing jeep ride through the jungle. Hitting big chug holes, Marty and I bounced a few inches in the air. I peered over the side of our open-air jeep to see how far we'd fall, estimated the speed, and then calculated the brush burns and head trauma caused by such a fall. I had become expert at imagining the gore before it even happened. I also took in all the adults laughing and talking over one another. I calculated who would notice if I fell out.

I could have been no more pleased to have the soil of the earth safely under my feet when we arrived at the Yagua Village. The tribe, who painted their faces red, surrounded the vehicle. My mother pushed me forward and told me to give the kids the candy. A trickle of young boys and girls the color of cacao beans gathered expectantly. Why would they want this cheap, cruddy candy? I thought. But, boy, did they.

The moment I opened the plastic bag, the kids lined up in front of me. A sort of trick-or-treat handout, only I played the part of the lady at the door to the house, and they were the trick-or-treaters dressed in costumes. The little boys wore grass skirts like their fathers, and the little girls wore red cotton wraparound miniskirts.

After I'd given out all the hard candy and caramels, the kids ran inside their beehive-shaped hut, then quickly returned. Three of them pulled along an old wooden chair and set it in the middle of the cleared area in front of the main hut. A few others grabbed me by the arms and tugged me over to the chair.

"Go on," Suzanne said, and I thought, *traitor*. I didn't want to leave my family's side. When I sat down, the remaining kids gathered in a circle around me, spoke in their own language, and with their little hands, raised a string of beads over my head. They christened me with a long necklace made of the flaming red huayruro beads and giant deer's eye seedpods as big as, well, a deer's eye. Then they stepped back. I guess they were waiting for my acceptance speech. As I had none, I scurried back to the safety of my gringo family.

"They just made you a Yagua princess," my mother said.

That's it? That's all you get for being a princess—a seed necklace? I didn't feel like a princess, and the whole thing felt like a setup. Candy for a title.

"Say thank you," Mom instructed.

I was a fat girl dressed in yellow stretch knit, I was no princess. Did Mom really fall for this stuff? I was starting to see there were multiple sides to situations. Not everything was as it appeared. Or was exactly as it appeared. I just had to figure out which. I would have to learn to maneuver.

Across the way, the Yagua chief lifted a long pole to his mouth to demonstrate to my father how to use the blowgun or *pucuna.* Long and thin, the eight-foot hollow pole seemed lightweight at a glance. It reminded me of the spear that Dubbie, my cousin in Texas, used for gigging bullfrogs. The Yaguas held the hollow pole up to their mouths and with a short, powerful puff, a thin, sharp dart propelled greater than a hundred meters, hitting birds or monkeys high in trees. A *pucuna* shot can go farther than any shotgun and in complete silence, unlike the loud blast of the gun.

It was painful to watch my father try to lift the pole to his mouth. "It's heavy," he said, imitating a weakling who can't lift a barbell. Everyone laughed. His John Wayne image was tarnished. An Indian who stood no higher than my father's waist took the dart gun from Dad's hands, lifted it with no effort and showed him again how it was done. The quiver had a piranha jaw hanging off the top where the darts could be sharpened between the razor teeth.

BACK AT THE LODGE, THE LODGE LADY MADE US DINNER AND served it family-style, which I preferred, because I could take seconds. As I reached for more fried yucca, my huayruro bead necklace clanked against the table edge. For dessert we had fried bananas with honey. What more could a pudgy princess in stretch knit desire?

After dinner Mom said I needed to take a nap. A nap?! In ten days I'd be ten years old. A discussion about whether or not I could stay up for New Year's with the adults had occurred without my input, and it had been decided I would need a nap first.

I was shooed off to the bunkhouse.

The rainforest floor at dusk was soft. The tapir still stood at the bottom of the veranda as though he hadn't moved all day. Perhaps he knew his plight and chose boredom and regular feedings over being alligator lunch or becoming a rug for someone's den. The parrots must have been off having their own dinner. Alone on the trail, I began to notice the jungle sounds for the first time. Frogs croaked, monkeys leapt across creaking branches overhead. I sensed I was being followed.

At the bunkhouse, all the beds looked alike. Through cot after cot wrapped in white netting, I made my way down the center aisle. Finally I spied my tan Barbie carry-on where I left it at the foot of the cot.

Napping was not going to happen. So, as at home with my stuffed animals in my room, I just played under the mosquito net. With a flourish, I flung back the opening to let in my pretend guests. I served them tea, as we (my imaginary visitors and I) all sat cross-legged on the cot. It tended to be a bit crowded, but no one minded, as we had a lovely conversation about the day and my coronation. Then they said they had to leave, so I flung back the fluttering mosquito net for them again. And bid them adios.

"¡Ciao!" I said.

Then I was alone again.

I lay back on my bed to wait. The room had grown dim. The only light came from a buzzing, long fluorescent bulb speckled with dead insects. With just enough light from the fluorescent at the end, I pulled my book from my bag—*The Velvet Room*, about a girl who moves to a migrant camp with her parents to pick peaches. As she wanders the property alone, she finds an abandoned house with an upstairs room filled with fuchsia velvet furniture, where she can hide out and read all day. She relishes the idea no one knows where she is, that she can escape to her own world. I had read it two times before, but I couldn't get enough of the story. It was like this girl and I were friends. Like we understood each other.

But the light was too dim, so I tried readjusting myself on my tiny pillow. The buzzing night sounds carried through the open roof. In the distance, I could hear the grown-up chatter and a radio that had been turned on, music for the party. New Year's Eve. I could probably go back over there, I figured. Surely my nap should be over by now. Surely someone would come to get me. They had said they would. They wouldn't forget me. Although I knew they probably would.

A breeze brushed open the bottom of the hut's curtained entrance. Then it traveled along the floor whipping up the netting on the first few bunks. It stopped before it got to mine.

I sat stark still.

Then I heard a cry. Like a scared baby. I laid my body out as flat and inconspicuous as I could. My eyes didn't blink as I scanned the dark room. I heard it again, a moan, a wail, long and sad. I regretted that I hadn't gotten up and gone to the party before now. Now I was too scared to get out of my mosquito netting. The scream continued. It had to be a baby dying. I lay as still as possible. They, whoever they were, would get me next. I waited. It screamed again. I closed my eyes and pretended to be asleep. The impending attack was agony. I pictured everyone coming back from the party, finding me in my bunk, the mosquito netting splattered with blood. I teared up when I thought about how sad my Mom would be, and maybe everyone else. I stifled my tears and my labored breathing not to alert the evil nearby. I listened harder to see how close it was. It sounded like the crying came from above me, high in the ceiling.

How long would I have to wait?!

Across the room footsteps headed my direction from the doorway. Voices rose as the room started to fill. I squinted my eyes open enough to see someone walking toward me. A small person. My mother!!

"Why aren't you sleeping?" she said as she approached my cot.

"Because of all the screaming," I whispered.

"The party is just about over," she said. "Then it will quiet down."

"No," I said, "It's screaming in the ceiling."

Other people started to straggle in. I became shy and embarrassed when my mom told them I heard screaming in the ceiling. Everyone looked up. Mr. Estes, who was also staying at the lodge, laughed.

"Look, he said. He pointed up at the ceiling. "An owl." He turned to Mrs. Estes. "And you said I was snoring last night."

The brown-and-white owl sat snug in the corner of the ceiling, no bigger than the beer mug Marty set on the floor by his bed.

"Amy, put on your warmest clothes." Everyone was putting on jackets and sweaters.

"Why?" I sat up and threw open my mosquito netting again. I felt safe to be a princess in my head again.

"We're going crocodile hunting," Marty said.

Crocodiles would be much safer than sitting here in my bunk waiting for the owl to attack me. I always preferred to go when invited along with the adults. In this instance, it was simple logic: if I got eaten, it would be with another family member. Together we would be devoured.

Crocodile hunting consisted of floating down the pitch black Amazon night in two canoes. Of course, my parents were in the other canoe. Silence was absolutely required. Only the sound of our rudders in the murky river could be heard, and the occasional zip-zip of a nylon jacket as we rearranged ourselves on the uncomfortable canoe seats and fidgeted. I worried about capsizing and strained to see my folks' shadows in the canoe behind me.

"Watch for two red dots in the darkness," our canoe driver had instructed, "then shine your assigned flashlights in their direction." The two red dots were the eyes of the crocodile. The drifting boatload of silent gringos and the lulling whoosh of the water made me drowsy, but I tried to be alert in the silent darkness. Then a man behind me tapped me on the shoulder. I looked where he pointed. Two red dots! I listened for breathing, hot breathing like a dragon would expel. Suzanne, sitting next to me, lurched onto her knees and switched on her flashlight. A crocodile on the mossy riverbank stared directly at us, not moving. Murmurs came from everyone. I checked in all directions to make sure another caiman didn't attack us from behind while everyone was distracted. Boas could drop from the black canopy of trees, anacondas could snap off a hand trailing in the water. No one was paying attention.

The crocodile caught on to the flashlight trick, turned slowly and crept back into the jungle darkness.

The canoe was turned around, and we headed back to camp. I was relieved. I preferred land.

AS WE REMINISCE, I ASK MY MOTHER ON THE PHONE, "DO you remember the jaguar?"

"The jaguar?" She hesitates.

She doesn't remember, as she doesn't remember the body in the grave. It will come to her.

I remember it well.

Other than our arrival with all the animals, all my Amazon memories are related to nighttime. Maybe it was when my imagination was most active, or maybe the nocturnal jungle rallied fears that sustained my most vivid images, or maybe it was when I felt least protected. It was, after all, when I was most alone.

But the last night of the expedition I wasn't alone.

It was deep in the middle of the night. Frogs were having a party with throaty trills on their deep banjos. A few feet away someone, maybe my dad, maybe another gringo, let out a scratchy snore. The owl had returned and hooted, but it didn't provoke the same anxiety now that I knew it was an owl. Now that others were in the bunkhouse with me.

I had been awake for a few minutes contemplating a dilemma: I had to pee. The outhouse was down a long, dark path through the jungle brush. Finally my bladder had reached a point where I needed to ask for help.

"Mommy," I whispered. Her bunk was next to mine. Nothing. "Mommy," I tried again.

"What is it, Amy?" Suzanne, on my other side, asked, sounding groggy.

"I have to go to the bathroom."

"Now?" she asked.

"What's the matter?" Mom woke up.

"I have to go," I said. I had waited until I was desperate, and now I needed to hurry.

"Are you sure?" she asked, her voice thick with sleep. I heard Suzanne's sheet rustle as she turned over to go back to sleep.

"Mom, I really gotta go."

With her flashlight, Mom and I made our way outside to the other side of the bunk hut, then to a smaller hut where inside two toilets sat on a raised platform. An outhouse of the regal sort.

Holding my breath from the stench, I hesitated when I reached the throne. Marty had told me snakes lived in the toilets.

"You go first, Mommy," I said. Why not sacrifice my mother before risking my own life?

"I don't need to go, Amy." She wiggled her flashlight beam over the wooden seat to the detritus below.

"How will I know if there are snakes or not?" I stayed a safe distance away, but my bladder did not like this new plan, so I hopped on alternating feet in my flip-flops.

"Here, I'll shine the flashlight on the toilet. Snakes don't like light, so they'll stay away." She waved her flashlight around.

"What if the snake is *inside* the toilet?"

"I'll look first." She leaned over and shone her beam directly into the stinky filth. A little green frog no bigger than my thumbnail jumped out from behind the seat, and we both let out little screams.

"There are no snakes, Amy." Her tone was now irritated. But I still didn't feel right about sitting on that dark cavity.

"Are you sure?"

"I thought you had to go, Amy?" The beam of her flashlight dipped.

"I do! I'm just ascared of snakes, that's all." I tried to convince myself. I knew I couldn't go back to bed, I'd wet the mattress if I fell asleep, and I could hardly hold it in any longer. I thought I might wet my pants right there.

"I'm losing my patience," Mom said. "I'm going to go back to our hut." She pointed her light toward the door and made to leave.

"NO! Wait. I'll go now. I think it's okay." I wiggled my panties down. She shone the flashlight for me. I tinkled as fast as I could, considering I was so clenched for fear a snake would bite me midstream. Finally I finished, hopped off the seat, and pulled up my panties.

I tugged my nightgown back over my bum, and we stepped off the platform and back into the sweet, fresh air of the jungle. The sounds around us had died down. We stepped out into silence. Then to my right, a sound like a flutter of wings broke the quiet like quills clacking together or a maybe a low purr.

We stopped dead still. "What is it?" I whispered to Mom, but she didn't answer. My ears piqued. The jungle moisture dripped around us but otherwise, silence still.

Then, invisible in the dark, it hummed close enough we could reach out and touch it. This time it was clear the sound was not a low purr, but a guttural growl. I thought I next would feel the warmth of its breath. I waited for Mom to shine her flashlight in its eyes or try to freeze the animal in the beam. Instead, she leaned into me, pushing against my shoulder, trying to get closer.

I wanted to whisper "Mom" again, to get direction, to be reassured. I wanted her to snatch my hand, irritated I was so unnecessarily scared. I wanted her to walk me back to the bunk. But I got nothing except heavy breathing on my earlobe. "Do something!" I wanted to scream. This was not the time to be making loud noises that might startle jungle animals, I surmised.

The click click and growl, like a gas burner catching flame, came again, and now I was certain it was in the underbrush next to the doorway to the outhouse. My heart beat inside my eardrums. My mom's weight leaned harder. The growl, long, low, and ceaseless.

Self-preservation is instinctual, but shrewdness and whom to trust is learned. There is no real protection, my dad had said. I didn't have time to wait or to think about what we should do. I just did it. I grabbed Mom's hand, and with a little tug to get her to budge, we ran.

My flashlight beam bounced around on the path's dark loam in front of us. Tiny, silent frogs hopped out of our way. The path narrowed, and I let Mom run in front. I held her hand tight, her knuckles crunching against mine like she did when scared. I pushed against her lower back with my palm to rush her. Faster, I wanted to tell her, but was afraid to make a noise more than the padding of our feet. She picked up the pace but seemed drugged or in a trance. I pushed harder. I would catch her if she fell, I thought. I was there for her. I pushed and pushed. Neither of us looked back. We just ran, and we didn't stop until we'd passed through the entrance to the bunkhouse.

"Was it a lion?" I asked as we stepped inside the door.

"I don't know," Mom whispered, breathing heavy, "but it was awfully close." She still held my hand, tightly. I walked her to her bunk. I wiped the chill off my back.

As we passed my dad's bed, in a hushed voice because the rest of the gringos were sleeping, he asked why we were out of breath.

"We heard a lion roar near the potties," I said.

"There aren't any lions in the South American jungle," he said.

"Whatever it was," my mother said to my dad, "it was close, and it sounded hungry."

"If it were going to make you its dinner, it wouldn't have announced its arrival," my dad replied.

"It was scary, Daddy!" I scream-whispered to him, because he clearly didn't understand.

"Maybe it was a jaguar or a puma," he said, sitting up.

"Do jaguars come out at night?" I asked. I had to speak in *voz alta*, because I was back at my own bunk, climbing in, and he was two bunks away. The rest of the room stirred.

"Yes," my father said, falling into his didactic role. "They sleep in the daytime and come out at night to hunt."

"Quit talking, Amy," Mom said, although it was pretty clear she meant both me and Dad. "You need to get back to sleep before morning."

"I can't sleep if a jaguar is outside." Really? Could anyone?

"They don't like the taste of little girls who eat Froot Loops," Marty said. Now we were all awake. The other tourists must have hated my chatty family.

"Well, everyone else is trying to sleep," Mom snapped. I would suffer the consequences if I said one more word.

I tucked in my mosquito netting all around me. The growl we'd heard still rattled in my head, along with Mom hiding behind me. I wondered what would have happened if I had waited for her to make up her mind on what to do? I lay down, my head on the tiny pillow, staring through the opaque netting at the dark ceiling where other creatures lurked. I could hear everyone else's throaty breathing, and I knew I would not fall asleep.

Passing the time, I considered all the different ways I could have died between the bunkhouse and the toilets. What if the jaguar did eat everyone but left me? I'd have to go live with my grandmother in Texas, and that made me start to cry because there was nothing on her TV except *As the World Turns.* At least, that's what she'd told me.

"DID YOU REALLY SEE A JAGUAR?" MY MOM ASKS ME ON THE phone from Texas.

"No," I tell her. Because I never did *see* it. Neither of us did.

I GOOGLE YAGUA AND FIND THEY ARE THE EXPERTS AND artists of the blowgun. They invented the poison *curare* made from a strychnine plant and venom. I read about how they are losing their language and culture because of the encroachment of the white man. I picture the blowgun that now hangs over the basement window in Texas as a curtain rod.

My dad bought the blowgun that he was unable to lift to his mouth, along with a quiver of darts and a nutshell of poison. A dollar bill goes a long way in making up for humiliating moments, the gringo recovery method.

Mom turned to him and said, "I don't know where you think you're going to put that thing."

So he handed it to my brother and made him carry it.

A jaguar pelt with a bullet hole in the rump hangs on the wall opposite the blowgun.

We had hunted crocodile with flashlights but weren't the gringos who hunted the Amazon black caiman to near extinction. Is that just because we didn't live a lifestyle that included crocodile boots and purses? Or had we just not been handed that opportunity as we had the Chancay pots?

I ask my dad if he hunted the jaguar that hung in the basement. Did he shoot it? He had been a hunter when we lived in the States, a deer every winter for our freezer. Javelina, pheasant, quail, he was a good shot.

"It was a gift," he says. "The jaguar came into our camp. Would have eaten one of us. One of my men shot it. He had the skin tanned and presented it to me, *el jefe*, the next time I went to the jungle."

ONCE UPON A TIME THERE LIVED A PRINCESS WHOSE FATHER, El Jefe, received offerings. Because of these offerings that weren't always his to take, a curse was placed on this family, and until that curse is broken, the little princess will live *all* alone.

The Butcher Gets Bigger

> History is moving pretty quickly these days, and
> the heroes and villains keep on changing parts.
>
> —Ian Fleming, author

I DON'T KNOW WHAT PROMPTED HIM THIS TIME. I WASN'T
probing. I didn't even bring up South America, or did I? I guess I
did inadvertently.

"Use dynamite," I tell my dad.

"Where am I going to get dynamite?" he asks.

"You used to have it all the time when you worked on the surveying
crews. Don't you have any spare sticks lying around?"

This is what I think prompted him. It was true, what I said. They
used dynamite in his job. We had spools of copper wire as big as
Quaker Oats canisters in our cabinet over the washing machine,
where we kept the gift wrap. The copper wire was used for fuses,
but sometimes we used it for ribbon when wrapping presents or for
better radio reception on the shortwave. I remember tablets of paper
kept by our phones for phone messages, promotional advertising for
Austin Powder Co. with its red diamond-shaped logo on the graph
paper, supplied to geologists like my dad. We used the pads for
notes to others in the household, like, "Gone to the grocery store."

Or "I'll be home around five." Or my favorite, "If I'm not home when you get here, aliens kidnapped me." The latter one—left by my mother—is another story for later.

I have called home, just a regular check-in call. My dad's retired now, but he doesn't just sit around watching TV. He is preparing to build a greenhouse.

"Your dad has been reading the instruction book for three days. I don't know if he's ever going to build it. I think he's just going to read the instructions," my mom said before she put him on the phone.

He bought a kit to build a greenhouse on the back of their property. "Should have built it twenty years ago when I could still bend over," he jokes. They retired on seven acres in Texas Hill Country, where in the springtime bluebonnets blanket the backyard. The wide, spiny, five-fingered leaves break through rocks and thin layers of topsoil, and the spires of purple flowers whorl upward.

"Just the fact that you're eighty-three and can still drive the seventy miles to San Antonio to buy the kit is pretty impressive," I tell him.

His problem, he says, is he can't find a level place where the construction of the greenhouse would be feasible. "I guess it will go by the fish pond," he says. He built a fish pond twenty years ago, and a green heron comes regularly and eats all his koi. So he just keeps buying more of the giant goldfish at the pet store. "All the rock keeps me from finding a place level or that can be leveled." Hill Country sits on a dome of granite. The topsoil is thin, and underneath is solid granite and limestone. This is why nothing grows except sage, cactus, and bluebonnets.

I am joking about the dynamite, but I'd run into a similar problem with how to build greenhouses on hillsides, which made me think of it. About fifteen years ago I worked on a Bolivian maternal and child health program's garden project for the villages. I tell my dad about the similar problem we had and how the villagers solved it. So I've brought up South America, but it is the Latin America of my adulthood, not my childhood. It is he who takes it back to that other time.

I tell him how successful our gardens were in the villages around Cochabamba, the same town we had lived in when I was ten. "In Quillacollo our outdoor gardens grew so successfully we decided to expand to Potosí," I said. Potosí sits at thirteen thousand feet above sea level. The mountain was at one time the richest mountain in the world. "Made of" silver, the Spaniards said. "One is worth a potosí" means one is worth a million. Many Spanish miners died from the unfit conditions and the extreme plundering of the silver metal, so they used local Incans to do the menial work, until they gradually began to die off too.

When I was a kid, my dad and I had visited a museum in downtown Potosí, a small museum, no bigger than my living room. He would take me to museums and point out things like the mummies in glass cases or in this instance the wooden cart used to transport the dead bodies out from the mines. As an adult working on the projects in Bolivia, I found the facts, the statistics, more bewildering than when I was a kid. Back then the idea of a wooden cart, something to ride around on, intrigued me more. But the importation of slaves, thirty thousand slaves in 1603 from Spain to replenish the depleted human labor, this stabs at my memory now on the phone call, of how the Spaniards then began to import African slaves when the Incans died off. The Africans met with the same fate—the wooden cart as transportation out of the mine.

But I digress from the project and how it applies to my dad's greenhouse conundrum. Because of the cold temperatures at thirteen thousand feet of elevation, when we were setting up the garden project, we realized we would have to turn the gardens into a greenhouse project instead.

"On the mountain, we had the same problem—finding a level spot," I relay to my dad on the other end of the phone. "But the locals found a solution," I tell him. "It wasn't the solution that we encouraged, but it worked."

"What was that?" he asks, hoping it will help him out in Kerrville, Texas.

"The miners all have access to dynamite," I say, "so the families who wanted a garden just blew out a big chunk of the mountain behind their houses. We provided the clear plastic tarp, and with some wooden poles, they built their greenhouses right up against the wall of the mountain. *Cerro de Potosí.*"

The one fact that I remember most of all about Potosí, when I visited it as an adult, was that due to all the mining, all the tunnels built inside, all the heavy metals that have been removed (the silver is depleted, and now just tin is mined there), the mountain is expected to implode eventually. We were told this as we donned those mining caps with headlamps, just before we hiked inside to see the miners' working conditions. Or maybe the memory that sticks with me more is the little girl, maybe ten years old, who told me she had been into the village of Potosí only once. Her biggest surprise: the cars were so big! From the mountaintop, they look so small, she thought she could hold them in her hand. Her perspective switched when brought down to reality. She had never been down from the mine before that time.

The miners start work at daybreak with no breakfast. They come out about fifteen hours later and have potato soup for dinner. They chew coca leaves to suppress their appetite. This is why we needed to help them get the vitamins from their greenhouse gardens.

"Dynamite, Dad, that's all you need to build your greenhouse."

Somehow the conversation shifts. Was it the dynamite? I don't know, but the conversation shifts to an old memory of his.

"The fellow at the party by the record player, he was changing the record. I remember the record player," my dad begins. I know the story instantly, because he has told it often. But this time it doesn't so much change as grow larger.

"I went up to him while he stood at the record player. I put my arm around him to pat him on the back." I know this part too. He will feel a gun. "My hand felt the holster under his sport coat. He wore a gun, concealed."

I wonder, didn't others find this gun when they patted their friend on the back too? But I don't ask this because it's the story of my father and the butcher.

"'Jim,' he said, 'we'll talk later.' So, I didn't ask any questions."

This is when the story starts to not change but fill in. In my mind, Tom Jones is the record on the reel-to-reel tape player. "What's New Pussycat?" This is my own creation. How I remember their parties. Somewhat lascivious. Husbands in turtlenecks, flirting with other men's wives. The wives in low-cut, long dresses, wearing thick gold chains around their necks, the gold rope as thick as my #2 pencils at school, with gold Peruvian ten-sole coins as pendants. Green lime daiquiris filled punch bowls, golden scotch swirled in silver-rimmed low-ball glasses. They drank, they danced, and sometimes one of the men would ask ten-year-old me to dance too. We'd shimmy and wiggle on the dance floor, where the coffee table had been scooched out of the way and throw rugs had been rolled up to reveal the slick marble sashaying surface. I would have a sip of daiquiri, and if I were good, I could stay downstairs until the end. Or until I fell asleep on the couch.

"Later," my dad continues his story, "I was standing across the room, and he crossed over as though he were bringing me a drink." *Was* he bringing you a drink? I want to ask. Was he bringing you a drink, but you didn't need a drink, but he used it as an excuse? "He said, 'Tomorrow come by my place.' He was the meat cutter. He had a shop. He and his wife."

"Sure, I remember," I say. "He was the butcher we all went to." His shop was down the street from our house. A small bodega. My mom bought meat from him. All the American wives did. As part of the agrarian reform of the nationalization policies of President Velasco in 1969, meat was sold only two weeks out of every month. We would have to buy enough meat in those two weeks to freeze and keep for the entire month.

"He tells me to take all the meat I want," my dad says. "To take everything. They are emptying the place out. He and his wife will be gone the next day. That's what he tells me when I go by."

The story has changed. In the first version of this story, all of this happened at the record player. The butcher said he was leaving, and then he was gone. Dad never mentioned going to his shop before.

"His wife was undercover. He was undercover. They both were." That's how he said it. Separate. I remember his wife as Peruvian. And I don't remember her being in his story before. I remember the butcher never in a sport coat but a starched apron with brown handprints smeared on the front. The wife could be Peruvian and still be undercover, I think. All the better cover. But the wife never appeared in the story before.

"He worked for the Treasury Department, back then they didn't have a DEA, but the Treasury Department tracked all the drug dealers in Peru." This is when I stop and really wonder why he is telling me this story. Why he adds on this detail. I know better than to ask him, to point out what he is revealing, because he will stop. Never before, never before the age of eighty would he talk about any of his secrets.

I have researched the DEA well before this conversation. My suspicions about my dad's possible undercover work made me wonder about which agency he worked for. I thought maybe the DEA didn't even exist, and that it was all just my crazy imagination coming up with these stories as explanations for the unexplainable. When I had asked him about his collusion with the CIA and he said no, so precisely, so certain, and yet he had hinted at his friends' connections in another story, I couldn't help but wonder if he was covering up his own contribution. But now, here, my dad, who does not know that I know that the DEA did not yet exist as the DEA until 1973, is telling me the same. The Treasury Department, by instruction from Richard Nixon, had started a new program to stop drug trafficking. The countries they had infiltrated first were Peru, Venezuela, and Colombia. When my father wasn't in the jungle searching for oil, he had "meetings" in Caracas and Bogota. Often we went with him. I have little emerald earrings from Colombia. I can still recall looking out at the Caribbean from the shore in Caracas. I wondered how two bodies of water like the Atlantic Ocean and the Caribbean could still be considered separate when the water is all the same water. It goes back and forth between any drawn boundaries and still tastes like salt. This Treasury Department program my dad is referring to would eventually become what is known today as the Drug Enforcement Agency, the DEA.

"They worked undercover. Both of them." The wife has taken on a bigger role in this unabridged version of the story. "'We will be leaving tomorrow,' the meat cutter told me," Dad continued. "'We have to be out of here. I've turned in the name of the city official who is in cahoots with the drug lords. He will be publically denounced. So we have to get out of here.'"

A city official! Now details are showing up. I keep quiet, let him talk. I lie on my couch with my cats snuggled up against me, phone tight against my ear, waiting for what would come next.

"They left," Dad said. "No one ever heard of the butcher and his wife again. I don't know where they went."

"They had exposed the city guy, so they had to flee," I said. I'm part of the movie now. I'm helping to write the script. Is it a script? Or is it the truth?

"The State Department stopped that," my dad tells me. "The embassy stopped the Treasury Department from letting the name go public. So no one ever knew who the city official was, or no one outside the U.S. government." And was my dad on the inside? How did he know the State Department stopped it? Did the butcher reveal the name at his shop that day before he left? When he asked my dad to come by? To take everything. *Did* my dad take everything?

I know this about the State Department in overseas offices: the diplomats in the embassy keep the cool with the host country. When I worked in Bolivia, we had to get approval from the State Department for all our U.S. Government AID projects. The embassy approved when and where we could work, not DC.

Why does my father tell me this story with more detail now? Why does he add the part about going to the butcher's house the next day? About how the butcher came up to him later at the party? Is it true? Is it added for decoration? To make a better story? Does it make him sound special, that he was chosen as the confidant of the butcher? But why would the butcher, if he was so undercover, so deep in this mystery, why would he confide in my father? Unless my father was somehow involved. But why would my father tell me?

Because I asked. I ask all the time for him to tell me these stories. I ask about questionable details. I ask if he was involved. Like bedtime stories, I love to hear them repeated. I love to hear about his job, the dangers, the antics, the adventures. If I ask too much, he stops. So I've learned when to just listen. To wait for him to tell me what he wants to reveal. A Burt Bacharach tune is always playing in the background of my head. On the record player. Side A. Then Side B. "What the World Needs Now."

I have no idea what is true. But I have an inkling.

PART 3

BOLIVIA

I always tell the truth, even when I lie.

—Tony Montana played by Al Pacino in *Scarface*

Taking Flight

> Constant togetherness is fine—but only for Siamese twins.
>
> —Victoria Billings

PERU, UNDER A NATIONALIST GOVERNMENT, HAD OTHER plans for finding resources under the earth, and asked the American oil companies not to let the door hit them on the ass on the way out.

I packed up my stuffed animals, my dollhouse, and its contents, while Mom packed up our house, the furniture, and the collection from the Chancay grave. I put Pretty Bird in his little yellow cage and slid him under the airplane seat in front of me, as we'd been transferred to Cochabamba, Bolivia.

In Bolivia we stayed in another hotel until our shipment arrived via ground over the Andes. The Gran Hotel Cochabamba was much more modest than the Hotel Country Club in Lima. The Hotel Coch (pronounced *coach*) had been a convent in its original days. The nuns were no longer housed in the convent, but the Catholic church next door still thrived. The bell that tolled every hour on the hour, much to our sleeping dismay, turned out to be a recorded broadcast belched through speakers from the belfry. During Carnival, I and other expat kids climbed the bell tower's long steps, wiping away spider webs. At the top we leaned out the arched openings to drop water balloons on the unsuspecting passersby below. All the while, the Virgin Mary statue on the plaza in front of us seemed to watch with discontent.

No rose garden pathway led to the foyer at the Hotel Cochabamba. The street noises echoed off the cracked honeycomb mosaic tile floor of the entrance. Our rooms sat just at the top of the stairs facing a courtyard. The horseshoe-shaped convent wrapped around a broken-down domed adobe gazebo surrounded by scraggly, swaying palm trees and an empty pool.

Exploration for oil and gas in Bolivia was new, so only a few expats lived in Cochabamba. Dad spent most of his time in the jungle again. But I was relieved to have another petroleum company employee's family move into the hotel a few months after we did. The family had two boys, Marc and David. Marc was two years older, and David a year older than I was. But they rode the bus with me, and their hotel room sat just doors down at the end of the mosaic mezzanine.

After school one day Marc asked me to come over to their room to listen to tapes. The three of us stretched out on the two twin beds we'd shoved together. I brought my Panasonic cassette player over to listen to the tape they had brought from the States. It was a comedy tape by someone named Bill Cosby. He was popular in the U.S., but I'd never heard of him. Our giggles turned us inside out as Mr. Cosby told stories about serving chocolate cake to his kids for breakfast and going to the dentist. Even though the funny faces didn't come through on the Panasonic cassette player, the nubby wool blanket bedspread scrunched up underneath us as we listened to the blubbery sound effects of Bill's novocained bottom lip hanging in his lap.

We didn't have TV in Cochabamba. Any day now, they told us, the TV station would be built. Any day. In the meantime Cochabambinos, the wealthy ones, bought television sets and set them up in their living rooms. The eternal optimists. Without TV we had to visualize the Bill Cosby routine.

I left Marc and David's room with my ribs hurting. I carried my cassette player back to my room two doors down. The tile floor cooled my socked feet as I walked along the entresol. A flower planter bordered the half-wall of the cloister's mezzanine. Just outside my room, Pretty Bird's yellow cage balanced on the planter. He'd been so used to the atrium in Lima with all the space and open air that I didn't like to keep him in my stuffy room, which had no windows.

But now the jade puffball didn't jump around inside the cage as I walked up. Only a second later did I realize the spindly cage door hung open. I checked the bottom of his cage, both hoping to find him and not to find him. With some relief I saw only the splotched *Los Tiempos* newspaper lining the bottom. I glanced up and down the planter, all around, and along the cracked ocher tile floor. Had I left the little wire cage door open? A simple vertical slide latch; could I have been so negligent?

Since he couldn't fly, I searched the ground carefully around all the wrought iron tables and chairs in front of the rooms on the veranda. My fingers came away stained by the moist, brown dirt as I riffled through the geraniums in the planter along the half-wall, lifting stiff leaves and soft red flower petals. Marc and David came out and were looking in hidey spots between tiles big enough for a softball to fit in. "Look in even smaller holes," I said. "He can curl up to smaller than my fist when he wants."

I spotted my mother two stories below in the courtyard. She took in the sun, head tilted back to absorb the rays, sitting in one of the curlicue wrought iron chairs circling the gazebo.

"Mom!" I shouted. She raised her head slowly, too slowly. She did not like being disturbed when she napped.

"What is it, Amy?"

"Pretty Bird's gone!" The shadows from the palm trees grew long along the grass garden, crisscrossing the gunmetal gray flagstone paths from the hotel's first-floor rooms to the gazebo.

"What do you mean gone?" She sat up, holding one hand in a salute across her forehead to block the sun. I knew what she meant—he couldn't fly, how could he have left? "He's around here somewhere."

"I can't find him. I need you to help me."

With his clipped wings, Pretty Bird's mode of transportation was either a side-to-side waddle or a hop. From high places I'd seen him hop off the edge, then glide through the air with his maimed, green wings spread open. He couldn't get lift, but he could coast down. Maybe he had jumped off the ledge where his cage sat.

Down below, my mom was poking in the bushes. Even the hotel waiters in their white jackets who brought us Coca-Cola and Inca Kola in the courtyard were bent over in search position. Max, the bartender of the Whiskeria, who knew us kids from cocktail hour when the folks ordered pisco sours and we had Cokes at the bar, had just come on duty. He laid his maroon tuxedo jacket in its dry cleaner bag on a wrought iron garden chair while he too joined the pursuit. I ran downstairs after finding nothing upstairs, not even one of the chalky blue feathers from under his wings. Pretty Bird had to be somewhere; he had to be nearby.

"He could pull that little latch up by himself," my mother reminded me. It was true: he'd seen us do it, and he would reach one claw out through the thin metal bars of the cage, and with one talon push the latch up and out from its cylinder. Had I not paid enough attention to him? I'd been so busy with Marc and David and Bill Cosby when I came home from school. I didn't sit and play with him as I did in Lima. Now I had friends, and he'd run away.

My mother enlisted any person who walked past the gazebo in the hunt for Pretty Bird. All the maids, the waiters, the bartender, the manager, even a few other hotel guests scrambled around the hotel grounds.

I did everything I could to keep from crying. I held my breath. I thought of Bill Cosby and his blubbery bottom lip at the dentist's office. "Loob ab my fabebe," he said to the dentist. "I don't understand," the dentist said. "Loob! Ab! My! Fabe!" Mr. Cosby pleaded again. I even pulled up my favorite routine where he said he and his brother thought their names growing up were "Jesus Christ" and "Damn it," because that's what his father yelled out the front door. But my throat held onto something the size of a parrot egg, and my eyes turned into rushing water pipes. So I looked up to the clean blue sky with the whitest threads of cirrus clouds to reverse the drainage and tried once more to be distracted. I couldn't stand the thought of losing my downy pet. His little head butts against my chin, his masticating my fingertip and chirping his name PRETTY BIRD, PRETTY BIRD.

I felt something more than just losing my best friend. Whomever I loved left. It didn't matter who or how. Even Mom had said malaria comes back. I couldn't predict when or why anybody left. I wanted some say in the matter. I wanted it to stop.

Then I heard the purl, and my ears perked up. The all-too-familiar chirp, chirp, squawk that said Pretty Bird needed me to talk to him, came from above.

In the sky, as high as the red tile rooftop of the hotel, I spied a flash of green flap-flapping hard and slow across the courtyard.

"Pretty Bird!" I screamed. "He's flying!" I could tell he heard me because he floated back down a couple of feet.

"Where?" my mom said, her sandals clacking on the stone as she ran across the courtyard. I pointed up, and she looked.

"He can fly," she said.

All the searchers turned their heads heavenward and watched Pretty Bird flutter his wings.

"He's gone," Mom said.

"No!" I said. No, no, no. I would not let this be. No.

"He's free, Amy." She shook her head as we watched him fly, his flapping uncoordinated as far as I was concerned. He couldn't leave me. Freedom? What good was that? Freedom was for the birds, so to speak. And Pretty Bird wasn't a bird, but *my* parrot.

"It's better for him," my mother said. Her hands were grimy from digging around in the bushes. She wiped them on her hips. "Birds are supposed to fly."

Of course, I understood this, as on some level I knew letting him go was the right thing, the just thing, the proper and fair way to be. But I quickly stuffed those thoughts away and went back to wanting him to come back, to be mine. Pretty Bird would stay with me. This was one relationship where I had the say. When it was convenient for me, we would play; if he was set free I wanted to be the one who determined this. With Pretty Bird in my life, I was never alone. I would not let him go. I couldn't. No.

I let the waterworks go full force. Snot and tears streamed down my face, my cheeks blotchy and my nostrils flared. I wanted Pretty Bird. I thought he had wanted to be with me.

"Oh, Amy," Mom said. "He'll be okay. He'll join the other parrots." Green flocks of squawking parrots circled the hotel every day.

"No, he won't," I explained. I knew how it worked. He'd be the strange parrot trying to fit in with the Bolivian parrots, a darker, greener breed. His softer jade would stand out. The parrot flocks would shun him. He might think they would be his friends, but he'd find out they really weren't. No, Pretty Bird needed me to protect him, and I began to chase him, to follow his serpentine flight pattern, arms outstretched overhead. "Pretty Bird, Pretty Bird," I hollered to the sky. He squawked back, and to me, he sounded scared. Maybe he wanted to be rescued from this thing called Freedom. Freedom, I knew, was not all it was cracked up to be. I ran and ran and waved my arms, never letting them down in case he wanted to sit on my finger. He thought I was playing. So he would scoop close, then swoop back out of reach. This was no time for play. "Get down here," I scolded.

A hotel guest in a brown suit, wearing a bowler hat, started to walk across the courtyard to his room when he saw the commotion and asked my mother what was going on. "Her parrot got loose," she said. "I'm afraid he's gone for good." I hated her for saying that. She gave up too easily. She couldn't understand.

The man stepped out near the domed gazebo, stood in the shadow of a pillar, and when Pretty Bird flew by the gazebo, he reached up with his bowler then pulled it to the ground so swiftly I couldn't tell what had happened. He slowly lifted the hat's brim off the ground, then stuck his hand underneath.

Wrapped in his thick, cigarlike fingers, Pretty Bird's head poked out, looking dazed. He opened his curved beak as he did when he wanted to step onto my finger.

My heart slowed to a sprint. With my two smaller hands, I took Pretty Bird from the man in the bowler, then held him to my cheek and rubbed his downy head on my skin. Not wanting him to fly off again, I kept my hands tight, the tiny bones and quills poking at my palm. I held him up to my face, and he headbutted my jawbone. Once, then twice. "Pretty . . . " he warbled, mellow and trite.

This is how it should be, I thought, holding on tight.

When my father came home that evening, Pretty Bird was safely back in his cage, and I relayed the afternoon's excitement to him.

"We'll have to trim his wings again," he said. "They apparently grew back."

"They can do that?" I asked. Wings grow back?

"Like fingernails," he said, "They keep growing."

I double-checked the wire around the lock before going to bed, and I put his cage on my nightstand. All night I could hear him shuffling around, restless. But I pretended not to hear.

Tabloids and Cigarettes

> If you don't read the newspaper, you're
> uninformed. If you read the newspaper,
> you're mis-informed.
>
> —Mark Twain

THINGS WERE LOOKING UP IN COCHABAMBA. WE HAD MOVED
into a smaller house. I roller-skated with the street kids on our sidewalk
out front. And I had a new friend from school. Marianne, the Dutch
girl, and I became fast friends. I had my first girl crush.

Marianne and I had been bebopping in her living room all morning. We'd listened to cassettes on her dad's stereo, wiggling our bodies
in some semblance of teenagers dancing. I had a snazzy dance step
that I thought looked cool.

I waved my arms over my head, shimmied to the right a couple
of times, then to the left, all the while weaving my head around in
semicircles. When I caught sight of the phantom reflection in the
plate glass window of a chubby girl wearing bell-bottoms creaking
around stiff legged, I realized I was not the sexy, jazzy girl in my mind.
I stopped twirling my long hair immediately, turned my back to the
window, and choreographed an entirely new dance step that involved
straighter posture.

Marianne and I played the same two songs over and over. Three Dog Night singing "Black and White" was my favorite, but Marianne preferred "Seasons in the Sun." We listened to both songs so many times that I knew every word and found myself singing one beat ahead just to show off my memory.

We'd played the cassette over and over. I held my fist up to my mouth as a microphone, closing my eyes, swaying. "Seasons in the Sun's" chorus gave me a chance to wiggle my butt, but I wished I could ignore the lyrics.

Goodbye to you, my trusted friend.

I hated goodbyes, and here I was with the best friend I'd had in my ten-year life, and I didn't want to sing this sappy song. But because my best girlfriend ever liked the song, I did too.

I'd belt out the chorus to rid my mind of all the morbid thoughts.

We had seasons in the sun!

The music slowed, and the last line made me wonder whether it referred to someone dead.

As the final words faded, I collapsed on the sofa, feigning exhaustion because I didn't want to hear the song again. Marianne had been dancing on the coffee table, and in her rhumba to the music she'd knocked the newspapers to the floor in front of the gold velveteen couch. The tabloid newspaper in Dutch had been pulled apart in sections. I flipped through to find the horoscopes.

"What sign are you?" I asked Marianne.

"Gemini," she said. "The twins. I have two personalities," she said proudly.

I did know a bit about astrology because my mother had me read Linda Goodman's "Sun Signs" book. She'd bookmarked the Capricorn Child section and placed the sapphire blue paperback in my hands. "This is you to a T," she'd said. "Even down to the not washing your ears." I didn't realize until that moment that I rarely cleaned my ears. "You could grow potatoes in there, they are so dirty," she told me. "Sun Signs" and Shirley MacLaine had become my mom's canons.

"I can't understand this," I said to Marianne, who now sat shoulder to shoulder with me on the couch.

"I don't read Dutch that well," she said. Reading wasn't Marianne's forte, but she could illustrate the most detailed veins of a cordate leaf or give the finest of eyelashes to our handmade, blue-lined notebook paper dolls.

"Try to read it," I encouraged. I wanted to know my Dutch future.

"What are you?" She folded the paper over so just the horoscopes were displayed. My dad did that—folded the newspaper into smaller squares. "What's your sign, baby?"

Her hippy come-on made me turn up my nose.

"It's an expression," she told me.

"Capricorn," I said and scooted closer to look over her shoulder as she read my future.

"It says," she hesitated to figure out the words, "You're going to see the world in a new way today."

Boring. I always wanted it to be more specific, to say something more like, *Today you will finally receive the Barbie camper and new Malibu Ken doll you asked for.*

"Read yours," I said.

"You dream wide, but walk skinny," she recited.

"I think you mean narrow," I corrected her.

She rolled her eyes and slapped the paper down. She hated it when I corrected her English.

The paper fell open to what had previously been folded over. But her mood changed quickly as she saw what the newspaper revealed. "Wow! Look at this," Marianne said. She opened the paper toward my face.

"What is that?" I said. "What are they doing? Read it. Read it!"

The double-page spread lay scattered with photos of bloody men and women, apparently at a party. Closer examination revealed that the blood had oozed from their heads. In the next photo a man pointed a power drill at his own head; another showed the man

pointing the drill at a woman's temple, and she appeared to be screaming out in agony.

"Come on, read what it says." I had to know what was going on at
this party.

Marianne tamped at the bottom of the paper to get it to flatten out
fully. She read silently at first, driving me nuts. "It's a party."

"I can see that. What kind of party?" I was both creeped out and
extremely curious. I pulled my knees up under me, to lean in closer.

"A drug party." She read further, her lips moving, but not giving
me any clues.

I had heard about the danger of drugs. I knew my dad's friends
tried to stop the drug lords. When some teenagers at our school were
caught smuggling, I figured that had been my closest encounter to
drugs. One teenage girl always liked to brag about how "high" she
was, her eyes rolling around in her head. This Dutch party, it had
to be the photographed version of what happens. All the blood had
me scared, so scared I didn't even want to touch the edge of the
tabloid newspaper.

"An ambulance had to come," she said. I could tell she was piecing
it all together the way I did when I read Spanish and didn't understand all the words.

"Why did they do it?" I asked. "Why would anyone drill into their
own head?" The partygoers were about our parents' age. Is that what
adults did at parties? My parents went to parties every weekend, or
they had their own parties. I was afraid for my parents. The photos
looked as if it had been any ordinary dinner party with adults gone
astray. What if my parents went to a party and didn't know this was
going to happen? What if they felt they had to do it because everyone
else was doing it? I was always doing things I didn't want to do because
everyone else was. If you didn't, you got ridiculed. But in this case, it
would be better to be ridiculed than drill a hole in your head.

"It was cocaine," Marianne said. "They were out of their minds."

"Did they die?" Maybe they just wanted to find out how far the drill bit would have to go in before they hit blood? But once they got started there was no stopping. They weren't thinking clearly.

I was thinking *too* clearly. I was thinking constantly about ways that my parents, my family could die. Their departure happened so readily, so easily, our togetherness was always tenuous. Any minute their image, their physical essence could fade. A visit home from Suzanne and Marty soon meant a goodbye. My mom had almost died, and even when she came back, she never fully came back. Juana was still writing letters from Peru, honing in on what I considered my spot in the family lineup. If Daddy was home, his suitcase would sit in the hallway prepared to leave again for the jungle. Everyone was like a slippery bar of soap, I would just get to hold them, and they'd slide out of my grasp. But the one thing I couldn't fathom, that I knew would take them away from me for good, was death. I'd gone from a fear of abandonment to a fear of death. Theirs.

I not only had to protect myself, I had to protect them too. No one seemed capable of this except me.

A bush scratched against the plate glass window across from us. I glanced up and was greeted by our reflection: two girls, one concentrating, the other too easily distracted. "Did they die?" I asked again, turning my attention away from the reflection.

"I don't think it says," she replied, her finger following the text slowly. Too slowly.

"You don't think it says because you can't read it, or you can't find it?" They had to die. How do you survive that much blood loss?

Marianne quit reading and slammed the paper down on the coffee table. "You can read it, if you want to know."

"I don't know Dutch." I was too worried about their fate, especially the guy who had the most holes in his head, to realize I had pissed off Marianne. I leaned and gaped at the pictures. Stupefied, I tried to figure out a few words to no avail. The party had taken place in a modern apartment, a home not too different than our own. The yellow walls in the kitchen were splattered with blood, the linoleum had rivulets running between the welts. One drill-game participant slumped over a kitchen chair not too unlike the yellow kitchenette set my mom had bought in Miami.

"The story is trying to make an impression drugs are bad," Marianne said. She had crossed her arms across her chest. I'd hurt her feelings, but I really needed to know some answers about this drill party, or I couldn't go on.

"I get that," I said. I just needed to know if they died. My parents didn't do drugs, but they had plenty of cocktail and dinner parties. They'd been partyers since Nevada. I needed to know whether I should worry that my parents would die at one of these parties, or if perhaps they would just be terribly injured with drill holes, like pox scars on their heads, like the gooey, pink welt on my shoulder I got in kindergarten after the vaccination.

I would have to warn them. I would have to be vigilant.

It never occurred to me that it was all staged. That the magazine had photographed actors. It didn't dawn on me that the fancy appliances and the otherwise spick-and-span house was not a drug den. That the glasses of whiskey and lines of coke and the perfectly arranged apartment were photo studio props. In one picture the camera pulled back and got a shot of all the partyers slumped here and there, Phillips and DeWalt drills still in their hands, trickles of blood flowing down their foreheads, ears, and necks. It never dawned on me how odd it would have been to have a newspaper photographer handy while doing these heinous activities.

I knew only the one girl in our school who did drugs. I knew her because her parents knew my parents. "No one ever knows," she told me on the bus one day, "because it's just a tiny pill or a piece of paper sometimes," she told me. "Parents don't pay attention." Then she disappeared.

This is what I worried about—that no one was paying attention but me!

Somehow somebody did find out about the girl's drug use. She got deported. Her father was in the military, and they found out she was sending drugs back and forth in the U.S. mail to her boyfriend in the States.

I would never do drugs, I thought. I must remember, I scolded myself, never to do what others told me.

Marianne had walked away from the sofa and now stood behind me. "Come on, let's go smoke a cigarette."

"Where you going to get a cigarette?" I asked.

"My mom's." She slid open a kitchen drawer and pulled out a package of Winstons, the same brand my dad smoked. She popped the edge of the pack against her thumb as though she'd done it before, pushing one white, slender cigarette from the foil and cellophane package. The menthol wafted up to my nose. My dad never smoked menthols. Those were lady cigarettes, he told me when he sent me to the bodega to buy him more. With a book of matches from Taquiña brewery and restaurant where my folks liked to go for Sunday dinner, we stepped outside Marianne's back door and lit up. We each took a puff.

"Hold it like this," Marianne said, pointing her two fingers forward in a peace sign. I thought I'd feel cooler than I did. I felt like a dork.

The screen door creaked open, and I jumped. To get caught smoking a cigarette—the punishment could be bad. Marianne quickly put the cigarette behind her back. But it was only Helmi, her older and cooler sister. Helmi wore her hair in a short brown shag, and a swath of embroidered red and yellow flowers grew across her denim bell-bottoms' backside as if wildflower seeds had been sprinkled around her back pockets.

"What are you doing?" Helmi asked. Her jeans sat just below her hips and her tiny belly button showed off beneath her midriff T-shirt. She stared at Marianne's elbow. Marianne pulled out the cigarette and purposefully took another drag.

"None of your business," Marianne said. Helmi and Marianne stood at the same height even though Helmi was two years older, four years older than I was. I wanted to be Helmi when I grew up, although I knew I would outgrow her in no time. I'd never be a petite person. But I also wanted to be Marianne, to be able to do what I wanted without being so afraid. To stand my ground. Whatever that was.

"You stole one of Mom's smokes. She's going to be mad."

"How will she know it was me? You do it all the time." Marianne handed me the cigarette, and I took it reluctantly. I realized I was supposed to take a puff, but I pretended I was not in a hurry and waved it in the air instead.

"Peter and Berche are here," Helmi informed us.

"So," Marianne said, taking the cigarette back from me, letting it droop from her pursed lips.

"Let's play spin the bottle," Helmi said. She always had something going on, a party of some sort.

The cigarette passed back to me, I put the paper-wrapped stick to my lips, only instead of inhaling I exhaled and it made the smoke flutter around my face.

Marianne took the stick from me and dropped it on the ground where she stomped it out with her foot. As she and Helmi made their way inside, I put my foot over the flattened cigarette butt and squashed it even further with a rotated ankle flourish, making sure to swivel my hips a little too. I may not have been very good at smoking, but I could practice my sexy extinguishing.

Once inside we walked through the living room, and Marianne snatched the tabloid off the coffee table. "Look at this, Helmi."

"Can you tell us what it says?" I asked. Helmi's Dutch was better than Marianne's.

"That's Mom's crap. Don't read that," she said, brushing the newspaper aside. How could she be so nonchalant?

"Just tell us what it says," I asked.

She scanned it for a minute. "Gross. It was a pact. They all made a pact. They wanted to try it, but only if they all did it."

As I walked down the hall to play spin the bottle with the group in the back bedroom, I still couldn't get my head around why someone would follow through with a pact when you saw the damage done. Had they been such good friends that they could make a promise and have to keep it? Were they that close? The dark side of being connected to people that closely revealed itself. A group could collectively lose its mind. My parents' group of friends, did they do drugs? I knew they drank a lot. That they partied with daiquiris and gin and tonics, rum and cokes. How would I talk to my parents about this?

Solo, I could be more aware. Safer. I could make my own decisions. Maybe it was better not to be part of a group.

I sat cross-legged among the circle of kids hoping the bottle wouldn't land on me. I needed to get home, check on my mom.

Politicians in the Living Room

She's not a girl who misses much . . .

—John Lennon, "Happiness Is a Warm Gun"

AN EMAIL FROM MY MOTHER READS, *MAYBE WE COULD RENT God's house. Wouldn't that be wonderful? Maybe they still have those opera records.* I pause, not getting it at first. We have been lamenting the current political fiasco, and I suggested we could escape to Cochabamba. Oh yes, God's house—it's what we called the castle behind our house. The random mansion with turrets and a cupola owned by the Bolivian newspaper magnate. The same family that rented us our house behind it. I reply: *Yes, I remember the dining room now—like Downton Abbey.* From God's house poured music every afternoon.

WHEN I WALKED IN THE FRONT DOOR, I SAW MY FATHER doing something curious in the living room, something I had never seen him do before. Above the fireplace on the wall, a frigate ship was sculpted out of alabaster. The soot from the smoke of years' worth of fires had accumulated on the bottom third of the sculpture. The effect made the ship look as though it tossed in a black-and-gray sea of tumultuous waters—the depths of the waves at the blackest part, the tips of the waves fading to gray, the ship, like a ghost ship, the white of alabaster.

My mother sat on the gold velvet couch across from the fireplace watching my father. She appeared most concerned about his soot-covered hands, which he kept placing on the chalky white mantelpiece. As his left hand's black-stained fingers held onto a white sail of the ship, he said to my mother, "Hand me the needle-nose pliers." Then he stuck his head back up the chimney.

My mother reached into the toolbox with most of its guts strewn out on the tan shag carpeting. She extracted the requested tool, stepped precariously through the rubble, and handed the pliers to my dad. Then she returned to her seat in the center of the sofa.

My mother and father both appeared too serious for me to come right out and ask what was going on. From out of the chimney, my dad pulled a length of dangling cap wire normally used as a fuse for dynamite. He pulled it across the room to the small black leather-encased shortwave radio sitting on the gray-and-silver veined white marble coffee table. The cap wire now ran from the radio, midair through the living room, and up the dark chimney.

FOUR YEARS EARLIER, A GROUP OF RIGHT-WING GENERALS from the Bolivian military gathered in the same living room. One of them was Rogelio Miranda, and they would become known as the Mirandistas. Together they planned a coup d'etat. This would be the 186th coup in the 146 years Bolivia had been a country.

I have heard my father say a coup was strategized in our Cochabamba living room—in the little house behind God's house. The details I have to google. As I research the coup, this is how I imagine it went down:

A man with a round forehead, thinning black hair, and wire-rimmed glasses hosts the evening. I assume it's evening because it seems appropriate that coups are planned after the clandestine setting of the sun. This I know: the host's father is the owner of the Bolivian newspaper,

Los Tiempos. And another son, the brother of the owner of our house, is also in attendance.

This I envision: these newspaper men and high-ranking military officers sit in the living room, smoking cigarettes and drinking beer from the local brewery.

Fact: Cerveceria Taquiña was built by Nazis who had disappeared to Bolivia after World War II.

The room, usually well lit, has the linen curtains drawn and feels stone-cold without a fire in the fireplace, the fireplace with the alabaster ship sculpture. The men don't notice the chill in the room. Entranced by their own conversation and heated by the occasional strategizing arguments and decision-making, their blood runs warm.

Fact: at least one man in the room will be exiled from Bolivia and especially this living room. One man is to become president of Bolivia, though only for two days.

The men don't lean back comfortably in the brown-and-gold velvet-upholstered furniture. Instead, they sit precariously on the edge of the cushions, talking with their hands, waving their cigarettes and planning a revolution of the people.

Fact: just three years earlier almost to the date, the host's brother was one of the four journalists to travel to Vallegrande in the jungle to identify Che Guevara's body. "He looked alive in death," he said.

This leads me to believe the U.S. government was in contact with the men who owned our house. This is my one clue.

Fact: Miranda, the designated leader, the present government's commander of the army, would lead the military to revolt on October 5, 1970.

FOUR YEARS LATER, ON AUGUST 9, 1974, MY FAMILY SAT IN the same living room, as my father laced the room with cap wire. When his task was completed, the wire ran from every corner and upper crevice toward the encyclopedia-sized radio on the coffee table. The wire spanned the room like copper spider webbing.

My dad noticed me standing in the doorway and told me to come in. "We are going to listen to a radio broadcast from the States." I had noticed the leather-bound shortwave radio we have owned for most of our overseas life.

The United States and what it had to do with me was so far away now; it was not just another hemisphere away, but another world.

My father turned the knobs on the radio; the whirring and buzz of the shortwave reception picked up voices way off in the distance, and then slowly they came in closer and closer.

"What are we listening to?" I asked.

"Shh," my dad said with his ear to the radio speaker, straining to hear the garbled words that gradually became clearer.

The man on the radio was talking about war and about peace and about future generations. All three of us leaned forward to listen, to hear every word. I thought I heard a wobble in his voice, as though he choked up a bit. Yes, I remember this, a hesitation in his voice, in his speech, in his well wishes to our nation. Their nation. Mine?

When the speech ended, when my father began rolling up the cap wire and chucking the tools into the tool box, and my mother left the room to check on what Lucia had planned for dinner, I sat cross-legged on the alpaca rug under the cross-hatching of dynamite wire. I was only ten, but when I heard Nixon's quavering voice, the shame and embarrassment in his speech, a grown man like my father, being shamed, it didn't sit right with me. I didn't even really know what he had done except that he had lied.

Under my hands I felt the softness of the alpaca fur. The marble of the fireless fireplace made the room cold, as did my mother's empty little blue velvet chair. My chest heaved, and my body trembled so noisily my dad noticed. "What's wrong?" he asked.

This man on the radio who I had never heard of before, he talked about his intentions and how this Congress, which I had also never heard of before, would keep him from doing what he needed to do for the nation. He had tried, but was stifled. I heard it. He sounded so sad. So weary. "I'm sad for him." I pointed to the radio.

"Nixon?" My dad said, sounding satisfied. "He's a liar and a crook. Just another ousted leader."

A spiral of smoke twirled from my father's forgotten cigarette sitting in the ashtray on the coffee table.

I didn't cry for Nixon, I cried because the voice on the radio, Voice of America, sounded betrayed. America had been betrayed. The people. The country. The coups were so common in Bolivia that we often had to take detours to get home. Who was right and who was wrong? Who were the betrayers? Did grown-ups even know?

FACT: IT TOOK TWO DAYS TO PLAN, BUT THOSE WHO STARTED the coup d'etat in October 1970 were defeated in less than forty-eight hours. Another party that wasn't even planning a coup, but jumped at the opportunity, took over the government instead.

As TIME magazine reported, "Even for Bolivia [this coup] was high comic opera."

THIS IS WHERE MY IMAGINATION AND MY MEMORY HAVE collided. Or maybe my memory has slipped, or my parents' stories have crashed into my memories.

My parents' fancy dinner parties. Daiquiris were served by the gallons. Crudités pushed on trays. I wish I could tell you the album The Butcher put on the record player when my dad spoke to him. I surmise from what I do know about my parents and their frequent parties at our house and at other friends' that the music had to have been Burt Bacharach's "Raindrops Keep Falling on My Head" or Tom Jones singing "What's New Pussycat?" Whoa ah whoa ah . . . I can still sing it.

When I think about my whole childhood and where we lived, I can pinpoint a drug enforcement reason we lived there. To me, my suspicions are becoming truth. I tell these stories to my friends, the same ones my dad tells, my own stories as well. I count the reasons, the proof on my fingers. I want it all to be true—for the sake of story.

I don't know anymore if this next part is a memory or if it has been told to me so many times that it is now my memory. I don't think I was there because Burt Bacharach is not playing on the record player, and Tom Jones isn't singing "What's New Pussycat?" It was not the kind of party where nine-year-olds danced. This time it's a sit-down dinner party. I'm not sure if we were in Peru or Bolivia. It must have been Bolivia because of the ending, which I know is my own real memory.

Everyone sits seriously at a long dining room table, dinner has moved into dessert. If I had to guess, I would say VSOP cognac had been served in the fat glasses I loved to look at in the cabinet, where all the fancy dishes sat waiting for the next entertaining event. Or maybe it was the thick, dark green crème de menthe in the thin glasses. On their saucers are the tiny black paper slips that hold After Eight dinner mints. This evening's dinner guests are an interesting mixture of young and old. The helicopter pilots, who work for my dad, have been invited. They wear black leather bomber jackets instead of the sport coats and turtlenecks the older men, like my dad, wear. The helicopter pilots are Vietnam Vets. My dad hires them to transport him and his seismograph equipment around the dense Amazon jungle. Carving a road would take months. The jungle vegetation grows so fast that the task is Sisyphean since when you reach the end, the beginning has already grown over and covered its tracks.

These young American men have one superb skill, and it brings them to South America: flying choppers. The helicopter pilots know their way around the jungle like no one else. They bring young American wives with them to South America. One is my fourth-grade teacher. The wives have not been invited to the dinner party.

The doorbell rings while dinner is still underway. There's a shuffling, and conversation is silenced in the dining room. Then the loud screech as chairs are scooted out, and everyone is trying to stand. The pilots are escorted out. The men at the door—Americans wearing dark suits. The pilots, so good at their jobs, jungle flight, that they have been moonlighting for the drug cartels. Tonight they have been busted.

My teacher, Mrs. Estes, is not at school the next day. When my friend Marianne and I go to her house to visit her, as we sometimes did after school, her boxer growls at us through the gate. She tames him and lets us in. Her red-rimmed eyes tell us she's been crying. She says that she is home alone, her husband is out of town, so she has let the dog off the roof to keep her company. She tells us she has to go back to the States. When we ask why, she looks the other way and says she just does. "No, don't go," we say, "you're our favorite teacher."

We have a substitute the rest of the school year.

The Chicken-Wire Menagerie

> People are not so dreadful once you get to
> know them.
>
> —Jim O'Connor in Tennessee Williams's *The
> Glass Menagerie*

MARTY HAD BARELY WALKED IN THE DOOR FROM THE AIRPORT
when I pulled him by the arm, guiding him outside to show him my
menagerie. He already knew Pretty Bird, of course. But he'd never
met the other two birds. Dad had brought home two more parrots
from the jungle.

"I haven't come up with their names yet," I said. "They are kind
of mean to Pretty Bird."

When he saw the identical brothers flapping around the cage,
he said, "How about the Flying Karamazov Brothers?" I had no idea
he was suggesting the name of a popular juggling comedy troupe.
Little did I know that the brothers didn't have a funny quill between
them and would prove to be more like Dostoyevsky's brothers of
the same name.

"How do you say it again?" I asked. I had to practice "Karamazov"
a few times until I got it right.

Then I took Marty by the hand and pulled him to the back of the house where the rabbit cage sat. We had to hurry. The sky had meta-morphosed into the deep purple that leads to black night. Once the sun set at eight thousand feet above sea level, no matter how warm the sun had been, the air turned icy.

The cage sat on the pathway between Lucia's quarters and the brick back wall of our house. I lifted the plywood door on top. The glow from Lucia's porch lamp shed shadowed white light on the cage. I couldn't see their faces well, but both rabbits lay on their sides dead still. "They must be sleeping," I said. I scooped up Charlie with my hands, and he dangled limply.

"Nah," Marty said, his head shaking. "I don't think they sleep with their eyes open."

The yellow bulb behind us revealed Charlie's blue eyes.

"Here, hold Charlie." I thought he'd wake up when Marty held him. That he'd be as excited to see my brother as I was. I then tried picking up Blanki, and she had the same slinky effect. Her ruby eyes just stared.

"I don't think they're sleeping," Marty said again. He sounded serious, and I knew I couldn't look at him because I didn't want to know what his face would tell me. My ribs tightened.

"Maybe they are just sick," I said. "Why else wouldn't they move? They love getting out of their cage." *Don't we all want to stay in bed when we don't feel well?* I reasoned. Besides, it was dark, maybe we couldn't really see. I wanted them to hop around, back legs tilting them for-ward into a bounce.

Marty laid Charlie back down gently on the chicken-wire cage bot-tom. A pile of tiny black pellets had climbed up through one corner of the wire, and I thought about how negligent I was at cleaning their cage. Maybe whatever was making them sick wouldn't have happened if I'd taken better care.

"I'm sorry, Amy," Marty said. He put one hand on the top of my head, as he always did, and mussed my hair.

I stared at Charlie and Blanki, lying on their sides, side-by-side. Blanki's scary red eyes stared back at me. Maybe, I thought, I'll close the cage lid, go away, then come back in the morning, and they'll be hopping around, their little toe pads getting caught in the wire bottom of the cage. I was frozen. Time needed to reverse. This couldn't be true. My rabbits could not be dead.

"Come on, Amy," Marty said. "Let's go back inside. It's getting chilly."

I just stared. Everything I had ever dreaded—the stillness, the silence, the separation—lay limp across the chicken wire. My heart beat so loud, I knew Marty must be able to hear it.

The next day I was home alone. Marty had gone on an errand, Dad was at work, and I didn't know where Mom was.

I created the graveyard at the back of the house.

Just past the rabbit cage was Lucia's maid's quarters. I usually never went back there, especially since she sometimes left her bathroom door open, and I could see inside to the most frightening showerhead. My father explained to me that the electrical wires spiraling out of it heated the water. An electric showerhead. All I could think of was how water and electricity did not mix. It only made me think that someday Lucia would be electrocuted.

The rabbits had come from *la cancha*, where we bought everything from firewood to chicken necks. I put Blanki in Mom's white Thom McAn shoebox, and Charlie's coffin was Dad's Hush Puppies box with the gold trim. Charlie, the larger rabbit, didn't quite fit, and I had to squeeze him into the box. The shoeboxes felt leaden in my hands. I neatly arranged round river rocks I collected from the yard, rows of rocks the size of a baby's fist across the top of each grave. I had plans to paint their names on bigger flatter rocks as headstones, but I hadn't found the appropriate stones yet.

I crouched next to their graves and waited. I felt something should happen. Something would rip through my rib cage. Something would crawl out of my ears. Something would move somewhere it shouldn't. Because nothing felt right, nothing inside or outside. Everything was wrong. I watched the stones, each placed neatly, purposefully. I watched as though they'd rise with a small breath.

But nothing moved. This, I thought, this was death. Just as I had imagined it so many times before. Complete stillness. Complete quiet. Completely alone. I thought of my bunnies, how limp their bodies had been, how they looked so sad, so helpless. That's what death was—being alone forever.

I WAS DONE BY LUNCHTIME, AND MARTY HAD RETURNED.
Every day at lunch Lucia served homemade soup. It was a Bolivian tradition to have soup for the midday meal. Sometimes we had chicken and vegetable, sometimes she'd used the leftover meat from dinner, and sometimes she'd make pumpkin soup, Mom's favorite. Dad would come home from the office, and we'd all sit at the table together.

Today it was just Marty and me.

"How do you say, where can I find a duck that's not dead?" he asked me.

He was always asking me to say crazy things in Spanish.

When I told him, he said, "That's what I thought. I took the bus to the market," he said. He'd gone stall to stall asking, *Donde esta un pato que no es muerto?* "I wanted to bring you a new pet."

I pictured the stone-covered graves I'd made. I thought of Blanki and Charlie alone forever. But Marty and the ducks took some of that away. He was trying to make me laugh, as he always did.

I am sure the only ducks he came across in his search were plucked, their orange feet strung up on clotheslines next to a side of beef, pig's head, and slab of bacon. All covered in flies at *la cancha.*

"You still have the parrots," Marty consoled me.

"The Kama-ra. The Brothers are not very nice though," I said.

WHEN MY DAD HAD BROUGHT HOME TWO MORE PARROTS from the jungle, Pretty Bird was not pleased. Suddenly he had to share his cage the size of a washing machine with two brothers with brilliant underwater green foliage and orange down around their beaks. The new brothers acted entitled and rather ferocious.

"They are from the same nest," my dad said, as though this would explain everything about them—their cliquishness, their matching outfits, their angry dispositions.

I thought the tension would die down, that eventually they would all get along. I could tell Pretty Bird's feelings were hurt. Hadn't he been mine first? I took him out of the cage as often as I could. I reached in the cage, forefinger outstretched. He loved having his chest rubbed. He nodded his head up and down and opened his beak wide like a yawn, wiggling his round tongue, as I stroked the feathers under his chin. He picked up one foot and shook it. Nudged me with his beak. Then he climbed onto my finger. Crawling up my arm to my shoulder, he nudged me with the rounded top of his hooked beak, a kiss. It was our dance.

When I reached inside the chicken-wire enclosure to take out the two brothers, they scooted up close to one another, squawking at me. I put my hand close, and they pecked and batted me with their wings. So I left the cage door open and let them wander out on their own. They ganged up together, so Pretty Bird and I learned to ignore them.

At the end of every day like this, I reluctantly put Pretty Bird back in the cage because he'd have to cower in a corner until I came to check on him. We never should have made them share a cage.

"They're from the same nest," my dad kept saying.

LUCIA SET A BOWL OF STEAMING SOUP IN FRONT OF MARTY.
"Karamazov Brothers," he said, "Maybe they'll come around. Pretty Bird was shy at first."

She set a bowl in front of me, along with a basket of *marraquetas*, the hard crusty bread I loved.

"But these birds are different," I told Marty. "Daddy says they are from the same nest." I didn't know what that meant, but as my dad used it as an excuse, I did too.

"Pretty Bird is a good guy," he said. "You gotta stick by the ones that stick by you."

I stirred the thin broth and tried to decipher the flavor. A few carrot pieces floated to the top. Some spinach wrapped itself around my spoon, and then a gray stringy lump bumped against the ladle of my spoon. Though reminiscent of my soup at school, this bowl did not contain any chicken feet.

Marty lifted his head from his bowl of soup. His spoon had hit against something odd as well. "What kind of soup is it?" he asked.

"I don't know," I said, pushing the gray blob against the side of the bowl and on to my spoon's ladle. "It looks like a thumb tip."

He looked at his and considered this possibility. Appendage soup. "I don't think it's a finger. I think it's an organ."

"Lucia!" Lucia came running to the table from the kitchen. "*Que sabor de sopa sirviste hoy?*" What flavor soup are we having today?

"*De pollo.*"

"*Y que es esto?*" What's this, I asked as I lifted my spoon to show her the tip of the thumb.

She leaned over and stared at my spoon for a moment. "*Corazon.*"

"Heart," I translated for Marty.

Lucia returned to the kitchen, since we had no more questions. Marty and I both slurped around the organ meat and ate only the carrot cubes, the squash bits, the cut-up potatoes. We dipped our bread in the salty broth, focusing only on our bowls, working our way through the rest of the ingredients. Marty reached the bottom before I did.

"I'm going to try it," he said, and he bit into his heart.

So I gave him mine.

THE NEXT DAY I STOPPED TO PAY A VISIT AT THE RABBIT cemetery. I found the rocks scattered and the gravesites in shambles.

"Julio," Mom said, referencing the gardener who had exiled my tortoises to the neighbor's garden, "decided the graves were too shallow. He said he put everything back the way it was."

"No, he didn't," I informed her. "I had made the cemetery very organized and pretty. Now it's just a rock pile."

"You can fix it, can't you?"

That wasn't the point. Too much tidying was going on. Didn't Mom see that? Julio wanted a perfect garden, and to get it he murdered my pets. Did Mom prefer the idea of perfect zinnias too? I was so mad, but no one would listen to me. There was nothing I could do, so I began realigning the rocks in rows.

All I knew of Julio was the look of his stooped-over back as he dead-headed the zinnias and geraniums that bordered the house. It was him or the tortoises, he had told Mom. My father had brought home a set of tortoises from the Chapare jungle too. One so big I could straddle its back and lumber around the yard. But after the tortoises' shovel feet dug divots through the grass lawn, Julio'd given his ultimatum. The tortoises went to live with the neighbors down the road.

Had he taken my rabbits' fate into his own hands too? Mom had hinted at possible poisoning. "The snail bait he scatters around, it can't be good for them."

I let Charlie and Blanki run free in the yard. They hopped along the edge of the flowerbeds, chomping on the orange and red zinnias. I never picked them up by their long ears as I'd seen in the movies. I ran my hand under their bellies then scooped their yellow-stained feet with my other hand. The top of their lush pelt would rub the underside of my chin, while the tender pads on their paws thumped in my hand. The rabbits never liked to be held long. They wanted to hop around, to chew on Julio's zinnias.

The only pets that Julio didn't despise, at least not to my knowledge, were the parrots. Maybe he figured they had their own murderous intent, and he didn't need to interfere.

AFTER MARTY WENT BACK TO SCHOOL, I THOUGHT ABOUT what he said. It was true. Pretty Bird was my buddy. And I should stand by him. Pretty Bird was quite a handsome parrot in his green feathers, with yellow and blue that peeked out around the edge of his wings. He appeared pleased to be told that he was pretty throughout the day. The way he cocked his head at me when I said "Pretty Bird" gave the impression he recognized the sounds. When he whistled and tweeted, it sounded as though he were saying his own name. Say it fast: *Pretty Bird.*

In the backyard, my father had built Pretty Bird and the Karamazov Brothers a bigger cage he covered in chicken wire. He propped sawed-off tree branches against the corners and balanced small limbs diagonally across the cage. Pretty Bird had plenty of room to climb and hop around and still ignore the other birds, so the tiny yellow cage was thrown away. But I still preferred to let him out as I had in Peru. "So he doesn't fly away, we have to keep his wings clipped," my father said. I certainly didn't want him to escape again, so I watched as Dad wrapped his hand gently around Pretty Bird's body, encasing the parrot's wings as he pulled him out the door. Pretty Bird's expression was perplexed. He was used to coming out of the cage on my finger, not inside the grip of a thick, albeit gentle, hand.

Outside the kitchen door sat a concrete chopping block that Lucia used to pound Bolivian beefsteak, *silpancho*, as thin as a magazine. My father laid Pretty Bird on his back, holding him down with one hand, then with the fingertips of the other hand, he unfolded a green wing, revealing the azure underfeathers. "Hold this," he said, as he took my little hand in his big hand and placed it on the top of Pretty Bird's splayed wing. The span of my hand equaled half the span of the wing. The vibration of the tiny body radiated up my arm. The concrete chopping block felt cold, but I knew it wasn't the cold that made Pretty Bird shudder. My father picked up a long, thick-bladed butcher knife, and I cried out, "NO!"

"Hold him still. You don't want Pretty Bird to fly away again, do you?"

"But it will hurt!" I couldn't breathe I was so afraid of what he would do with that knife.

My father could sense things from me at times. He put the blade behind his back. "I'm only going to trim the edges of his feathers. Just a tiny bit."

"But it will hurt," I said, looking at Pretty Bird, who stared at me from the one eye on my side. His pupils pinned open and closed as they did when he worried.

"It won't hurt at all," my dad said. "Does it hurt when you trim your fingernails?"

I bit my nails down to the nubbins; they bled and hurt all the time. But I wasn't sure it would be the same. Pretty Bird was made of all feathers, while my fingernails were just tiny little white moons.

"We will be very careful. If we trim too much it will be like cutting the quick on your nails, so you have to hold very still." Pretty Bird squirmed. "We should get it over with," he explained.

"Are you sure?"

"I promise, it won't hurt."

I watched as my father took the sharp edge of the knife, like a cleaver, and severed the bottom pieces of Pretty Bird's wings. The blade made small snaps as the feathers were blunted. I didn't move. Not even to breathe.

"Now the other side," my father said, and we folded the first wing in and pulled the other wing out, snapping the bottom edges off it as well. Snips of blue and green feathers scattered on the cutting board, then fluttered to the ground. We let Pretty Bird go, and he righted himself.

"Now we'll see if it worked," my father said, and he brushed his hand behind Pretty Bird's tail feathers. My parrot hopped along for a moment, then opened his newly clipped wings and floated the few feet to the ground. He flopped for a moment on the back patio concrete, unable to take flight for more than a few inches.

"We should do that regularly, so he doesn't leave again," my dad explained. I nodded. Pretty Bird must never leave. Wasn't he the one thing I loved that I could make stay?

I watched for any signs of hurt, but Pretty Bird fluttered his wings, poked around for a bit with his beak. Then he waddled off.

"Don't tell me when you do it," I said, picking a piece of green feather off my sleeve.

"You don't like it?" my father asked.

With his wings clipped, Pretty Bird could be let out of the cage to wander around the backyard, hopping and fluttering his wings in an attempt to fly. This made him like a chicken rather than the jungle parrot that he was. The wing-clipping procedure scared me, but I was glad he couldn't leave me. I was conflicted about my ability to care for him. Could I have a friend without clipping their wings?

"I just don't want to see it," I said.

FIG.5. Mom, Amy, and Dad on hilltop over Cochabamba, Bolivia. Courtesy of the author.

What I Do See

> Vision is the art of seeing what is invisible to others.
>
> —Jonathan Swift

MANY YEARS AGO I THOUGHT A HOUSE I LIVED IN WAS haunted. I went to the library and did research on ghosts. I learned that the noisy ghosts are officially "poltergeists" and are spirits stuck on this earthly plane because of a traumatic death. They don't know they are dead, so they are trying to reach out to get someone to notice them. If a spirit is encountered, this book on paranormal activity instructed, help the spirit by telling it to call to a dead family member to come help them to the other side.

The idea of being trapped in between worlds, of not being fully able to participate in either, sounds like banging on a glass window and no one on the other side paying any attention to you. I understand that feeling of looking out and tap, tap, tapping on the glass, seeing others just beyond my grasp, but not being able to get their attention. I wave frantically. Nothing. I scream, and no one hears me. I wonder, do the Chancay look for their belongings, their nice set of pottery dishes with the monkey handles that aren't in the grave where they'd been left, but are instead in my parents' living room? Maybe they are tapping on the glass of the other world wanting to know when we are going to give them back. Or are they watching us silently, curious how we live the way we do? Is the headless prince looking for his body? Surely he is banging on the glass. He should be the one screaming. I understand this searching, scanning for what isn't there. Looking in vain for what can't be. Wondering who we are.

Maybe I'm the noisy ghost. The poltergeist.

I HAVE A MEMORY OF A BENIGN, ORDINARY WEEKEND DAY, another weekend excursion, including a picnic that really isn't so ordinary at all. But I suppose none of our outings were as ordinary as I had once thought they were. I have begun to see that my family is extraordinary in its quirky denial, selective photographic memory, and provincial inattention. We are only ordinary in our origins.

My small family, Mom and Dad and I, had left for the day. We packed a picnic and drove to the countryside, up farther into the Andes, until we found a spot we liked, preferably a clearing with a view of the verdant, steep peaks and scenic plateaus. In the Bolivian mountains the brisk clouds moved in and out around us, often hiding our picnic spot at such high altitude, then burning off just as quickly with the sharp sun. We laid out a blanket and set out our sandwiches, a thermos of hot coffee, and the wax-paper-wrapped brownies Lucia had made from ground cacao beans Dad brought from the jungle. With rocks we weighted down the corners of the wool blanket to keep the wind from gathering it up with our belongings and tossing it over the side of the steep mountain. I liked to watch the misty air with its dampness and flecks of moisture that gathered on our alpaca sweaters like tiny reflectors.

We ate our sandwiches and brownies with abandon because the cloudy atmosphere moored the chill and kept us shivering. The landscape moved in and out like a camera lens adjusting to zoom and distance, as the nebula shifted and rearranged its position. At twelve or thirteen thousand feet above sea level, the sun warmed only the first layer of skin and couldn't seep down to our nearer-to-sea-level bones. I wrapped my arms around my shins and hugged myself to stay warm. I wouldn't dare say I was bored, as that would make me sound unappreciative of the Andean landscape.

For a moment the cloud cover broke open like an egg revealing the yolk of sun. And in that moment the jagged peaks across the valley from where we picnicked revealed to me what the line "purple mountains majesty" meant—that it wasn't just a place far, far away or a line in an anthem. I walked to the edge of the cliff to look closer, to see what it was that made those mountains really purple. I became conscious that the optical illusion worked like colored film over the distant vision. Purple mountains were a mirage. I observed how the clouds sat lower than the mountaintops, and when I paid attention, I saw how the mist closing in on me was the same cloud that sat below the peak across the valley. I'd been picnicking inside a cloud. That didn't sound boring at all. I pointed it out to my mom and dad, but they said they already knew that. The mist thickened and the clouds enveloped all of us overhead and all around.

A pack of vicuñas passed by in the brume. My small family hadn't even known the skittish descendants of the llama clambered just a few feet away. So rare to see the timid high-altitude vicuña. The fog ascended when a breeze rushing up the mountainside collided with the sun, and the tiny, long-necked camelids paused with surprise where they grazed within a few feet of us. With expedience, the vicuñas darted off the cliff. To us, it appeared as though they dove off, plummeting to their death, but their soft, padded ungulate feet helped them down the steep, rocky surface below the clouds. We, just three of us, had frightened them. Or had they frightened us?

The mist grew thicker and lower, and soon it seemed we were inside our own Styrofoam container. "It's too cold," my mom said, already wrapped in ruanas and ponchos. Across the road, the Land Rover began to disappear. With no view and the dense air now more wet than fog, we packed up our picnic and loaded it and ourselves into the vehicle. I was relieved to be inside the dry automobile, but wished we could have stayed on the mountaintop longer. I liked being inside

my own cloud. I imagined it was how birds felt. Like inside my head,
I played in the clouds.

   This is what that day on the mountain revealed: my family was there
when they were there. Then gone, just like that. Like the Andes behind
the clouds, when they showed up, when they were in the room with
me, I knew my family as whole. Then they'd be gone, poof, just like
that. Gone until the next time they chose to make an appearance.
Gone until the sun shone and burned away the cloud. I couldn't con-
jure my family members on my own; I had to wait until they wanted
to show themselves. Like ghosts, like apparitions that I had only to
believe in, but could never sustain. I could never know when they
would appear and when they would disappear. I never knew if they
would show themselves again. The joy I felt when they were there, the
elation, the unbelievable happiness, was fleeting. And I came to know
that it was fleeting, that the apparition, be it mother, father, sister, or
brother, would be present only for an instant, and then they would
leave again. So I learned to make every moment count, every memory.
When no one was around, when I was waiting, I was alone. I waited
not knowing whether they, one of them, all of them, might show up
again. Always, always in the back of my mind was the possibility that
what I had seen before was just a figment of my imagination.

BACK DOWN THE MOUNTAIN, MY FATHER PULLED THE LAND
Rover up to the white gates of our house. I knew my role, whether
pouring rain or sun; I hopped out of the rear door of the vehicle and
ran to unlock the gate padlock. In the pouring rain, I pushed half
of the gate to the side of the driveway, then ran the other half back
to the opposite side. I stood against the gate, holding it open, but
looked down at the driveway's concrete cracks. Toads liked to hide in
the cracks, but in a downpour they ventured out. One especially fat
one squeezed itself out of the concrete and hopped in the soggy grass.

   The Land Rover pulled past me, but I was entranced by the toads
and the rain.

   Lucia waited at the front door. I could hear my mom over my

shoulder as I pulled the gate closed and replaced the padlock. "It's your day off, Lucia, what are you doing here?"

"*Lo siento, Señora,*" she said.

Lucia handed me a cylindrical cardboard container. I recognized it as the box for a sixty-watt lightbulb. I could see the light green feathers poking through the bottom opening.

The birds from the same nest, Lucia told the story, rushed the one that was not their brother, pecked, batted their wings, lunged, dive-bombed and mobbed him. She had heard the squawking, the screeching, but was back at her apartment (where the electric showerhead was, I thought) and had arrived too late.

In the big cage on the back porch the Brothers Karamazov hopped from branch to branch, unremorseful of their murderous tendencies. My dad stood behind me as I looked at their dark green feathers, the way they groomed each other, nudged their beaks on the other.

"They came from the same nest," my dad said. "They weren't accepting of another bird that wasn't like them. Birds of a feather . . ."

Pretty Bird had been my flock, and I had not looked out for him.

I BURIED PRETTY BIRD IN HIS SIXTY-WATT COFFIN NEXT TO Charlie and Blanki in the cemetery, just past Lucia's electrocution showerhead.

Soon after, Dad announced we'd been transferred again. When we moved back to the States, Lucia said she would find a new home for the Karamazov Brothers. The cages were dismantled and thrown away.

BOLIVIA IS STILL MY FAVORITE COUNTRY. I THINK IF THAT song is correct, that we really can leave our heart somewhere, mine is in Cochabamba. I recall sitting in our courtyard with Mom, eating the brownies Lucia made from the cacao beans Dad brought from the jungle, Pretty Bird climbing the wrought iron chairs to get a peck of brownie from our fingers, opera music wafting over the fence that separated us from God's house.

When I was in my thirties and still searching for what I wanted to do in my life, I worked in Bolivia for an American nonprofit helping to build gardens for the families in Cochabamba and Potosí, a mountain town. One of my favorite moments in that job was when the families who owned the gardens threw me a party to thank me and my organization for the gift of fresh vegetables. I stepped outside to find long tables sitting slanted on the mountain slope, covered in white table cloths. Twenty folding chairs sat at the table as they were serving all of us dinner, sirloin steak with fresh salad, of course. These steaks, I knew, were a month's salary for them. The catch: I was a California vegetarian. But how could I not eat the steak they had prepared for me? How could I be so unaccepting? I knew Bolivians would not understand my vegetarianism.

I ate the steak. And I haven't been a vegetarian since.

PART 4

REENTRY

If you don't believe in ghosts, you've never
been to a family reunion.

—Ashleigh Brilliant

Helter Skelter

Look out helter skelter
She's coming down fast.

—Lennon and McCartney, "Helter Skelter"

THE PHILLIPS HOTEL SAT LIKE A GIANT FLESH-TONE WART in downtown Bartlesville, Oklahoma. Bartlesville was also the home of Phillips Petroleum Company's headquarters. The 1950s mushroom-colored brick Soviet-housing-esque building was home to business travelers and displaced families like mine. The five-story building was our home for nine months while we waited for our new house to be built. We moved from room to room, floor to floor, until after about a month we finally settled in a hotel-apartment. One wall displayed the kitchenette. That wall faced the living area, where a closet held the drop-out-of-the-wall Murphy bed where I slept. Down a small hallway was a separate bedroom where Mom and Dad slept.

Not an especially roomy apartment: I had to sit on the floor and lean against one end of the couch, partially in the living room and partially in the hallway, to watch the twelve-inch color TV, our first TV in two years and our first English-language TV in over five years.

American TV was fantastic! Fat Albert and Pink Panther cartoons on Saturday mornings and sitcoms every night, and then these made-for-TV movies about true stories. Who needed friends when you had a TV to watch? So when the made-for-TV movie came on about the Manson Family murders, I was not going to miss it.

The first night of the TV miniseries *Helter Skelter* began with Charles Manson slicing off a follower's ear with a sword. I was glued to the end of the couch in our hotel room. The brutal and bloody murders of the LaBianca and Tate households had me riveted to the tufted carpeting. On the refrigerator doors of the Tate home, one of the Manson Family members wrote, "Helter Skelter." I had no idea what the words meant, or why someone would paint them in blood on the household appliance of a murder victim. I certainly didn't know a thing about the Four Horsemen of the Apocalypse and Revelations in the Bible and how Charles Manson interpreted the Beatles song "Helter Skelter" to be a message that the blacks were starting a race war. I just saw some crazy hippies attacking people with knives. The Manson Family members called Charlie "Jesus Christ," and I did see a resemblance to the color photo of Jesus that hung over the refreshment counter in the First United Methodist Church basement. I'd seen the movie *Jesus Christ Superstar*, played the cassette tapes and sang songs at the top of my lungs, and I recalled Jesus being really pissed off, turning over tables in the market. This was not too dissimilar from Charlie Manson. Could Mom be right about reincarnation?

By the end of the first night of the two-part series I was gripped. The question of how anyone could fall under a spell that grotesque had me walloped. And what if he really was Jesus Christ? How would we know? Lots of people didn't believe Jesus the first time either. I was torn. A part of me was afraid if I believed the possibility, I too could be falling under Manson's spell. "What if?" kept buzzing in my head after that first episode. I knew the second night would answer all my questions.

Mom and I were joined at the hip when we moved to Bartlesville. Yet her presence, I sensed, was still nebulous. She could leave me on a whim. Just the week before we'd pulled into one of those newfangled ATMs, and Dad had jumped out of the car to get some cash. Mom whipped around to face me where I sat in the backseat. "I'm leaving!" she said. "As soon as I get a job, I'm getting my own apartment, and I'm leaving!" Had they had a fight?

I couldn't be more frightened. Blood rushed in my ears, and my heart pumped so fast that it felt as if it had expanded to three times its size and would explode. Kaboom. I couldn't breathe. Surely she saw the look on my face, my eyes had to have been wide, giant, pleading.

My dad hopped back in the car, and my mom turned to face the front. Nothing more was mentioned.

The nightmares started then and continued for years—my mother leaving, me staying behind. As I had always imagined it would work.

I would be left behind. Too frozen to ask, too scared to even think I could mention it. What if I asked, and the answer was no. What if she said she couldn't take me? What if she said I was selfish for asking? See, Mom, I'm fine. You don't need to worry about me. I'll be no trouble. I can take care of myself. This is what I thought I should feel.

WHILE THE MANSON MURDERS WERE ON TV, DAD WAS OUT of town again, so after Mom and I ate our favorite dinner of Banquet frozen fried chicken, a new American food, I set myself up with a bed pillow and a chocolate Snack Pack pudding for dessert. After all the blood and gore of last night's first night of the TV movie, I had myself prepared for more of the same, only this episode would surely reveal the answer to how this horror could happen.

THEN MOM SAID I COULDN'T WATCH THE SECOND HALF.

What???????

"You can stay in the bedroom and do your homework," she said.

"I don't have any homework. I did it already." I wasn't an academic superstar, but I was no procrastinator. Mom wasn't really going to ban me from the second half, was she?

"You can read then. Or listen to the radio." Mom and Dad had a clock radio that woke us up every morning—another newfangled American appliance with which we were enraptured.

"Nothing but church talk on the radio," I said. It was true, Monday night radio in Bartlesville played all the around-town preachers' sermons in case anyone had missed anything on Sunday morning. "What are you going to watch?"

"I'm an adult, I can watch the second half." Mom looked at the ground when she said it, then over at the spick-and-span kitchenette countertop.

"No way!" I said. "How can you do this to me?"

"It's not appropriate for children. It says so at the beginning." Now she was going to be a concerned parent? She picked up my propped-up pillow and put it on the couch where she usually sat.

"You let me watch the first half last night. How can you change your mind?" This couldn't be. I had to know what happened. If I didn't find out why the disciples were so taken with this creepy man, I might be unable to detect when it was happening to me.

"Amy, are you talking back to me?" Mom's tone turned up to the level that said she was done, that there would be no more discussion. What would happen if I pushed beyond that level, I didn't know because I never had tried. I was taking no chances that I might lose the one person that stayed fairly steady in my life.

So I took my pudding and went to the bedroom while she prepared to watch *Helter Skelter* in the living room. I was angry that not only had she banned me from TV after a two-year hiatus, she had also stopped me from seeing the conclusion of a movie I had already started. I wouldn't know what kept the Manson Family a family. I paced back and forth in the small space between the double bed and the highboy dresser. It wasn't like I was going to go out and hack people up! But how would I ever know why those crazy hippies did what they were told? Maybe she thought the gory stuff would scare me. I yelled out the door down the short hallway. "I'm not scared. Remember when we used to watch scary movies in Ely? I wasn't even the least bit scared. And I was only five then." When we'd lived in Nevada, if Marty was babysitting me, we would stay up late watching scary movies. I remember several: one about the ivy that grew over the castle and trapped all the people inside, one about the zombies that climbed out of the lake covered in moss, and another about bandage-wrapped mummies who took over the town.

"I said 'no' and I mean it," Mom said from the living room. In no uncertain terms was I going to watch the second night of *Helter Skelter*.

"I don't understand why!" I whined.

"It's too violent." Who was she kidding? I'd seen more violence in my life without a TV screen and diode transmitting the images.

"Mom! Please!" I cried out from the little bedroom's doorjamb boundary at the end of the hallway. But she ignored me. She wouldn't say anymore, I knew from trying. She just quit the back and forth. I cried big fat baby tears, although I didn't like to think of myself as a baby or even a kid. I was eleven. That space between child and teenager. I wanted to skip teenager and just be an adult.

As the commercials played, and I could hear, "Coming up next . . ." teasing me, I flopped down on the double-sized bed. Teeth gritted, arms and legs flailing, I pounded the mattress with all my might. When that didn't satisfy me enough, and garnered neither attention nor sympathy from my mom, I grabbed the cheap white chenille bedspread on their bed, then stifling a good scream, I pulled at the spread as hard as my frustration would allow. When the thin cotton cloth began to rip, it felt so good—the relief, the satisfaction of destroying something. Of being bad. My tears subsided, and I dried my eyes on the corner of the spread where I had laid out on the bed. When I calmed down, I realized what I'd done, and I stared at the hole in the torn bedspread revealing the yellow fleece blanket underneath. Big trouble. My heart began to pound harder.

The TV in the other room began playing the *Helter Skelter* theme song, a grating electric guitar crescendo. With my head at the foot of the bed, I saw the red credits flash on the screen. I could see the TV from this diagonally-across-the-bed twisted position! What a find. But I had to do something about the torn bedspread. I tried positioning the two sides of the rip together as neatly as possible and imagined pretending nothing had happened, but I could tell that wouldn't fly.

As the "previously on *Helter Skelter* scenes" started to flash on the TV screen, I remembered the sewing kit Mom kept in the top dresser drawer. I got up and dug around inside the metal candy tin where she kept various colors of thread and needles. The metal tin lid was hard to remove and clinked against the maple of the dresser.

"Amy?" Mom called from the living room.

"I'm sewing!" I said. My heart pounded harder and faster, worrying she'd come in the room and discover what I'd done.

I found a spool of white thread. The electric guitar zinged as I poked one end of thread through the eye of the needle, remembering what I'd learned in the sewing class I'd taken a few weeks before at the YWCA. I arranged myself so I could catch a slanted sliver of the twelve-inch TV screen. I turned the bedspread over and stitched from the underside. Mom never called out again, but I'd hesitate if I heard her rustling in the next room, readjusting herself on the couch or getting up to go to the kitchenette. In between stitches, I looked out the door to see what was happening on the TV. Mom had turned the sound down, but I knew enough from the first night to follow along. More stabbings, the women who did what Manson told them to do, the malevolent gaze in their eyes, the vicious smiles. I pulled the thread taut through the fabric till the knot caught and tugged.

The trailer before the movie had said Manson offered his followers love and family. Is that what made them do these heinous acts? I looked down to stitch one stitch at a time, then stared at the TV.

The tear in the bedspread was about six inches long, and I was no more a seamstress than a singer, but I steadily sealed the hole I had made, continuously looking up to see more flashes of stabbings or Manson's cunning face and eyes. The Frankenstein of stitches across the end of the bedspread looked so mangled that I knew Mom eventually would denounce me for it. I tried tugging the cotton to smooth it out, but the movie had me riveted. What bothered me most was that this group from the commune called themselves a "family." Manson offered love in exchange for murder. The deal was no one could leave, no matter how badly they were treated. Once you were part of "The Family," you had to stay. The murders kept them together. You had to kill to prove you wouldn't betray the others. It looked so easy to end up in a place like that, doing what someone told you to do without realizing you were brainwashed until it was too late, or never at all. But they were a family that stuck together. Despite my family's transiency, it was the ephemera that held us together, like ectoplasm. The anticipation, the appreciation, and even the apprehension of each visit—when would they be back and how soon till they left—had led me to see my family as a special treat. We didn't make promises, we weren't together enough to betray, and best of all there was no carnage, no slashing off of ears. Mom's refrigerator, spick-and-span, no weird phrases written in blood.

When the red credits began to roll at the end, I smoothed out the area I had stitched as best I could, then flipped over on my back with my head against the pillows. I pretended I was reading a sappy Nancy Drew. When my mother came in, I tried not to look at the end of the bed where my handiwork bunched up with bulky stitches at my feet. Instead I asked, "What happened?"

"It was just courtroom scenes. Boring, really."

"How long will he be in jail?" I asked.

"He's up for parole in twenty years." She pulled her pajamas out of the drawer where I'd taken the thread from the candy tin.

Twenty years—I added in my head—I'd be thirty-one. "What will happen when he gets out?"

"He won't get out. They don't parole someone like him."

"They could, though," I said.

"They could," she said.

I slipped under the covers on Mom's bed. Dad was out of town, so there was no way I was going to sleep out on the living room's Murphy bed by myself. I would sleep with Mom.

"Can I sleep in here tonight?"

She smiled.

"I won't move. I'll be so still you won't know I'm here."

"You can keep me company," she said.

Yes, yes, I would.

Images on a Paper Soul

Whatever satisfies the soul is truth.

—Walt Whitman

THIS TIME MY BROTHER CALLS ME. HE IS WRITING HIS WILL.
"I don't have much, but anything you want?"

"Yes," I say. I know exactly what I want.

Great Grandpa Schultz's stony face with its sharp-pointed beard
looks out from a mahogany frame, the matte tinged brown with age.
His face appears hostile, with black eyes that travel around the room.
When we were kids, visiting Mommom and Papa, all of us were frightened of the photo. His eyes followed us as though watching our every
move.

"He knows what you're thinking!" we would whisper. "He's looking
at you!" Then we'd scream and run across the room, jump on a bed
with a pile of cousins to see whether we could divert his attention.
But it never worked; he kept an eye on all of us. Even after the lights
were out.

A cousin had told me that the photo contained his soul, that's
why his eyes still moved. Marty had said it was Grandpa Schultz in
that space between the cardboard backing and piece of glass. That
he wanted out.

A trick of the light, the way the image ended up on the photographer's film, or how the lens captured the perspective of the eye, that's what caused the photo's subject to follow you. I was a logical child and wanted a reason, I wanted it to make sense. "There's nothing to be afraid of," my mom told me, but everything made me afraid, so why wouldn't a pair of moving one-hundred-year-old paper eyes frighten me?

"That's all I want," I told Marty on the phone. "Grandpa Schultz's picture." He had taken it when our grandparents died.

When photography was first being invented, the small wooden box with a lens at one end projected a scene onto a piece of frosted glass at the back, where the artist could trace the outlines on thin paper. They called these fairy pictures, creations of a moment but destined as rapidly to fade away, the images left only to our memories. Artists traced the pictures until experiments with writing paper brushed with salt, a thin coating of silver nitrate, and the right amount of sun caused these natural images to imprint themselves durably and remain fixed upon the paper.

Permanent memories.

What Remains

You say goodbye and I say hello.

—Lennon and McCartney, "Hello, Goodbye"

THIS TIME, INSTEAD OF A PHONE CALL, I AM VISITING MY
folks in Texas. I want to touch the pottery, read the *Daily Sun* articles,
flip through photo albums.

In the doorway of the den, my parents stand and watch me as I ravage the cabinets where all the smaller memorabilia is stored. Albums
stuffed with all my letters from Papa, our visas, Dad's signed contracts
with witch doctors to allow him to traverse the tribal lands—I rifle
through all of it—the paraphernalia of our lives.

I open a small drawer in the middle of the oak cabinet built in
Lima to hold our stereo equipment.

"What's this?" I ask, holding up a plastic baggy so old and opaque
that I have to open it to see what's inside. A poof of dust escapes as
I unzip it. I have to tilt my head back to let it pass. The last ghost?

I pour out a handful of metal pieces, some an inch square, flat
but curved, some just fingernail-sized, patina covered like dead moss.

"That's the crown," my dad replies.

I pause. I'm having a hard time thinking this is what I think it is.

"From the skull?" I ask. Marty's skull, I want to say. The skull that belonged to a man who lived over one thousand years ago.

"Yeah," my dad says, "When I gave the skull to the movers, I took the crown off. It's silver."

"You kept the crown?" My disbelief twines itself around all the brittle pieces in the palm of my hand. He not only robbed a grave, but denuded the skull? He robbed the prince? He just had to keep the crown?

"It proves he was a prince," my dad says.

I don't mention that the skull the crown wrapped around is missing. That the prince is scattered. That there is no prince to prove a prince. There is no body, as my mom would say.

Yet, it's not really about the body. When I watched the body being unraveled, I really expected there to be no body under the *tela*. That's why I had to keep confirming. I expected nobody.

It's not the physical. It's none of this paraphernalia in the room I stand in.

It's the fleeting emotions. The fragility of their thereness. One swipe of my arm for a hug, and they could turn to dust or thin air. But my memories, those are like bone. Their love is dust, but memory is bone. My memory is all I have, so it must remain. Even if it's remembering the dust.

As I hold out my hand with the crown pieces, the tiny, almost invisible scars across my top knuckles remind me of my mother's lips so softly on my fingers. At Papa's funeral, when I was twelve, in the hot parking lot, I had slammed my hand in the car door. Mom took my hand and kissed each fingertip with her soft lips. I liked that she was kissing my fingers so gently, her manicured fingers wrapped around mine. It hurt, but I liked it. Then, without warning, I started to cry. My whole chest cavity and my abdomen sucked in and out with each wail. Mom told me, she promised me, it would all be okay. She cried, and I cried, as the hearse pulled out onto the road toward the cemetery.

Mom bent my fingers one at a time, slowly back and forth, to see whether they could move. Her coral-colored nails at the tips of each

finger rocked mine back and forth to see whether they were broken.
I passed muster on each finger. But I didn't want her to stop. Then
she put her arms around me. "I'm so sorry," she said, "there's nothing wrong, you don't need to cry." I was disappointed that my fingers
weren't hurt worse. I wanted to cry some more. I wanted my mom to
hold me longer.

Now I look at my hand and the crown disintegrates in my palm.

THESE MEMORIES ARE MY INHERITANCE, NOT THE POTS, OBVIOUSLY
not the skull or the crown. Who we were, is in these memories. Were
we hideous people? That changes with perspective, with time, with
holes filled, holes dug. Who we *are*, that will always be what remains.

ACKNOWLEDGMENTS

MY GRATITUDE COVERS DECADES OF PEOPLE AND PLACES:

Many years ago in a class with Phillip Lopate, he sat me down and told me to look at my family with a wider lens, cast a view from experience, not innocence.

Then enter my graduate school teacher Laurie Alberts, who first called it memoir.

Sue William Silverman. What can I say, but she opened doors, both on the page and in the world for me. It would take a memoir to tell what all she has done for me.

Rachel Groves, my fiction friend who isn't fictional at all, but who read more drafts than a person ever should and still remains a friend. Rachel, the other funny one here.

Katie Scott Crawford, my hiking buddy through grad school, who always saw the bright side, even when there wasn't one. She has the biggest heart of everyone combined.

Over twenty years some version made a pass through all my writing groups. Thank you for reading in various forms, Judi (Yudi) Hendricks, Janet Fitch, Emil Wilson, Judy Reeves, Lavina Blossom, Lisa Loop, Beverly Magid, Denise Nicholas, Rita Williams, Victoria Clayton-Alexander, Jodi Hauber, Lola Willoughby, Rochelle Low, Anita Santiago, Nancy

Spiller, Hope Edelman, Liz Berman, Christine Schwab, Amy Friedman, Samantha Dunn, and so many others.

Meredith Resnick sat beside me in my first nonfiction class, writing and laughing, and meeting me halfway to write more drafts, to share our writing woes, for many years.

Holly Robinson, a long-distance friend whom I met along the way, made me laugh and pointed out a crucial element was missing from the manuscript.

Patty Santana who highlighted the parts I didn't fully understand and said, "This is where the heart is, do more of that."

Susan Henderson, who got excited about a gothic memoir and read an early draft, who willingly and enthusiastically asked if she could.

All my students who, it's been said before but it's true, inspire me. They persevere and then persevere some more.

David Ulin, workshop partner and who handed me a shovel and told me to keep digging. Check out our manuscript workshops!

Mark Drew, *Gettysburg Review* editor, for publishing an excerpt and making me think this story really could be something the outside world would be interested in.

Monica Holloway for giving me insight on telling family stories.

Mary Gordon for enlightening and inspiring me on the ways of telling our fathers' secrets with our walks in Saratoga Springs and her own memoir, *Shadow Man*.

Bob and Peg Boyers for all their love and support (and dinners!).

New York State Summer Writers Institute for the time and space and literary atmosphere that inspired me to ache for so much more in my writing, where this and other stories were penned. All the Institute colleagues and students where conversations are endlessly inspiring. Most especially Claire Messud—when we compared our stories of lives overseas as children and our parents who took us there I knew I wasn't alone.

Alicia Christiansen, Emily Wendell, Patty Beutler, editors extraordinaire, and all the folk at UNP who helped make this a book worth reading.

Lee Martin for suggesting the obvious question, which gave me the answers.

The newest members of my family, Neil and Elisse, and Adam with his kindred song, "Ghost Town."

Eber, who made certain I didn't die inside my writer's attic, served me hot meals, put up with me and walked the dog. The person who never wavered in his belief even when I wanted to give it all up and start a pie shop instead.

Fred, Elmo, Mr. B, and Hazel, I couldn't have done it without you walking across my desk (or keyboard—thanks Fred, the greatest ghost of all).

To order or obtain more information on these or other University of Nebraska Press titles, visit nebraskapress.unl.edu.

CPSIA information can be obtained
at www.ICGtesting.com
Printed in the USA
LVOW03s1928160418
573665LV00001B/65/P